To Ric
Enjoy

xo

THE YELLOWHEAD PAPERS: A JOURNEY

November 1998. Beginnings. We stop at a greasy spoon in Kitwanga, British Columbia, for breakfast. I discover I'm a minority here. The first peoples outnumber the second. The discovery is a refreshing vibe, a revelation, another stop on the road to finding more about myself and the country of Canada.

I'm sat at a window seat with a pal watching skeins of wispy fog drift across a nearby highway, as strange large birds glide on currents of invisible waves above obscenely high majestic treetops, when a memory comes to mind, a pleasant, smile-inducing memory of another pal trying to interest me in Jack Kerouac and his Dharma Bums, but at the time I was more interested in Stephen King and tight bums. I succumbed eventually and read *On the Road* and a quote from the book fits this moment in time: *The only people for me are the mad ones...mad to live, mad to talk, mad to be saved, desirous of everything at the same time, the ones who never yawn, or say a commonplace thing, but burn, burn, burn like the fabulous yellow candles exploding like spiders across the stars...you see the blue centre light pop and everything goes, 'Awww!'*

Is this what I have lost, hidden away with my vinyl records and black leather motorcycle jacket? Does it matter that with forty years under my belt I look more like a member of the Village People than Gene Vincent when wearing the jacket? Am I guilty of masking my vehement spirit to become vegetative and venerable? Is this what this journey is all about, to prise myself off the couch and rediscover what got me this far in the first place?

If so, its a movie responsible. A movie starring a miserable French chap pursuing a miserable French woman through the corridors and compartments of VIA Rail's flagship train the Canadian...and someone tried to commit suicide by jumping from the train and eventually the guy got the girl in the baggage car and that was that. I was hooked. It got me thinking about trains and travel and how much I needed to get off that damned couch.

The movie was on again the following week with subtitles, and off we went through picturesque scenes of awe-inspiring landscapes and sultry people chasing each other only this time I could read what they were saying. I dropped the remote and made a note to drop hints as to what I wanted to do for my birthday. Lordy, Lordy, he's about to turn forty!

Mouvements De Desir, was born in 1993 according to the telly-bible, and starred Valerie Kaprinsky, Jean Francois Pichette and Jolianne L'Allier-Matteau, and I'm reminded of the movie that started it all as I sit here on the Canadian adding to my journal. Scribbling away as obnoxious passengers amuse themselves by imitating the conductor-come chef-come comedian when he slips from English to French over the intercom as this train crosses the Manitoba border, '*...Ladies and gentlemen, please remain in your seats, except of course all non-citizens of the province of Manitoba. The rest of you please produce passports upon request, sil vous plait. Merci!*'

He's good, a natural, I like him, and I reach instinctively for something to defend myself with when it dawns on me that this train isn't about to be stopped and boarded by pock-faced men in leather trench coats snapping orders to sit down and produce passports; no snarling dogs, sirens or searchlights for this is a Canadian border, and a conductor verbally sparring with a few passengers straining at the leash from too much caffeine and lack of nicotine is all we have to deal with in that regard; Cold Wars to us Canadians mean winter weather, hockey and flu shots, we are Canadian!

Thoughts of past travels whizz about my head as the conductor keeps up his spiel. Memories pop and I feel the need to record them. I'm a traveller, I've travelled before, I'm a veteran of inter-continental and territorial travel. I rode an Air Canada plane from Toronto to Montreal for a wedding once, hitch-hiked to Wales twice, and rode a Crosville bus into Liverpool town centre on more than one occasion.

Wales: Bingo, leaky tin can caravans surrounded by leaky tin can caravans filled with mouldy holiday makers, penned in by rusted barbed wire. Bingo, sunburn, the runs, cheese & onion sandwiches devoured on rain-lashed beaches dotted with stinging jelly-fish. Bingo, ice-cream, salt and vinegar crisps, beans on toast, the smell of gas, a wooden match put to flame. Bingo, falling for your best mate's older sister, spin the bottle, chapped lips, blue balls, and the flu. Bingo, the flash of black and white photos snapped in tiny kiosks, pocket money, knobbly-knee contests, naughty postcards, candy-floss, toffee-apples, brown ale and No6 cigarettes. I loved Wales. Cymru meant more to me thanCaernarvon Castle and the eimage of Prince Charles on plates.

The television news show, Granada Reports, showed up at our house in 1974 after one memorable week in Wales, when my mum blew the whistle on a dodgy travel agent for renting condemned caravans to honest, working-class folk. '*You should have seen the muck! It was disgusting!*' she told the north-west of England in her best posh accent as I sat on the couch with my sisters, sweating and squirming beneath the lights and a half-arsed afro haircut. Frank and Sally Sutton never did get their money back despite the five minutes of fame, and I was off school with the die-hoory-hi-ho-hey for a week.

Montreal: Smoked-meat sandwiches, poutine, hairy bikers, The Mob, Mordechai Richler, Leonard Cohen, Oscar Peterson, Guy LaFleur, Jean Chretien, Rene Levesque, tobacco smoke, Sainte Catherine Street, the Expo's, St. Lawrence river, '76 Olympics, the Canadians, Give Peace a Chance and the bed-in. I loved Montreal. I might not have left home if I had been born in Wales or Quebec. Don't get me wrong, I loved my hometown too, but Maggie Thatcher was annihilating it without remorse and Canada was calling. The Nationalist Plaid Cymru and Parti Quebecois might have grabbed me as hard as Punk and New Wave did. *'What are you rebelling against, monsewer Paulie?'*

'Whatta ya got, boyo?'

'God save the fucking Queen!'

'That'll do!'

'Smash it up la!'

I once appreciated the soothing sound of a pilot's pleasantly educated baritone once on a jumbo jet somewhere over the Atlantic, as fellow passengers laughed, pulled faces, and made up jokes on the spot when he morphed into French. *'Ladies and gentlemen, this is your captain, Captain Trips speaking. Welcome aboard, we are now traveling at the speed of light and have managed to shake the alien spaceship that had been tailing us since Ireland. Only joking!'* Big claps!88

Feigning offence at foreign things is a time honoured tradition with the British abroad, or aboard travelling things, as they sup complimentary wine and I loved it at the time, but at this moment in time I'm researching what Canada is all about regards size; as in 3,553,300 square miles (9,203,054 square kilometres) of mostly wilderness and practically devoid of human settlement, extending north into the Arctic Ocean to within 410 miles (660 kilometres) of the North Pole at Ellesmere Island. A country that reaches 83° North latitude and sprawls south to the American border, eastward to the Atlantic and westward to the Pacific, which boasts 171 species of trees,

163 different kinds of mammals, and 518 species of birds that raise their young on the Tundra, in forests, along coasts and on Prairies. 42 species of reptiles and amphibians, 12,000 species of fish and 117 species of mammals inhabit Canada, which has more coastline than any other nation on Earth. 36,357 miles (58,509 kilometres) not counting islands and offshore waters full of whales, porpoises, dolphins, seals, sharks, cod, tuna and salmon, as well as lobster, shrimp, crab, clams and oysters. Beetles, mosquitoes, black flies, hornets, wasps, bees and Don Cherry abound, all related to the first sea spiders and primitives that emerged during the Silurian period of the Paleozoic era 360 million years ago. 30 million humans inhabit Canada and I consider myself lucky and proud to be counted among them, plus I love Beetles.

Nuts, bolts and screws: 11:30am, Tuesday, November 3rd. Toronto, Ontario. Cold, damp and dull. Return ticket to Prince Rupert. Backpack, laptop bag minus laptop. Trail mix, oranges, apples, toffee squares, Halloween peanuts, three joints, waterproofed matches and a pack of mint chewing gum. Bank card, $60 Canadian. Maps, Bell Calling Card, camera, four rolls of film, uni-nocular, Swiss army knife, three pens, three note-books, and a silver St. Christopher medal on a silver chain. Steel-toed boots, ripped jeans, heavy plaid shirt with black vest, long sleeve T-shirt, socks, ball-cap; spare jeans, two teeshirts, long-johns, undies, two toques, gloves, hooded sweatshirt, poncho, long coat, running shoes, and way too many books and magazines.

I'm using red ink to establish how close I came to having a coronary in the van on the way here as we sat dormant, behind schedule, on the traffic-snarled Queensway. The VIA sign out front of Union Station beckoned as we sat idle amidst snarling traffic. Stuck in the middle with you. Just another traffic congested day in the life of the big city of Toronto, one of the reasons we bailed for the rolling hills and fresh air of Orangeville five years ago. Just another trip in the van with dad for the kids.

'They should all be banned these drivers! What happened to bikes?'

'Dad!'

'I hate cars. Imagine a world without cars. Let me out, I'll walk!'

'Dad!'

'Look at that idiot! *Got your license in a box of corn flakes did you?'*

'Paul!'

'What? This windows broke it won't wind back up.'

'Dad!'

'Alright, I know, I'm sorry.'

The offspring would be better off left at home alone than in the van with me and their vocabulary would be better for starters...which brings me back to the point of this exercise. After a lovely pre-trip birthday celebration with the family I'm off to see the wizard, or as much of Canada as I can.

Caged dogs in the baggage car ahead howl their contempt for jailers in blue VIA uniforms, and compete for attention with a snot-nosed kid across the aisle who voices his contempt for his harassed mother. Luckily for all his baby sister sleeps, for now.

My ticket has been checked by a conductor who informed me of the whereabouts of the Dome Car andmore importantly the Bar Car. Food smells waft temptingly from the Dining Car bringing my heart rate down to a reasonable four on the floor drum beat allowing me to finally relax and the pen to run out.

No problem. Back to black!

'Everyday while I'm away I'm thinking of you.' - Slade

I'm wondering why none of my farewells go as planned. No stills from Casablanca for me. No scenes of billowing steam engulfing my beloved, her dress, her make-up, her tears, as I disappear slowly into the foggy distance, waving pain-faced from an open train window, slow-burning cigarette in hand.

I vow to do my best to rectify this in future, but windows on trains aren't allowed to open anymore. Possibly to stop people from trying to escape. They've stopped using coal as fuel too and it's a $50 fine for smoking. So instead I got to stand in front of Union Station waving an envelope full of tickets in direction of a departing family van in full view of a fleet of cabs, whose idling drivers took to honking horns in protest that the driver of the van, my wife, would dare use their taxi stand to drop me off at.

Beep-beep, honk-honk, beep-beeppp! went the Bowie in Berlin tune as I stood there smiling and waving at the arse of the van as it melded slowly into more traffic chaos and I swear I saw it heave a sigh of relief as it went. I let my arm fall slowly back to my side, took a deep breath, and brought it back up with two fingers bared in majestic salute. Take that, I laughed and swept that salute back and forth across the idle fleet. Sid Vicious would have loved it, I thought, as I turned and staggered towards the station entrance beneath the weight of a backpack that weighed a ton.

Union Station drew me into its dark vastness as a cacophony of taxi horns piped me in like an out-of-tune Bangladeshi Bagpipe Band. 'I think they like me.' I told a gang of porters stood there laughing. 'Give us a ride, will yis,' I begged, as I wobbled past like a Weeble that wouldn't fall down. One old porter offered me his back which cracked us up further. 'Farewell Toronto, I knew thee well,' I sang, and staggered off in the direction of a long line of people weighed down with food parcels and sleeping bag paraphenalia. *All Aboard who's going aboard*!

By sheer good luck I've picked a perfect time of year to take this trip. Bald trees fail to hide vistas of farms and small villages.

I haven't a clue where we are, I should retrieve my map from the pack at my feet but I'm scared to move as that Olde English schoolboy thing strikes me for the first time in years: Fear of making a fool of oneself in front of strangers.

I'm glad I brought the trail mix as my furnace is starting to rumble a mean Bossanova. Was probably a bad move to leave the Halloween peanuts with the kids. The VIA guide found in a seat pouch indicates no swing towards Montreal. My father-in-law was right. We aim northwest towards Sudbury.

I'm hoping to find a copy of Pierre Berton's *The Last Spike* or *The Great Railway* on my travels. I've searched high and low in bookstores and on the internet for both but they appear to be out of print.

2:30pm: Washago, beautiful cottage country, the sun attacks the left side of my face. Leaves that still cling to indifferent trees glow red, gold and orange. I spot a gang of hairy Rambo types skulking about in the bush decked out in orange clothes like cross-dressing Denver Bronco cheerleaders, carrying guns, they look to be intent on killing wildlife and trains. Instead of shooting innocent deer maybe they could take out their bloodlust on howling dogs in the baggage car or, better still, the Devil's spawn tantalising his mother across the aisle.

Endless views of beautiful lakes and wilderness pass by my window, it's funny to sit here thinking about the '*big shitty*' hassles this morning. All this land and people prefer to live inToronto, Vancouver and Montreal. I realise that's where the jobs are but you should see this!

I also realise that I should have brought a sleeping bag. My wife Janice assured me that pillows and blankets would be available like on planes, and I'm hoping they are, but who can sleep in this car with crying, abandoned horrors wandering the aisle left to their own devices. I'm thinking of opening the door to the baggage car, the hungry dogs might thank me.

At Reynolds, Ontario, my reflection in the window reveals a sunburned face. One side red face, that's me. Despite the racket I've managed to settle and lose myself in *The Wasp Factory* by Iain Banks, resurfacing only to watch the youngest child smear green snot down the left leg of an annoyed looking passenger to my right. I smile at him and make gunslinger poses, he glares back.

3:10pm: Our first stop is Parry Sound on Georgian Bay, where laughing kids wearing school uniforms wave at us from the street below. I wave back with a big smile before being driven from my seat by the smell as a diaper is changed across the aisle. What a stink! Eldest child screams at mother who screams back louder before youngest joins in to win the competition as I head for the door; that's it I'm getting off at the next stop!

A sobering walk in direction of the observation car three carriages to the rear finds passengers curled-up sleeping or reading books in peaceful, heavenly silence. Yep, the curse has struck again. Planes, the subway, the movies, banks and grocery store line-ups. They find me eventually, these crazies and their offspring.

First Dome experience: I'm sat quietly in a back seat enjoying the silence and relative safety as I observe and scribble. The Dome is bright and spacious and affords mostly unobstructed views through windows almost clean. Air conditioned to the point of frostbite and situated above the smoking section, galley stairs lead up from and down into an inferno of cigarette smoke, which gamely tries to join us but is driven back by said-air conditioning. *Ha-ha. Get back, damned nicotine. Back, I say*! The Dome is a place of refuge and I'm waiting for the 'Back in Five' sign on the caged door of the kitchen to ring true so that I can purchase a cold beer. But, oh no, *It's* found me. The curse of steerage has followed me up here and is rolling my way wearing a grimly fiendish smile, kids in tow. Where's my gun, a blunt spoon, anything, too late, I'm done, they engulf me!

I had the urge to finish them off with the dead red pen there but managed to escape intact to purchase a warm $3.50 beer from a stern faced Uncle Fester lookalike steward, who warned me that due to company policy regards coach. I have to drink the beer back in my seat, and no, they don't stock Guinness only domestic. I take a sly swig on the way back and it tastes like boiled shite. There seems to be a theme developing here.

The sun is finally setting on a beautiful fall day in Northwestern Ontario and the Dome is the place to be as the world turns a bright shade of golden orange. Unfortunately a conductor warned me not to bring a backpack or blanket up here as company rules don't permit sleeping in the Dome, blah-blah! No chance of moving far from the maddening crowd. VIA rule makers have ripped a page from the ancient book of the Raj according to me, which states that first class can do what they like, second class almost can but with restraint, and those in coach can jolly well fuck off.

I caught a passing glimpse (and I reckon all glimpses will be of a passing kind from now on) of a log cabin nestled in the woods, not far from the track, emblazoned with a large sign announcing *Billy O Hunting* or something above the front door. A large bloody carcass lay on the ground surrounded by a gang of laughing men sporting guns dressed in camouflage gear guzzling beer and posturing for the cameras, the sight made more gruesome by the setting sun. *Love Shack*, it wasn't man.

Northern Ontario at this time of day is something to behold through the window of a train, city dwellers. What must Ojibway or Cree have thought as they watched the white man lay ribbons of steel through bush, swamp and rock. I can't imagine them thinking it a great idea before dashing off to build cedar picnic tables and place them in sun-sheltered spots for rail workers to rest at as they drank earthenware jugs of cold, fresh water from pristine lakes and rivers. I wonder how many passengers on the this train think Northern Ontario was created Jurassic Park style? Ontario, yours to discover....

The Specials song ska's through my head again, *What am I doing here?* As I watch passengers go through the motions and rigmaroles of smoking from up here. You have your rumblers, your hackers and your wheezers all in search of a smelly high as they go about the business of clearing tarred and feathered lungs, a reminder that the first fag of the day was always the worst. The rituals are what grabbed me though. The stainless steel lighter and the brand with the black cat on the cover, the bobs and weaves of the head and the dip of a shoulder as a fresh smoke is pulled from the pack. The cupped palm and the flare of blue flame to the burner hanging from the corner of a mouth in emulation of hoods and hoodlums seen on film. Walter Raleigh really was a silly get. *'Eee! The smells all over my clothes and I was only in there for ten minutes!'*

We must be near Sudbury, I reckon. We're stopped in a siding and have been allowed to disembark for five minutes for fresh air and a leg stretch. Five minutes only, the guards remind us as we stumble down steel steps. Its pitch black as I chat and practice knee-bends indiscriminately with the smokers. A tall, pleasant young man with a thick head of hair tells me he's from Halifax, Nova Scotia, and that we are in Capreol, not far from Sudbury. Turns out he's headed to Prince Rupert as well. He tells me to call him Quint, 'Short for Quentin.' He's twenty-one years old, dresses conservatively, loves books, and is one hell of a good listener. As we board into the light we discover we are neighbours and it was him having snot smeared down his pant leg. Small world!

I am the passenger and I ride and I ride. I ride through the city's backsides. I see the stars come out of the sky. Yeah, the bright and hollow sky. You know it looks so good tonight! - Iggy Pop

Wednesday, November4th. I'm awakened from a troubled sleep at a place named Nakina after a long night of jolting stops and starts at various, identical snow-blown towns. Its early morning, Drowning River is close by according to my map, and its one of many drowning rivers that abound up here in Desolationville.

And they called it lonesome town, runs through my throbbing head. It's hot in here. I'm thirsty. Would Drowning River enjoy another victim in search of a mouthful of cool clear water? I'm wrapped like a sore thumb in a regulation VIA blanket, uncomfortable as hell, my head jammed against a window, my window, as I follow the beam from the engine as it seeks out the track through pitch darkness like a giant flashlight. We take curves and bends and race along straights and it all reminds me of a projector in a movie theatre, only in this theatre the eyes of wild animals can be seen glinting through veils of hard blowing snow.

I haven't a clue what time it is, my belly is howling to be fed, but the food car doesn't open until noon, Quint tells me. He's huddled in his blanket feet stuck out in the aisle making an obstacle course for passengers on the night prowl. He has a K-Mart price sticker on the heel of one sock. 'Surely we must be able to get something to eat before noon?' I moan. 'Are we on British rail or wha'?' He looks puzzled. 'Hang on...we can't be. I still have my wallet!' and he laughs along as he checks his back pocket. A nosey-parker informs us that the dining car opens at approximately seven eh em and we thank him. Ha, lots of time, so I stretch and take a look around to find steerage resembling the aftermath of a travelling party. Smelly, sleeping, twitching bodies with clothes and blankets in disarray, some with mouths wide open, others snoring, the rest performing gaseous explosions to the detriment of partners and neighbours. A thief's paradise with nothing stolen except deep breaths and time.

Canada. I love it!

By the look of some out-of-shape contortionists on here there's bound to be complaints of stiff necks and backs, a Chiropractors dream. I'm fine though, thanks to years of sleeping on tiny couches or in lumpy beds. I'm well prepared and I'm patting myself on the well-muscled back when a leg cramp attacks, so I take a stroll to walk off the pain and bump into a man in uniform who tells me we are scheduled to stop at Winnipeg soon, for an hour, to change staff and replenish supplies before embarking on another overnighter to Edmonton. He asks how I'm enjoying the trip so far so I tell him it's been a fucking laugh riot and push him in a cupboard and jam the door with a chair. To hold off consumption I purchase a steaming cup of coffee from the snack bar and try to extract the correct time from grumpy half-asleep revellers milling in the corridor waiting for breakfast. 'It's 6:30am!' a miserable fat man tells me and continues sulking. I thank him and head back to the sanctuary of the Dome.

We're heading straight into a bashful full moon which hides behind red-black clouds and banks of mist, that envelopes tall trees that stand on guard as the moon waits and stares with an egg yolk eye; the watcher. Images of First World War photo's recently viewed in a magazine come to mind, and for a moment there, I was transported to Belgium and frozen trenches. Complete desolation and stark realism combine despite lack of tanks and howitzers, maggot-ridden bodies, and shell-holes. Light returns slowly, revealing ice-crusted surfaces of small lakes, and frost covered emptiness as The Canadian sails North West through barren terrain. Would my bleached, gnawed bones be found come spring if I were to step from this train at the next stop? Believe it or not we're still in Ontario and not due to exit until around 3pm Train Time. I still haven't a clue what time it is now but learn that all timepieces will be synchronized in Manitoba at a town called Collins. But for now we wait in a siding at a charming town that goes by the name of Armstrong on Lake Nipigon south of Caribou Lake. Below us Thunder Bay and the shores of Lake Superior. Toronto is fourteen hundred kilometres southeast, and no, I can't see the CN Tower from here.

Armstrong, like Nikina, stands isolated in the middle of nowhere. I can make out a tiny store, a chapel, a bar, and a sign that boasts of an *Attack Base.* What's to be attacked and who will be doing the attacking? I'm searching for missile silos and jet planes when the moment is spoiled by the arrival of mother of the year and creepy offspring. I escape to the dining car in search of a much-needed breakfast, where a fellow journal-filler-inner, who I'm slightly familiar with from The Dome, points to an empty seat at his table and insists that I join him. So I do, eagerly, this being the first chance of real human contact for hours.

Terry is in his late twenties and stands tall and rail-thin with a head of short wiry hair. He's an animated scribbler and likes to talk...a lot. This I don't mind, as he has an interesting, well-practiced repertoire of anecdotes and stories to amuse. He's a playwright/actor on a get away from a lost love tour of the country and he's from St. John's, Newfoundland, he tells me with much pride. I tell him he looks, sounds, and dresses like a Newfoundlander despite the army coat and habit of wearing his boots on the right feet. He laughs and records the compliment in his journal. His destination is Kamloops, British Columbia, where he intends to spend some recreational time with friends. He chats, I listen, and we swap email addresses over a large plate of *Egg Scrambler* and umpteen cups of coffee.

The food is good, well worth the expense. Terry tells me he was watching and writing about me last night as I searched high and low for the bar car. I'm famous! He thought it was a funny scene, skips back a hundred pages or so to find it, and reads aloud from his journal - to the amusement of Scary Mother, who has sniffed me out again ir seems. She lurks at a table behind us, observing, laughing, and eating, occasionly stopping to throw scraps to her offspring; the youngest of which has a shoe in its snot smeared mouth. The owner of which is not amused as his foot is still in it.

I feel like I'm being interviewed as Terry records our conversation in ink because he left his camera behind at a going-away party in Ontario after guzzling gallons of Irish whisky, but I don't mind, as its obvious that we're destined to spend the next couple of days together scribbling like demented travelers on the run.

Collins comes and goes without further incident, just a mad rush of time-changers congregating in the aisles, watches and fingers poised. 'So far so good?' I ask a worried looking man as we stop for fuel and a breath of fresh air at Sioux Lookout just west of Savant Lake on Lake Minnitaki. 'It's 10:30am!' He replies, checks his watch again, and scurries off down the corridor towards First Class scratching his head and looking baffled. At least he didn't tap the watch as he went, that may have been a bit too much even at this hour.

Sioux Lookout looks interesting, so I grab the camera and disembark to investigate a 'historic' train station and the town that surveys it from atop a steep hill and enjoy the northern fresh air while lining up a shot of downtown with my camera, which refuses to work again, so I smack its bottom and berate it like the naughty camera it is, as a crowd of locals pass a bottle in front of a row of rundown stores. 'Bottled heat, they call that here,' an American passenger informs me, amused at my camera skills. 'Who hasn't done that, eh?' I reply, and he nods in agreement and wonders off down the platform sniffing the air.

This place has a *feeling* to it and I can't decide if it's one of danger. I want to know more about the place and inquire amongst milling rail staff if I have time to meet the locals. 'No, there's no time for walkabouts. We are slightly behind schedule,' a stiff necked conductor informs me. 'People have been know to miss trains here,' the American leans in to tell me, flashing a smile of conspiracy. He's back! 'Thanks for telling me,' I laugh, and slip him a wink.

'No problem!' He replies, and wanders off again, just as the camera decides to function and take an unexpected and unwanted shot of an ice covered train bogie.

The rest of my short stay in Sioux Lookout is spent watching a brick shithouse of a male biker trying to coax a large white ferocious looking dog back into the baggage car after taking it for an obviously much-needed plop at the base of the downtown hill. Other dogs cavort, bark, and follow suit all over the place as his dog takes to ground cowering and shivering his owner tries in vain to coax it back aboard the baggage car the poor thing has been howling to get the hell out of since Toronto. The dog seeks revenge by refusing to move and then barking and snapping at its bemused owner in view of an amused and shivering audience. Being a mainly Canadian audience nobody causes a scene or laughs too loud - we just stand there kicking stones and heels and fall further behind schedule, until a brave conductor steps in, calms the terrified dog, and hands it over to the keeper of the baggage car to scattered applause as the biker scowls in the background.

That's it for Sioux Lookout. However I was told by the American that First Nations are discouraged from entering VIA property due to past episodes of first class patrons being hassled for money.

'Barred from their own country then?' I ask, disgusted.

'It looks that way,' he replies. At this I boot a large stone onto the track and board the train. It seems the Empire is still alive and well in Canada, and on that note we depart Calcutta, I mean Sioux Lookout, and head west towards Winnipeg, or 'Winter-peg' as the conductor calls it. He informs me that we are now travelling on Central Standard Time and laughs at my expression.

Miles of untouched wilderness on both sides of the Canadian, as we pass through Red Lake Road, Canyon, Minaki, and Malachi (sounds like the McCourt family) all desolate and untouchable. I take shot after shot of Johnny Cash scenes, the old train coming down the track and round the bend and all that, as we roar through tunnels blown and bored through iron rock with barely a foot of clearance all round.

'Testing, one, two, three! Will all non-Canadian citizens please remain seated with passports at the ready, please! We are about to cross the Ontario-Manitoba border...thank you!...clunk-whinnnnnnnnnnnnne-whistle.'

The East-Coasters are having a laugh at him and at my expense because Terry has brought my travelin' man attire to their attention. 'That Englishman's dressed more Canadian than the rest of us put together b'y!' I blush for Canada and they get the same treatment as the cab drivers outside Union Station. 'Take that yer bastards!'

3:20pm: Somewhere between Rice Lake and Winnitoba a line of camera-wielding passengers groan as one when they realise the conductor has been up to his tricks again. He's had them stood waiting to take photos of a 'historic' sign that announces the Manitoba border, which of course doesn't exist. Terry tells me there is such a sign. A man listening in disagrees. I watch them argue.

The conductor has been a welcome breath of fresh compared to the rest of the staff. Rumours are rife that this is their last trip, some are to be laid off. The listening-in man tells me they are always miserable to members of steerage, the opposite to First Class. I leave Terry beind agreeing and defer thoughts on the subject for now to find a free window to survey an endless landscape beneath a great blue sky.

The great ocean itself does not present more infinite variety than does this prairie ocean of which we speak. In winter, a dazzling surface of purest snow; in early summer, a vast expanse of grass and pale pink roses; in autumn, too often a wild sea of raging fire. No ocean of water in the world can vie with its gorgeous sunsets; no solitude can equal the loneliness of a night-shadowed prairie; one feels the stillness and hears the silence, the wail of the prowling wolf makes the voice of solitude audible, the stars look down through infinite silence upon a silence almost as intense. This ocean has no past-time has been nought to it; and men have come and gone, leaving behind them no track, no vestige, of their presence. - William Francis Butler, Adventurer, RCMP founder.

Butler penned that in 1871 after crossing the prairies during winter with a Metis guide. They traveled by snowshoe, horse and dogsled. No crying babies or First Class to bother them two, steerage all the way baby!

Winnipeg. The Canadian is to be re-stocked here. Passengers have an hour to do the same only quicker. It's a cold Winnipeg that greets us as we pull into its historic Station. A station built in 1911 and designed by the same folk who created New York's Grand Central. Like its cousin the place has great atmosphere, with cozy waiting rooms and a bright and breezy lobby, however, the walls of this building are faced with Tyndall limestone loaded with prehistoric fossils, seaweed, crab-shells and ammonites from ancient sea-beds that once covered the prairies.

Terry has been told by the conductor that a fast-food joint called Veejays does business across the road from the station and has the best burger and fries on the rail route. I decline the invitation and head for the phones. I need to talk to my family. Unfortunately, it takes fifteen minutes of tourist time to figure out how to use the mysterious Bell Calling Card, and when Janice picks up the phone I'm in a right state. Same state they left me in at the station she tells me, and the rest is lost to static.

'The kids are alright,' gets through, as does, 'watching *The Addams Family.*' I can hear them laughing in the background and this calms me down and we manage a quick, mushy chat. Upon hanging up I blow kisses at the receiver and a woman waiting to use the phone catches my eye and smiles. I blush like an angel and head off in search of The East-Coasters. Forty minutes left...

Sleepless & Stupid in Winnipeg: Like most passengers I left my backpack on the train and while on the phone I witnessed a hysterical woman telling blank-faced security guards that her handbag containing train tickets and money has gone missing, she left it on her seat. The guards didn't look too bothered or impressed so her boyfriend waded in with the histrionics which had no effect either. I'm sweating bullets, I knew I should have brought the pack with me but betrayed all instincts. Security won't let me back on the train either and I'm mad at myself for being careless. I'm cursing as I choke down a sweaty egg salad sandwich bought in the station lobby while Quint and Terry revel in their gourmet burger and fries and tell me not to worry, to take a chill-pill.

'What you got in the pack anyways b'y, smack?'

'Nah, just a photo of your ma.'

'Wha'!'

I leave them rubbing bellies and burping to poke my head out the main doors like a turtle and inhale a gob full of fresh Winnipeg air and hand a bum some change just to say I'd been there. 'Was that the call for the train?' I shout from the entrance.

'Nah, Quint farted.' Yelled Terry.

Winnipeganisms: The Cree named this meeting place of people and rivers Assiniboine, Red, and Seine, *Winni-nipi* which means muddy water. The rest called it *The Chicago of the North*, or just Winnipeg according to the fellow who sold me the egg salad sandwich. The city was laid out in a diagonal-type street plan instead of the grid system used by most western cities at the time. Settlers in chase of 'The Great Manitoba Land Boom' marked property lines like spokes on a wheel with rivers as hub.

'If there ever was a fool's paradise,' wrote George Ham, *'it sure was located in Winnipeg. Men made fortunes - mostly on paper - and life was one continuous joyride.'*

I bet none of them ever left backpacks on trains.

'The new Eldorado,' the Winnipeg Times, blurted in 1881, and in 1998 a brochure tells me as I wait in line, that, *'Winnipeg is home to more than fifty ethnic groups, an Art Gallery, the world's largest collection of Inuit sculpture and art, and the largest French-speaking community outside of Quebec!'*

I'm glad I missed it all by making a phone call!

The East-Coasters pick up on how pissed off at Bell Canada and myself I am and attempt to cheer me up by picking on security as we show tickets and passports in order to board the train. Something about the Titanic, the Irish, locked doors and drowning passengers in steerage. VIA staff don't find this at all amusing for some reason. I do, and after a long wait we poor sods are allowed to board to find everything intact only cleaner, even my belongings. Everything the same except the staff, who are all women, and very efficient women at that.

Following the moon to Saskatoon, and after observing several unpleasant exchanges between staff and passengers old and new, it appears that the next stage of the trip is going to be more eventful than the last. I'm wondering if this lot are about to be laid off as well or just in need of a good laugh. If so I know just the passengers to help them thaw out.

Talking of cold, it was freezing in Winnipeg, coldest stop so far. I'm trying to get stuck into *Swing Hammer Swing* by Glaswegian author Jeff Torrington, but can't get past the second page due to staff efficiency. I await a '*Ve are only vollowing orders,*' any minute, as they scare more passengers into submission.

The train is sold out, packed solid. Timid travelers sit all quiet and stiff next to strangers, bags on knees, not making eye contact like they do on the Toronto Transit System. New faces abound. Luggage is stowed in compartments above seats in silence and the temperature has shot up a notch due to the sardines and kippers like seating arrangements, and as per nobody wants to sit next to yours truly, ahem. I have my ways, trust me, I value my space.

In the confusion, I decide to go get myself a beer...only to get chased back to my seat by a Beer Nazi.

'*Vait in your seat pleeze. I vill be taking beverage orders az zoon az pozzible. Pleeze return to your zeat!*' he orders, nose twitching, and takes off down the aisle, arms gesticulating. I chance a glance at a neighbour but he's not playing. True to his word, Beer Nazi returns half an hour later to fulfill his promise, so I order and receive a warm Canadian, down it in three gulps, and request another as he comes back down the aisle waving an empty tray.

'*Vot! Anudder?*' he barks, and gives me the evil 'we have a drunk here' shiny monocled eye. All around are silent and intimidated but he doesn't frighten me. He doesn't know who he's dealing with. I know how to handle little Hitlers. 'Please sir, please may I have one more' I beg, Oliver style, and he's taken aback for several seconds, which invites giggles and coughing from dark corners and an outbreak of fidgeting from an elderly couple to my right. He glares at me but I hold my ground, and he takes off to return in record time with another warm beer to match his now sweating demeanour. He makes no eye contact as he pours, mumbles something about '*ze inglish*', and slinks off pushing his trolley loaded down with a handful of my loose change as passengers suddenly make themselves visible again.

It's warm like the beer in here, I'm feeling sleepy, looking through the window (the window to my heart, is the rain about to start?) its turned real dark and cold looking out there. Trees, tracks, and vista covered in blue-white snow. I must remain in character or the Beer Nazi will surely suss me out of that I'm sure. Here he comes now flexing his moustache...

'Spracken de Deutsch.'
'Nein Mein beerkellar.'
'Achtung! Achtung! Englisher svein on borden!'
'Schnell, Schnell...hiden in de shitenhausen!'

That's it I'm caught, but as the train slows to a halt, breaks squealing, I take a deep breath and flush myself clear to the track. The snow breaks my fall to the sound of barking dogs, the crack of a rifle shot; a bullet pings off the steel toe of my boot and ricochets into the night.

'Thank Gotten for K-Martens!' I whisper, (stay in character old chap) and spring like a cat over a signal box to slide down an embankment and dash to the safety of a forest of skinny pine. I lurch through inky darkness, lungs on fire, frozen branches trying to whip me into submission and impede my progress to the ice-fields ahead. Freedom is a spotlight in the distance and I'm scaling a barbed wire fence to reach it when from out of nowhere a Stormtrooper disguised as a male elk appears. He charges and I take his picture with my dodgy camera. The flash blinds him and he gores himself badly in the leg. It's a mortal wound, I can tell, as he screams and thrashes about in the snow which pools red with his blood. I leap from the top of the fence, pick up his discarded rifle and take aim with intention to put him out of his misery but he screams again, a long blood-curdling scream....

Which wakes me up, I'm awake, alive, hands over ears trying to keep out the demented squealing of steel wheels on a tortured track. A long swig on a water bottle soothes me back to reality. I compose myself, check for bullet holes through me or the boots bought on sale in K-Mart before I left, as the Canadian continues to carve a path through the outskirts of Siberia. Some dream that!

Train keeps-a-rollin', all night long!
- Tiny Bradshaw

Yes, we're all aboard 'The Night Train' heading northwest to Saskatoon, due in Edmonton at 9:20am. Portage la Prairie, Brandon North, and a town called Rivers pass by under cover of darkness. To the North sleeps Lake Manitoba and Riding Mountain, to the south, Fargo, Minnesota, the home of Paul Bunyon and a pregnant cop that says 'ayep!' a lot. I'm tired, knackered in fact. My window to the Prairies has been turned off so I make like a pretzel in my blanket and drift off into another deep, dark sleep. The last thing I hear before entering the abyss is a frazzled neighbour enquiring about the cost of a sleeper from Helga, she-wolf of the night, as she makes her rounds.

SASKATOON, SASKATCHEWAN

Running back to Saskatoon...and jaysus, I've slobbered all over my shirt, where's my boots? Its 4:35am depending on whose watch you trust on this 5th day of November. *Light up the sky with Standard fireworks*! comes to mind. Amazing how advertising jingles stick like shit to new shoes isn't it, and away I go, remember, remember, remembering not a Womble but a snot-nosed soap-dodger stood shivering outside a smelly pub with his best mate jammed into his sisters pram pretending to be dead, begging for change from smelly drunks on the way home 'to bash the wife'.

Penny for the Guy please mister!

For North American readers this is similar to standing outside of Kelsey's with your best buddy in the Fall asking evening diners for a nickel for your man.

The British celebrate Guy (Guido) Fawkes every November 5th by burning his effigy on bonfires in blazing streets in which no shed, fence, sign or dog are safe. Fawkes was an English Catholic who tried to blow up the Houses of Parliament in 1605 with a little help from his friends, but they were caught and two of them were hung, drawn and quartered. Fawkes avoided the hanging bit by jumping to his death from the scaffold. Any excuse for a party. Can't wait for Easter!

Like I said last night before falling into the abyss, this train is headed to Edmonton and on to Jasper, where I intend to find a hot bath, big comfortable bed, gallon of Guinness and a juicy steak. I'll be looking for adventure as cabin fever has set-in big time. I had Terry and Quint in stitches last night with my ranting and raving regards 'laissez faire' attitude of staff towards us mangy dogs in steerage, which they loved and joined in with much vigour. I awoke afterwards shivering in my seat. For some reason we were stopped at a frozen town named Melville. Stopped dead with doors wide open. We must have been there for a while as I could hear teeth rattling like a Gene Krupa drum solo. Images of partisans attacking the train flashed across my addled bonce and my reflection in the window told me, *My shine ish Shcorpio shee*!

Something tells me I better get cleaned up before breakfast.

Scrub-a-dub-dub in Biggar, Saskatchewan, home of Schmirler the champion Curler; and after waiting in a line of dishevelled, head-scratching passengers for ages, I managed to commandeer the washroom for a soapy paper towel bath and much-needed foot scrub. There is something to be said regards bouncing bollock naked in a train washroom as the Prairies flash by through half frosted glass as you wash your bits brush your teeth and change undies and socks all at the same time as some fool whines at the locked door.

'Anyone in there?'

'No.'

'You've been in there for hours!'

'Here's Paulie!....'

Up in the Dome thinking of absent friends: Quint and Terry are still here but Psycho from Peterborough departed during the night somewhere on the Prairies. He wasn't too hard to miss as he stepped down from the train. Wild hair, manic grin, covered in tattoos, he spent the ride chatting mostly to a woman who resembled Katherine Hepburn, complete with wobbly head. When he wasn't talking to her he was reminiscing with me about drinking Black Label in the Red Dog pub in Peterborough, Ontario, though fifteen years apart. We both had an affinity for Stompin' Tom Connors, the Damned, the Cramps, the Clash, and the Sex Pistols.

Aussie Girl the first, has gone as well. Her rail-pass ran out at Winnipeg, so she took off down the road talking away to herself. She'd travelled across most of Canada by train and told me what was left of her intended to hitch-hike to Vancouver and busk the fare back home to Australia. Hope she makes it!

Ontario is Boring, is on his way to Medicine Hat and the oil rigs to fulfill a dream. He's a tall, dangerous looking country & western fan with a habit of claiming my seat as soon as I vacate it to use the washroom, the bastard.

The East-Coasters, or the Beer Coasters, intend to fall off the Canadian at Jasper and head to Banff for some 'wine, women, winter and song!' They invited me along but I said no despite the appeal. People on the move looking for adventure...there's more I could mention but won't for fear of litigation.

Unity sits all alone on the Saskatchewan prairie covered in Christmas lights. *A good town in a good district,* its motto. According to the map pilfered in Union Station we are knocking at the Alberta door, climbing northwest towards the mountains, the backbone of Canada.

Ayup! Almost forgot to mention Sexy English Chick who I met while waiting to board the train at Winnipeg Station. Stood there in line with us commoners she was, Union Jack boldly emblazoned on her backpack, chatting away with a balding and totally-enamoured little American. She was sharing a story in her best Sloane Ranger accent about a recent adventure through the rice paddies of China, as us Colonials pretended not to be listening. She knew she had a well-captured audience, none of whom had the nerve to strike up the band never mind conversation with her, but me being from 'up north', a minion in her presence, stood a respectful three paces behind scraping the toe of my boot on a cobblestone and doffed my cap each time she looked my way. My minion might have been hers for the taking but I was worn out out from all the cap doffing. I just passed her on my way to the washroom. She was fast asleep with manicured hands folded in her lap, long black silky hair framing angelic face as her light snores permeated the carriage; head back, mouth wide open, a silver puddle of drool on the collar of her winter coat.

Strange why she's not in First Class, which reminds me: Terry did some sneaking around last night and found himself in the land of pacemakers, wigs, and pearls. Being such an accomplished actor he was able to mingle and observe the wealthy and bulbous nibble on blue steak and devour bottomless glasses of fine wines. Elderly folk fresh from hot showers relaxed in spacious comfort and watched videos with feet up, shades down, totally uninterrupted by Helga and crew. Unfortunately, Terry was caught liberating a basket of fruit as scurvy has reached epidemic proportions in steerage. He was last seen being escorted down the aisle at a brisk pace by two stern-faced guards, protesting loudly to the end about the plight of the working classes, Joey Smallwood, Farley Mowat, and the decimation of the cod fish. God love Terry, a martyr to the end.

Talking of which, this passage from *Rails Across Canada, One*

Hundred and Fifty Years of Passenger Train History should give you an idea of what we are trapped and starving aboard:

CPR opted to purchase 173 stainless-steel cars from the Budd Company of Philadelphia for the Canadian, inaugurated on April 24th, 1955. This splendid transcontinental steam-liner not only reduced running time by 16 hours but offered accommodations second to none and a new concept in train travel across Canada. With its hand-painted murals, maps and heraldic designs, it became a veritable art gallery on wheels. Where else in the world could one gaze at an original painting by A.Y. Jackson or A.J. Casson while moving across the Canadian prairies at 75 miles per hour in air-conditioned comfort sipping one's favourite beverage?

Included in the order were 36 dome cars. It was somehow appropriate that CPR would order these as it had invented this type of sightseeing vehicle way back in 1902. Seating 66 passengers in a glass-enclosed observation room and raised cupolas, these striking cars provided fantastic views of the glaciers and mountains in Rogers Pass.

Throughout the new cars a Canadian theme dominated the interiors, with original murals, plaques, coats of arms, maps and scenes depicting the varied activities of the country. The most beautiful cars were the 'Park' series of dome lounges, named for Canadian national and provincial parks. In the intimate Mural lounge under the dome, were ten foot by four foot paintings reproducing the unspoiled beauty of each park. Created by Canada's leading artists, sponsored by the Royal Canadian Academy of Art, these works are currently on tour. Park flowers were artistically portrayed in glass etchings and carved linoleum panels on the bar. In the curved rear lounge of these cars were three by five foot maps of each park and a descriptive nameplate.

The interiors of the Skyline dome coffee shop cars were also quite striking. In the coach section were hand-painted, coloured and animated maps of Canada. In the small cosy dining room under the dome were large photographic reproductions of Canadian scenes from coast to coast. The coffee shop area featured carved murals tracing the development of transportation in Canada, running the artistic gamut from birch bark canoes, kayaks, dog sleds, stagecoaches and wood burning locomotives. Canadian provincial and federal coats of arms and Parliament buildings were displayed in carved linoleum renderings.

Dining cars on the Canadian presented a new approach to the enjoyment of meals on wheels. Each car was named for a distinguished dining room, public room or lounge of a Canadian Pacific hotel. Representative Canadian birds were portrayed on etched glass partitions, while provincial flowers appeared on hand-carved coloured linoleum wall panels.

One type of sleeping car featured the names of English manor houses while the name of a well-known French chateau adorned each car of another type. A descriptive nameplate explained each name and the interiors were painted in shades of Banff blue, Alberta green, Prairie gold, Empress rose, French gray or Atlantic turquoise.

And after reading that I can't help but wander about the train bumping into passengers and uttering awestruck comments like, *Wow, will you look at the etchings on that, what a rendering!*

In the real world, smokers are gathering to a crescendo of coughing, signalling the hour of 6am. I should make an attempt to reset the watch my son William loaned me as the alarm went off last night at 2am again to a chorus of tutting, growling, and boo's. It's also time to purchase a coffee from the Beer Nazi masquerading as a chef in the kitchen. Be brave old boy, think of David Niven!

The Alberta border is crossed without further fanfare, and no, there was no sign. On the good news front, my belly roll is disappearing, leaving in its wake a prominent six-pack which will be more prominent after some much-needed exercise in

Jasper. Talking of belly fat I have to wait an extra thirty minutes for breakfast because we are now on Mountain Time, which causes me to expire slowly in the corridor whistling the theme from The Beverly Hillbillies.

Terry and Quint join in the vigil and serenade me with a rousing, *Whisky you're the devil, you're leading me astray, over hills and mountains, and to Amerikay. You're the sweetness from the Bleachner, and spunkier than tea, oh whisky you're my darling drunk or soberrrr!*

We're pumped now, ready for battle, anything, but decide to let them all live and sit down to breakfast in a bright, sun-swept dining car, table tops bedecked with gleaming cutlery and fine china cups with saucers. I'm impressed. Crisp white cotton tablecloths and napkins are about to be covered in ketchup. A smiling waiter delivers three *Eggs Scramblers* as the Canadian sits waiting at a siding in scenic Wainwright, Alberta. He re-appears from the galley to re-fill empty cups with black treacle-like coffee and listen to our compliments with a smile; life is good again!

Five minutes silence for chewing is interrupted by the arrival of a recent acquaintance of Terry's, who on his way to first class stops to say hello. By jove, I exclaim, It's the American from Sioux Lookout! He pretends not to recognise me but is convinced by the nature and humour of our conversation to join us. He introduces himself in a broad Boston accent, divulges his name is Eric, and that he's working on an article for Rail News magazine regards crossing the continent by train, but facts get lost in accented conversations on books, heritage and scurvy, hookers, cabbages and kings.

A well read, well-traveled man, Eric is easily amused by us court jesters talking expertly through our arses. He takes an interest in the Jeff Torrington book I have with me and is impressed by the critic's comparisons to James Joyce on the cover, so we make an appointment to meet for a quick Guinness at Jasper before he heads off to Vancouver. He retires back to the land of soap, showers and seclusion and we three scruffs head back home. 'Hey Eric, send some fruit back here will yer, the scurvy's killin us!' I beg him, in my best John Lennon imitation, which cracks him up and he promises to do so. Good food, good company, good times. The shape of things to come?

Scurvy, for those not in the know, is a dietary disorder caused by a lack of Vitamin C that inflicts on sufferers extreme weakness, spongy gums and death. Americans have been known to use the word 'Limey' because the Royal Navy once issued citrus fruits to its sailors to combat the scourge during the early Empire wars with the lesser peoples of the world, who didn't have scurvy because they were clever. Jacques Cartier and his crew where at deaths door back in 1535 and the Iroquois saved their lives by giving them the inner layer of white cedar bark (*Arbor Vitae*: The Tree Of Life) which contains Vitamin C, depending on the season, and I'll wager the Iroquois wish Cartier had visited Cuba instead.

7:45am on a foggy Alberta morning, where's Gordon Lightfoot when you need him? I tell you, this land, every muddy square inch of it, isn't ours, but I wish I could borrow it for a week in August. I can see for miles, and miles despite thick fog, as we cross Battle River and snake through Prairie towns like Irma and Kinsella, before coming to a halt at a surprised looking Viking.

Bruce, Holder, and Riley slip by, as we glide through now swirling fog towards Edmonton. *Hey, hey, it's a big boned gal,* plays on the record player in my head, but, so far, no sign of kd lang.

Beavers galore swim and play in scattered streams and ponds that surround, none wearing cowboy hats. 'Lots of hungry beaver round these parts, eh boys!' cackles a young man sat on the

Dome stairs. The response is frightening. *Castor Canadensis* get no respect at this moment in time and I'm not telling anyone joining in that beaver were known as 'hairy bank-notes' back in the fur trading days.

9:20am, Edmonton, Alberta, is damp and chilly as we step down from the train and head inside the station for a 'spot' of free tea while the Canadian waits patiently to be re-supplied. Quint goes in search of a wicket to buy a ticket to Prince Rupert and a copy of the Edmonton Sun, leaving me to have a chat with Eric about Canada's Festival City, which boasts a population of just under one million. A rollicking boomtown since the Yukon gold rush, Edmonton covers more territory than any other Canadian city and is famous for its hockey team and the West Edmonton Mall, which gets seven mentions in the Guinness Book of Records. Eric tells me that two rival fur trading forts, Augustus and Edmonton House, formed Edmonton's roots, and the Klondike gold rush of 1897 put the town on the map, and made it the gateway to the north.

The railway arrived in 1905, Edmonton was established as a world class city, and here we are stood freezing, sipping tea and stamping frozen feet on a concrete platform, sharing knowledge as we watch VIA staff herd bleary-eyed passengers together to tell them it's only a quick stop and to stay close to the train. 'Don't run they might have guns!' shouts one accented wag from the safety of the mingling crowd, as guards patrol silently, walkie-talkies crackling orders in the cold still air. After being cooped up for so long it feels extra cold so to keep warm we take turns singing and taking photos of each other posing in front of the engine, where the other three find out that it's not really me on 'Thomas the Tank Engine'.

Eric is a wealth of information regards everything historical, railroad and geography, and I'm developing a headache as we stand rail-side chatting and performing knee-bends for the crowd. Tall, fit, middle-aged, he looks to have been around the block judging by the lines that criss-cross his weathered face. Then again, being Irish he may have been born like that. Breath and steam from hot tea billow away in the cold as he tells me why Edmonton station is in the middle of nowhere and not downtown as it once was. 'Its only a seven-dollar cab ride downtown if you want to have a look,' offers a grumpy guard after I inquire about getting downtown on my return journey.

'Nobody likes where this new station is located,' Eric tells me, as I pull faces behind the guards back. 'Most Edmontonians wanted to keep the old station as they hate coming out here and they fought it all the way.'

'So, how come they moved the station then?'

'Who knows, Paul, who knows?' he replies, with a chuckle. Sipping at his tea he diverts my attention from the Edmonton skyline, now half-eaten by fog, to a trickle of brackish water dripping onto the line from beneath a First Class rail car.

'What on *earth* is that?'
'Looks like a leak to me, Eric.'
At this, and with great drama, a passenger overhears me and panics. 'The train is leaking, the train is leaking. I hope it's only water!' he bleats.

'Get back, it might be fuel, *get back*!' warns his female companion, to great effect, which gets everybody's full attention as the overly inquisitive squat close to take a look as something mysterious and brown escapes with a *Splat* onto an oily rail tie.

'*Eeeeeuuuwwww*!' they sing in unison.
'Another one, Eric!' I laugh.
'Yes, Paul, another one, I'm afraid!'
'Fuel, eh?'
'I suppose one could use that for fuel, yes,' sniffs Eric, and off we wander in search of more entertainment. '*Please do not flush when train is stopped,*' is engraved on brass signs in every wash-

room on the Canadian, and I should know, even Mister Magoo can read them.

Just as I'm rounding up a few brave souls to nip across the fields to Edmonton for a quick pint, the guards round us up and shepherd us back to waiting seats quicker than you can say Dave Semenko. Various familiar faces have departed this mortal carriage. Scary Mother being one. Hurrahhh! She wheeled her offspring over in a stroller to give me high fives as I chatted with Eric earlier. She wanted to wish me a sheepish 'good trip,' as she lit up a Players Light, before steering the snow-suited kids toward an impatient father suddenly taken with a look of fear upon first sight of all three. Emotion, nah, doubt it!

Sat here back at my seat enjoying the quiet I recall the pleasure of meeting a charming old gentleman as we waited patiently for the Canadian to snail into Edmonton, surrounded on all sides by crews of idle rail guys. He appeared smiling mischievously at my table as I sat studying a map of Canada, and after some idle banter about where we were from and headed to, he disclosed with pride that he was eighty years old and used to drive a '33 Ford on the roads of Orangeville back in the late Thirties. 'Of course, it was a lot different back then, Paul,' and he took charge of my map to show me railways travelled as we swapped tales of places seen, missed, or heard about. He had loads of rail tales because he was forty-three years working on the railroad and in retirement he makes a habit of traveling the country by train visiting grandchildren and staying out of trouble, but he went and ruined it all by divulging in a hushed tone that he lived in North Bay and was good friends with Premier Doug Harris.

'Don't tell anybody I said that, eh,' he whispered, followed by a conspiratorial wink, and we talked trains some more as Edmonton loomed on the horizon. I never saw him again after we left the Dome to prepare for some Alberta fresh air. I can't recall if he told me his name, which makes me sad as I jot down, '*Trains*

and the traveler, eh! 'on a napkin as we cross McLeod River to leave Edson and its lighthouse behind.

The Dome is filled to capacity, the chatter of excited travellers and a sense of ending or completion in the air as we draw closer to Jasper. I'm enjoying a juicy green apple given to me by Eric to combat the you know what. He managed to smuggle a dozen into Canada and saved one just for me, thoughtful chap, and I tell him how much I appreciate it. We're joined by Terry and Quint, all four of us squished into a table seat marvelling at snow dusted scenery through muddied windows, debating books, music, movies and places seen and read about. Politics is a no-no in our gang.

It's too foggy to see the Rocky Mountains in all their glory, the tops are enveloped in thick mist, but we do catch a few glimpses. Exhilarating bridge scenes and flashing rivers bring the cameras out in force... *click, click, flash, flash!* Mountain goats and elk perch precariously on mountainside indents like paying customers - as they watch us ogle and point. I leave the party at this point to return to my seat with the excuse of getting my shit together for Jasper. The lads tell me it might be a bad idea as I'll miss so much but I'm tired and more than a bit irritable. Three days on the Canadian has made me a little punchy, besides, I'll get to see it all on the way back, and it was getting a bit daft at times up there in.

The first time Terry shouted '*DUCK!*' as a tunnel approached was funny because most people actually ducked, but the third time had me feeling cornered. I used to feel the same way aboard the top deck of the H8 bus as a teenager. Cigarette smoke choking and engine rattling bones as the old Crossville bus wound its way through council estates on the way home from school or into town. My mates would annoy hooligans, pensioners and drunks with similar tactics as we went under bridges, and sometimes an angry wasp of a conductor would throw us all off and we'd have to walk to our destination in the rain. I felt the same back then as I do now despite knowing I won't have to walk to Jasper in the fog, and well....in my attempts to put thoughts to paper, I'm being distracted by a young Brad Pitt look-a-like as he attempts to charm the drawers off an attractive young woman who is revelling in the attention. She pretends not to speak English to prolong the affection. I heard her talking to a conductor earlier without a problem. I'm impressed, startled in fact by this game. I can't get my thoughts together as Brad plants the first of many kisses to come, I'm sure. Things are getting steamy and I'm feeling like a bit of a voyeur of which I am, so I stand with a flourish worthy of Andre Previn with intention of departing the scene, and crack my head on the luggage rack. He catches my eye and smiles. I smile back and stroll coolly in direction of the Dome praying that the carriage door opens on the first try, and luckily for me it does.

The slow entrancing journey through Jasper National Park (The Gem of the Rockies) has to be seen to be believed, and I spend it in the Dome showing everyone the lump on my head. I couldn"t stand watching Romeo downstairs anymore, I tell my pals, who jeer and hit me with Viagra jokes. I tell them to take a powder and read this from a tourist leaflet instead, which shuts them up for a minute: *Jasper National Park is the largest park in the Canadian Rockies. Bighorn sheep, mountain goats, black bear and grizzly make their home here in the vicinity of Sunwapta Falls: Stoney Indian for 'turbulent river'. Jasper is named after Jasper Hawes, who built the original Jasper House in 1813 at Devona Siding, just north of Brule Lake, east of Snake Indian River, for his fur trading business. The Athabasca River meets up with the Rocky River to create Jasper Lake, which fills up in the summer and empties in the winter.*

Mount Roche a Perdrix, situated just south of the park gate, was part of an ancient seabed that created the Rockies 80 million years ago. The Miette Range of mountains and its hot springs are also close by. The Athabasca River, Canada's seventh longest river originates in the nearby Columbia Icefields and flows through the park into Lake

Athabasca.

No more fooling about from Terry after that. Herds of elk and deer are all over the shop, hawks and birds of all description dot the gray sky as we slowly follow the Athabasca River, the same river we've been following since just before Hinton. We sit goggle-eyed and silent for a change and I spot a red sports car on Highway 16 which startles me. It looks out of place and I wish it were gone, whisked away in the talons of a great eagle to feed its hungry young, and next thing the Canadian is making a grand bell-clanging entrance into Jasper station, belongings are gathered and backpacks loaded on keen backs.

Farewells abound as the train halts at a picturesque building sat Lego-like surrounded by mountains. Mountains that cause me to duck my head slightly as I step from the train, back-pack slapping my arse in synch with my feet as I head into whatever comes next. The Canadian will carry on overnight to Vancouver after a stop of one hour, and one hour only. I have to find the guys, so I say good-byes to the staff and ignore the Beer Nazi. It's warm enough to go without a winter coat and while searching for Quint I bump into Brad Pitt and girlfriend. He tells me with a cheeky smile that he's decided to stay in Jasper with her for a while. I laugh and wish him luck, the swine, and join the Three Mousketeers. A pub is spotted across the main road as large snowflakes fall slowly to melt at our feet. There stands Sexy English Chick waiting for a taxi, all alone and full of confidence. I ask her if she wants to come for a pint and she laughs. I was only kidding and she knows it. Terry calls me a naughty old man. 'He hasn't looked at a woman the whole trip and as soon as he gets near Jasper!' More laughs as we cross the road and enter the pub like old pals. Loud music is an alien assault to my ears, it's only 3:30pm, this passage from *Caesars of the Wilderness* may interest you while we find a place at the bar and I order the first round....

A day highly suggestive of the past, of fresh scenes, of perilous travel, of fatigues, excitement and of adventures by mountain and flood; the retrospect is full of charms; images of the morning breezes, the bright sky, the glowing sunrise, the rushing waters, the roaring cataract - the dark forest, the flowery plains, the impressive mountains in their pure white covering of snow, rise before me, at this moment, as vividly as ever and old as I am, my heart bounds at the bare collection of scenes I loved so well...I can recall nothing more delightful than our bivouac on a clear moonlit May night, near the Punch Bowls - the highest point of the Jasper Pass. The atmosphere was bright, sharp and bracing, the sun set in glorious splendour, bringing out the towering peaks and fantastic pinnacles dressed in purest white, into bold relief. Our camp was laid and our fire built, on the firm hard snow which was about twenty feet deep. As the daylight faded away, and the shades of night gathered over the Pass, a milder light shot up from behind the nearest Peak, with gradually increasing brilliancy until at last the full orbed moon rose in silent majesty from the mass of mountains shedding a mild radiance over the whole valley beneath.'

JASPER

What a spectacular view from a balcony to suffer a hangover. The mountains, the air, the elk, the Guinness! I'm stretched out on a bouncy clean bed in the comfortable confines of The Mountain Park Lodge hotel situated on Jasper's main drag, and it's still only 6pm.

The place we hit was called The Lava Lounge on Connaught Street, and after Eric and Terry left, Quint and I had a couple more 'Mother's Milks' before donning our packs and heading off in search of a place to stay, which unexpectedly took no time at all. Jasper must snooze this time of year as hotel rooms are a plenty.

We took a look at a few pricey joints but I don't think we were welcome after we fell over a pair of over-shoes in the lobby of the first one. We think the word spread fast on the ski-crowd bongos that the Canadian had dumped a couple of Irish/ Scottish lunatics in town. But after navigating herds of foraging elk we found the Mountain Park and they took us in, despite me asking the Jewel look-a-like behind the counter if Elke Sommers was in residence. She feigned ignorance and entered our information into a computer as we broke into fits of giggles while searching through pockets for wallets in suddenly hard-to-find pockets.

Nice clean room. Coffee maker, double beds, large bath, decent colour television with cable, bathroom loaded with fancy soaps and shampoo which I hide in my pack as soon as Quint leaves to phone his mum.

The view from the bay window is one of herds of elk arranged like figurines on grass verges and a main road. Some have taken over the disabled parking spot below our balcony, but I can't see anyone giving them a ticket with racks like that. Snow-capped Old Man Mountain dwarfs the station. Its misty and snowing out there all at the same time. The bay window frames all this as if a Paramount picture and any minute I expect to see Danny Kaye tap-dancing across from the next balcony.

Somewhere out there awaits the Maligne canyon, a restaurant, but first a hot bubble bath and a shave. After Quint does his bit in the bathroom we take off in search of the Athabasca Hotel, which looks from the outside to be a fancy joint but upon entering we find it a bit of a dump full of drunkards who yell stuff at us as we take a quick look around and leave. *Yahhh! Go ahead and leave then, yahhh!'*

So we did, across the hotel lobby to a more respectable joint with the lowest bar I've ever seen in my life. It must be all of three feet high, a bar built for Ken Dodd and his Diddymen. Quint eats, I partake of more liquids as I've decided to save money, as we fill out postcards and watch the Leafs get battered by Boston on a mute television above our heads. Jasper is dark and deserted on the way back to the hotel and we spot Brad and conquest making out in an open-air phone-booth. About to advise them to get a room as its cold, I have to run like a bastard due to a sudden attack of dysentery. Quint runs behind me laughing until we tear around a corner and straight into a herd of elk. Fortunately, we have the element of surprise on our side, but one big brute decides to give chase. We can hear hooves clattering on concrete behind us, smell his breath he's that close as we sprint for the hotel.

'Hurry up, quick its coming...arghhhh! '

'Gerroutthefuckinwayyyyyyyy!'

Quint steps on my boot heels as I almost pull the entrance door off its hinges and we scramble inside just in time to save us from a good goring. The glass fire door is slammed shut as fast as a pneumatic door will slam. 'Quick, hurry up and push, its gonna kill us!' and we put all of our weight into the job...but there is no elk pushing back, nothing there about to smash the glass and eat us as it looks like he shit himself and gave up the chase. We cheer, hug, make happy to be alive noises as I take the stairs two at a time and pray I have the right key to the right door, and to the sound of laughter echoing in the hall I burst in with no time to spare. Not again! Quint sleeps through the night and I spend it in there with the fan on. Bloody elk!

At first light I find a leaflet propped up on the television courtesy of Parks Canada: '*WARNING! ATTENTION! WARNING!* Both male and female elk may charge without warning. Keep your distance-stay back 35 metres or 3 bus lengths. Never approach a bear; remain in your vehicle. Be alert. Always drive safely.'

'We could've been killed, mate.' I tell my room mate as he jams belongings into an overflowing backpack, leaving a towel hanging from the overhead fan.

'Hey Paul, how big is a bus length?'

'As big as my bloody head feels right now, why?'

After a quick soak in the tub, I liberate a roll of toilet paper to be on the safe side and we leave bright and early to find something substantial to eat. Quint takes a photo of me stood there smiling like a dope beneath a sign that says 'Nature Calls' over the door of an old stone building on the way to find a restaurant.

'You should call your journal Shittin' Across Canada!' He yelled from across a busy road as he snapped away. 'Water off a duck's back to me that, mate,heard it all before!' And one bottle of Pepto Bismal and a Clubhouse sandwich later I'm ready for a good snoop around town. No more Guinness! We mail postcards and buy supplies for the journey to Prince George and take in the sights of downtown Jasper. A bookseller warns us to be careful in Prince George as it's a tough town and he should know as he was born there. I make a mental note as I search for Pierre Berton books without luck. Outside, Connaught Street has spectacular mountain views which have us tripping over untended bikes and kerbs while looking up to take photos of mountains. Safe in the knowledge that I'll be back next week to explore some more, I climb aboard an empty Skeena, VIA's Link to the West, with Quint, laughing about last night and prepare to face the next leg of the journey.

12:45pm, Friday, November 6th.'*Grizzly on the track! Grizzly on the track!...on the right folks, on the right! Too late, damn, he's gone!*' I'm stuck in limbo trying to find a window between mid-corridor and the Dome when the announcement came crackling over the intercom. I guess you could say I was caught between the Dome and a hard place. I knew I should have stayed in my seat but the conductor was annoying me again.

'Did you see it? Did you see it!' She asked, all excited, as I made my way up the stairs.

‘Nope, I missed it,’ I told her, as she passed me on the stairs like an experienced deck hand on a rolling ship.

‘Too bad, next time, eh?’ She fluffs her hair, straightens her tie and re-arranges leaflets on a table below before disappearing down the corridor, hopefully to bug Quint.

I share the Skeena - three cars and an engine - with a staff of four and about fifteen passengers sat hither and yon. I sit alone in a blue four-seater as we head Northwest through The Yellowhead Pass. Sat quietly nursing a hangover and scribbling events experienced since Toronto in my journal. There is nothing else to do other than write, read, relax and enjoy the scenery. I love it. This is by far the most comfortable and scenic stage of the trip so far. This is what I had in mind when they bought my ticket and to make things even better I found Berton’s book in a travel agents in Jasper Station after searching for it for weeks. I happened across it by accident while having a nose around, lost in the ambiance of the hot, stuffy old station. After leaving my pack on a wooden bench with a nice old couple I wandered after Quint who was checking out the price of a ticket to California in a tiny travel agents. I walked in and there it was sat on a top shelf amongst dusty travel books and I was prepared to fight anyone for rightful ownership or hand over the twenty dollars to buy it.

'Quint! Look, its the book!'

‘It's only a book Paul, what’s all the fuss about?’

‘Only a book? It’s *the* book I've been talking about since we met, soft lad,’ I fired back while searching my wallet for money.

‘Nice, you best buy it then!’ He advised, lost in a brochure as the happy for me travel agent searched a computer screen for flights to Lotus land. The strange thing, besides finding the book in there, is after convincing her that I was from Liverpool and not Quebec (accent thing, don't ask....) she sold it to me for fifteen dollars and looked quite happy about it. 'You're really happy about finding that book, eh!' And while I was dancing about the lobby clutching it to my chest Quint decided to stay the course to Prince Rupert after she told him the cost of a flight in search of his dream job in the sun. I was a happy man. 'Karma!' I told him as he went off to buy a ticket north.

Enough, I'll be crying in a minute. I see from my map that we crossed into British Columbia back at Yellowhead Pass (no sign) and are now following the 1,3000 kilometre long Fraser River, the longest river in British Columbia. We have changed time zones from Mountain to Pacific as well, but I could care less as I haven't looked at the watch for days, it's still on Toronto time as far as I know. I'll catch up eventually, I muse, sat back all comfortable with my feet up against the window in peaceful silence watching the country go by at a snail's pace.

Bliss!

The Skeena roll's on through Red Pass and winds its way through the wilds of British Columbia unmolested, unlike those who have gone before us (don't ask, I have no idea...) when the thought of trying to keep Terry in the bar for one more pint yesterday has me laughing out loud, which is fine with me as I'm the only one within laughing distance.

After the first Guinness hit his empty belly Terry fell head-over-heels for the heavily-pierced bartender who was serving dark pints and blushing at Terry's quest to count her tattoos - and thus the Shakespearian scene was set.

'Ah, the lady is beautiful, no?' he asked me, in his best card-carrying Shakespearean actor guise.

'Aye, but she's also a bit young, no?' I replied, in my best Liverpool policeman accent. It was at this point I noticed his ears were turning pink, as he stabbed me with an imaginary rapier.

'You don't want to be entertaining thoughts of sneaking her back to Newfoundland by plane either. Security alarms would be going off all over the place.' Quint warned him, but 'twas too late, for Sir Yappalot was truly infatuated as he made his way behind the bar to help the object of his affection pull more pints. 'You can always read her after...,' a stranger wearing flip-flops started in with but was cut off by a chorus of boo's and beer mats. 'Now, now, there's no need for that young feller' I admonished as I admired my Guinness moustache in a Kokanee mirror behind the bar where the love-birds had become deaf to everyone but themselves.

'Let's try and get him to stay. Think of the laugh we'll have!' Quint suggested. 'That sounds like a grand idea, mate. Can you imagine the look on Eric's face when he finds out he won't be having dinner with him. He'll owe us one.' I countered, as a lady of indeterminate age appeared from behind a curtain and attempted to shoo Terry from behind the bar and ask him who the hell he thought he was as she shoo'd. 'That's a daft question missus, I mean, even he doesn't know the answer.'

'Joseph Smallwood is the name, madam, and I'm sorry to have offended!' Terry told her with a flourish of an imaginary cape, and bowing low, made his way back to where he belonged. 'And that man there is James Joyce!' he announced, pointing at me with authority before resuming the attack on his pint. Eric was loving it.

'He's mad, take no notice,' I told her. 'I'm Margaret Atwood, and him there with the daft grin on his face is Farley Mowatt.' I pointed at a nodding Quint as he ordered another round, as Terry leaned over to ask me about his ears. 'Are my ears turning red yet, Margaret?' he stage-whispered and turned his head to reveal the reddest ears I've seen outside of a boxing match.

'No, they look alright,' I lied.

'That's a good thing then.'

'Why?'

'Because the redder they get the drunker I am!'

'Great mate, why don't you stay here with us and have a

laugh then?'

Eric had promised Terry a meal in first class as a treat, but didn't touch alcohol anymore and hadn't seen Terry with a drink in him before. As Eric finished off his Coke and shook hands with Quint and I, before heading back to catch his train we promised to stay in touch and gave him a send-off with the raising of the pints. I was sad to see him go but he was in his element back on that train. Terry told him he was right behind him but had to use the phone first.

'What's *he* doing?' the bartender asked.

'He's calling his mates in Kamloops to tell them he's staying here for a couple more days.' I told her. Quint was stifling a laugh as I was but had to to keep a straight face as I was the oldest. The look on her face!

'*He's not!*' she whispered from behind the bar. 'He is I'm afraid,' Quint told her, before heading to the front window for a breather.

'*I'm with someone!*'

'*Do they like red ears?*' I whispered back, and took off to the washroom for a much-needed laugh and a leak. It was quite the eclectic bathroom, I must mention, and upon my return, Terry told me he was sorry but he couldn't stay, he had to leave as the next train wasn't due for two days and his friends had a big party planned in Kamloops, he had to be there. I told him that was probably for the best but we'd miss him and we hugged before he finished off his pint. The music stopped and off he went after hugging Quint and chasing his muse around the bar (only kidding about that bit, but he was emotional saying his goodbyes.)

I imagined Eric looking at his watch safe in the knowledge that Terry wasn't going to be joining him for dinner. We heard train doors being slammed shut and we were all hopping on the spot pointing at the Canadian being made ready to roll.

'RUN TERRY, RUN!' we yelled, as he tore across Connaught

Avenue on wobbly legs, ears blazing. I thought he wasn't going to make it but a door popped open and a blue clad arm helped him aboard, and just like that Sir Yappalot was gone. We stood in the window and waved our pints as the Canadian departed for Vancouver, leaving behind empty luggage racks, barking crows, waving civilians and a grateful Jasper.

'Quiet, eh?'

'Yep, want another?'

'Might as well, my round, life will never be the same!' and we headed back to the bar where Quint wiped away imaginary tears and we consoled a relieved bartender and relieved her of more Guinness. (Eric told me in a letter that Terry had fallen asleep in his soup.) *The Four Decades*, we'd christened ourselves, we'd all been on the same page and if we were to reform Spinal Tap wouldn't stand a chance.

My God, what a long tunnel that was, I thought I'd gone blind there for a minute in attempts to record the sight that dwarfs us. Ladies and gentlemen, Mount Robson, the heavyweight champion of the Canadian Rockies. Well worth the price of admission because today we get two Mount Robson's for the price of one thanks to the reflection in a mirror-like Moose lake. Oh man, what a sight. Standing at 3,954 metres, *Yuh-hai-has-hun,* or *Mountain of the Spiral Road,* Robson gets its English name from fur trader Colin Robertson.

The Overlanders must have shit a brick when they set eyes on this behemoth in their quest to find the Pacific Ocean back in1862. The Skeena winds its way around the foot of Robson like a drowsy caterpillar and deftly skirts the lake it stands in. Plentiful beaver cavort for the cameras here. If you're quick enough you can capture beaver tails on film before they disappear from view with a splash.

Hello beaver, what must you think of this Great Iron Horse

as it intrudes on your playground? Modern trains aren't Iron Horses anymore, of course, more like Blue and Yellow Constrictors, and this constrictor is snaking through the history of the region...The Rockies, the Cariboo Mountains, the Selkirks, Rogers Pass, the Rocky Mountain Trench, Tete Jaune Cache and an Iroquois trapper known as Yellowhead, real name Pierre Hastination, or Bostonais depending on the source. Some literary sauce for you to put on your history and chips as I go in search of a coffee:

Competition between the Northwest Company (Nor'westers) and the Hudson's Bay Company increased as the H.B.C. pushed further and further into the trading territory previously held by the Northwest Company. In February of 1819 John Clarke, of the H.B.C.'s St. Mary's post on the Smoky-Peace River confluence, chose Jose Gaubin to lead an expedition with a band of Iroquois to cross the mountains into New Caledonia to see if the natives could be induced to trade with the Hudson's Bay Company. In December of 1819, Ignace Giasson began another H.B.C. push up the Smoky. Colin Robertson, man-in-charge of the Hudson's Bay Company's operations in the area, prepared written instructions specifying that the group be accompanied by a yellow-haired Iroquois guide. The group was to ascend to the Grand Forks of the Smoky where they were to meet another group of Iroquois, wait until Spring, and then cross the mountains (via Robson Pass) to make friends with the Shuswap Indians of the upper reaches of the Fraser. On June 10, 1820, James McDougal recorded in the Northwest Company's journal at Ft. St. James that he had heard "a report of there being at the Forks of Fraser's River one of the H.B.'s Co's clerks and three men.

Ha, what price a ticket back in time, eh? Beats television, video games, email and chat rooms, or searching through Blockbuster for the next box of tripe from Hollywood, doesn't it. I'd rather be with George myself:

Arrived at Tete Jaune Cache after encountering very hard travel. Three men were nearly exhausted, and one of them died of a vile dis-

ease. Tete Jaune Cache is a place where one Iroquois Indian half breed who was fair-haired, had made a fur cache, or a place to store his catch of furs and was known as Tete Jaune or Yellowhead. It is near the meeting of the Grand River which flows from the base of Mt. Robinson - and the Fraser River.

- George McDougal, April 25th, 1827

Duke Nukem, Doom and Quake have nothing on it -more levels too.

Tete Jaune continued trapping and trading in the area and by 1827 had relocated his cache from the Grand Fork of the Fraser to the vicinity of the Shuswap salmon fishing camp on the Fraser River where the town of Tete Jaune Cache stands today. The relocation was made to facilitate trading with Fort George. Unfortunately, Tete Jaune was not allowed to continue trapping. Sometime in 1828, near the headwaters of the Smoky River, he, his brother, their wives and children were murdered by the Beaver Indians for revenge on the Iroquois for their earlier encroachment into the Beaver's hunting territory.

Eventually, a pack trail was established through Tete Jaune's Pass. The leather passed through until 1830, when due to undescribed difficulties with passage through the pass, Simpson ordered the leather to be transported through the Peace River Country, and the Leather Pass fell into disuse. -Jeff Waugh, local historian.

Whoah! I'm jolted back to reality in the vicinity of Terry Fox Mountain by the loud voice of woman in blue demanding to see my ticket. See you later Tete Jaune, history lesson over for now, game saved.

The VIA conductor has nothing to do and no one to talk to so she picks on me. She thinks I'm a hooligan. She makes it clear from the start. I think she looks like Colleen Jones the curler but I don't say anything. She has that Jones sliding down the ice with demonic mouth and eye thing down pat.

'You look like you're up to no good,' she tells me, looking me up and down with obvious distaste, scribbling in her official VIA notepad and searching my pockets with darting eyes.

'I'm here to rob you of your train, missus. Hand it over,' I reply. Instead, she hands me back my autograph book and train tickets from a safe distance. The look on her face tells me she wants to be my official tour guide. For this I am grateful in a Catholic kind of way. I like to don a hair shirt as much as the next person when travelling long distances. On short journeys I sleep.

I peer through dirty glass at a waterfall, a dead something, a rainbow, and imagine Conductor Colleen screaming, Harder, HARD, HARDERRRRRRRRR! It's not hard to imagine as she sweeps the blue, well-worn VIA carpet clean with a ratty regulation broom, stopping only to point with a pen swished from behind a diamond studded ear at something visible only to her. I look, she explains, I blink, she coughs. I attempt to snap a photograph of something moving in the bush, a Windigo? But my camera refuses to co-operate again.

Her fuse shortens and during the lecture on batteries and back-up batteries I miss reams of Kodak Moments but that's okay, I'll be ready on the return journey unless I'm in jail for murder. I can see the front page of the Toronto Sun now.

More thoughts on Jasper as I'm swept onwards and upwards through mountain, hill, vale and back down again by the Skeena. Though a beautiful and friendly town, one thing that sticks to mind apart from the view from the hotel we stayed at, is how small and round elk droppings are. They remind me of chocolate Maltesers and Jasper has mounds piled willy-nilly all over town. Sidewalks, grass verges, roads, driveways, front gardens are covered in them. The town should be renamed Malteser, they'd make a fortune. See brightly dressed tourists on posters pulling elk tails like they do slot machine handles in

Vegas, fancy drinks in hand.

'Bingo, Doris. I've hit the Jackpot!'
'Way to go, Fred. My turn...'

Lost in such daft thoughts I sink back into my seat, feet up on its opposite number, as the Skeena slows and comes to a halt in a siding in the middle of nowhere again. Croydon Station, the sign says. Last time I was near a station in Croydon it was raining. It's raining here too. I catch my reflection in scratched, mud-flecked glass as I check for blemishes and wrinkles, pull a face and move sideways to see how far I can go without losing sight of myself - when, from out of the corner of a bloodshot eye a man appears. A tall man. He's dressed in dirty jeans, a blue checked shirt, big dirty leather gloves, and is stood going about the business of whatever it is he's doing to the track with a metal implement. I know he wants to look this way, so I wait. He looks. I wave. He waves back. I smile. He smiles back. I'm about to give him the old two-finger salute when it dawns on me that I'm trapped, playing silly buggers in the middle of nowhere, again.

He could be a nut. He might have a gun. Instead, he's winding his implement and whistling. He catches me looking again and smiles. I decide at this point that I need something important from the backpack at my feet. I feel my face redden the colour of the Muskoka Dinner Jacket I'm wearing as I dive into my bag and feel the heat from my face as I burrow for a book, a can of mace, a bazooka, anything!

The book draws me in and a sudden train jolt draws me back and I look up to find him gone and the train moving slowly forward as it starts to rain harder. I'm thinking *Ghosts of Run-over Rail Guys*, as we pull in to Dunster at the pace of a well-seasoned escargot. Dunster boasts a rare General Store and Post Office and rarer still it's open. The Mayors name, I think, is Herman and the station was built just before the Great War. It looks like it and is barren of all living things. A nice place to live for a nun, I muse, engulfed in The Wasp Factory, a fine book by Iain Banks that seems to fit the moment.

I'm glad I bought the trail mix, I'm starving. Warm water from a fountain on this side of the washroom wall holds back a bird-cage-bottom thirst and I'm losing power when the steel door that leads to the engine squeals open and crashes against its steel frame.

Heavy footsteps tramp up the aisle and Big Foot passes leaving behind the smell of oil and cigarette. It's him, the phantom waver. I watch as he makes his way at a fair pace towards the rear of the train slamming dividing doors behind him as he goes. Train robbers in face scarves in black and white scratchy films send Banks packing. I put him down and wait. A door in need of an oiling squeals. He's coming back. I sneak a peek. He's carrying something black in one hand and a steaming white plastic cup in the other so I strike up conversation to save my life as his knee draws even with my head. 'Hey their big fella, was that you back there before?'

'Before what,' he drawls. I laugh. He has a kind face but don't they all. I scratch my head and recall Karate lessons learned since the winter of 1974. The voice of a Dalek from the walkie-talkie in his hand screeches and blots out any further attempt at conversation. He barks a reply and thumbs the OFF button. Exterminate! He's not wearing his gloves I can relax. He's not going to strangle me with bare hands. My kids watch C.S.I.

'I was just changing the rails buddy, why?'

'Well, erm, I thought you were up to no good there for a minute,' I explain, and think logically about standing up because if I sit with my head back any longer it's going to lose all circulation. Like I said, he's tall. 'Thought maybe you were stalling for time until the rest of the gang showed up on horseback all barrels a-blazing.'

'Nope, nothing as exciting as that buddy, where's that accent from by the way?' I tell him the same place as me and stand up and try to make myself big like it said in that pamphlet in the hotel room in Jasper.

'You Irish?' he asks.

'No, I'm just bored, are you American?'

'No, I'm just Canadian.' He laughs, and hoists an oily boot to the seat next to mine and nods at my book. 'Good read?'

'Yeah, it's a good. You read?'

'Yes, I do. Write too! The names Don.'

'Paul.'

'Nice to meet you Paul.'

We shake. That's us bonded and talk of music, Guinness, travel and the Beatles kill miles of endless trees, as in scenery, until Colleen makes an unexpected appearance to check tickets and pulses. At this, Don excuses himself with a promise to come back later and winks slyly as he makes a quick exit before she nails him with her broom. When she starts in with the chatter I grasp both ears with clenched hands, open and close my mouth like a goldfish and pretend to have lost all hearing and she leaves, face pinched like a bunion.

I take the chance to catch up on much-needed sleep until Don wakes me bearing gifts: a box of earplugs and an invitation to travel up front. I accept both and wipe drool from my mouth.

'Could have used these back in the day,' I tell him, extracting two waxy stoppers from a small package. Do they come in threes?'

He laughs and points at door number one.

'Quick, before she comes back.'

He leads I follow.

'Will I need a coat, Don...my things?' He tells me to leave them, they'll be alright, so I do, except for my journal and pen; I check my wallet, decide to leave the camera as the door to the engine room slams. 'HANG ON! Wait!' and I follow him into the heart of Conrad.

Don's stood there in the dark talking into his walkie-talkie when I crash into him nearly losing an eye to the aerial.

'What you shouting for, I'm not deaf!' he yells.

'I'm blinded!' I yell back.

He warns me not to touch anything. I promise not too as we enter the engine room where angry machines crash whine and creak. Wind whistles, grabs at my ball cap and I'm deaf now as well as blind. Something my mother always told me. Hot, hot, heat hits me square in the gut as if I'm stood in front of a backline of Marshall amps at a concert. I shout, nothing comes back as I follow my leader careful not to fall into pumping heat spewing machinery. I catch a glimpse of Don's blue checked shirt as it disappears down a narrow aisle and bang my head on a low steel doorframe in my enthusiasm to catch up. Stars appear and I'm checking for blood as I waltz into the control room. Brightness melts my irises and two bemused men stood staring at me laughing.

One I recognise, the other offers me his hand. I shake it and Don motions for me to remove the earplugs to introduce the second engineer who goes about the business of recording numbers on a clipboard and driving the train. He moves a lunch-pail from a beat up leather seat behind him and motions for me to sit down. I sit where I'm told and gawk as coyotes clear a path and scurry to safety and coloured bird's dart back and forth across a silver track that stretches before me forever and chase each other from tree to tree. A deer stands motionless in a clearing bathed in orange from the setting sun. I feel like the girl who followed the white rabbit. The view is spectacular.

'Time to earn your keep, Paul, get on over here,' Don tells me and motions with his hand like he's waving away a sudden smell. 'I beg your pardon, I'm not like that.' They laugh and next thing I'm driving the train with Don at my shoulder giving advice and instruction: Keep one eye on the speed-gauge the other on the brake, you'll be alright. 'I'm cross-eyed Don!'

'Keep a close eye on Casey Jones here. I'm off for the coffee,' the second warns Don and heads for the door.

'Tea for me, please.' He tells me to keep an eye on the track and the hammering machinery takes him as Don keeps up a running commentary on occupants of shacks and lodges we pass in the mist. He's driving now, I only had a little go, and I find out that the '*Grizzly on the track*' warning earlier was him.

A big old grizzly has an elk or deer stashed in the bush, track-side, and has been spotted on numerous occasions when he shows up for a nibble. The food chain (cougar, eagle, coyote, fox and crow) wait patiently for him to finish his meal so they can fight over the leftovers. 'Colleen had me doing push-ups on my knuckles at the time so I missed it,' I tell him. He tells me he and a couple of pals drove into the bush last weekend with intentions to film the bear but it never showed up and he gives me the impression he's glad. 'It's the wrong animal to piss off,' he tells me and I believe him.

Handsome Ned sings, *On the Wrong Side of the Track,* in my countrified head as we head further on down the line towards McBride where a solitary figure stands smiling a cocky smile as he smokes and guards a stack of cardboard boxes tied up with string. 'Ha, it's Old Tom,' Don tells me, and waves. Tom waves back and flags us down. 'You should buy him a beer - he's full of tales,' he advises as we leave McBride behind.

A leaning, derelict, boarded-up shack sits alone on a

few acres of scrub surrounded by a herd of scraggy buffalo. It belongs to a crazy inbred hillbilly family from the Southern States, I'm told. They survive by breeding the buffalo for meat and fur and have a habit of riding around on horseback late at night brandishing guns and cussing neighbours. 'Land encroachments, garbage and noise, it'll all end in tears!'

'Sounds like Orangeville, Ontario,' I reply.

At Crescent Spur, a log 'cabin' complete with helicopter pad is spread all over an acre or two of tamed bush. The helicopter is used by wealthy Europeans as a base for ski jaunts into the mountains. Don slows the Skeena down and we wave as naked hot-tub bather's pop up like funfair targets to expose bronzed bodies that flash in the sun as they wave back.

'Can we stop for a bit, Don?'

No answer. I whimper, wave goodbye and he hits the gas. I watch him drive the train from Crescent Spur to Raush River Bridge to Goat River, studying dials and gauges that jump and dip behind glass cases as the ribbon of steel stretches on endlessly. The Deadman *buzzes* at regular intervals to drive away any idea's about falling asleep and Don has to hit a button to cut the *buzz* so the engine doesn't shut down.

At Goat River the second appears with refreshments, smiling and smelling of nicotine and fresh air. He hands me my tea. It's hot and much-needed and with boots up on the dash, I watch the big screen narrow slowly - taken by the twilight - as a solitary headlight burns a silver tunnel clean into the night. Orange and red lights flash like fireworks in the blackness of an endless tunnel that eventually spits us out at Mount Rider where I announce that I should be making tracks as I need to eat, one can't live on Trailmix alone.

The once thriving sawmills and settlements of Loos loom large and I'm escorted back to coach where Don and I sit and chat for a bit. He yawns and I follow suit. We shake hands and he tells me he'll look out for me at Prince George and leaves with a knowing smile.

My belongings are still there like he said they would be. I open my journal, click my pen and rub the wee lump on my forehead. '*The VIA conductor has nothing to do and no one to talk to so she picks on me. She thinks I'm a hooligan....*'

Upon waking I need to tell Quint about my big adventure, to let him know what he missed, so I hit the door handle between cars and go in search of him. The screech of steel wheels cause me to jump in my skin as I'm wound tighter than a bedspring. I only have three cars to search, he's in the Mural Lounge beneath the Dome, deep in conversation with Tom the logger who boarded at McBride (pop.720). Don told me he lives in a cabin deep in the bush near Penny and rides the rails once a month to McBride for supplies and a rendezvous with 'Fat Susan'.

Quint introduces us and Tom offers his right hand in greeting and grabs hold of my left bicep as he shakes. 'Hey Torch, he's a big one, give him a beer,' he tells the steward with a wink, and I spend the next five minutes trying to open the beer can with crushed fingers and a dead arm as the occupants of the Mural Lounge give me the eyes. He's a strong man is old Tom, and instead of telling Quint about driving the train I get to hear Tom tell tales of logging camp fights and whores and chopping down trees in all weathers.

'Eh, Scottie, d'ya think I look like James Dean?' he asks, and lights up an 'Export A' in pose of a teenage idol. 'Yeah, but he's dead mate,' I remind him.

'Is he? Well fuck me!' he replies, scratching his head and feigning surprise.

'No thanks Tom, you're too old and ugly!' Torch the bartender tells him from behind the relative safety of his tiny bar, which brings a deep, gravel-filled laugh and a flurry of air punches from Tom, followed by a long swig of beer and a deep drag on his cigarette. Silence reigns after as we all seem to take a breath and collect our thoughts. Quint squishes into his corner seat a bit more and the steward finds another glass to polish and Tom's off somewhere in his head and the rest of us are either studying beer cans or smoking. I take the opportunity to study the logger under the guise of scribbling something important in my journal.

He's short with a barrel chest and has hands like hamhocks that appear to be veterans of fisticuffs and sharp tools; his face boasts scars too and at the grand old age of 63 I'm thinking Tom is still not the guy you want to get into a fight with. With a thinning yellowy-grey greasy quiff and the way he cocks his head as he leans in to light his cigarette and leans back in his seat to exhale....that squint, the shrug of the shoulders, hmmm, maybe in the right light he did once look like James Dean.

‘Hey Tom, you wanna beer?'

‘Sure. I'll take one off you Scottie.’ He winks at Torch as I order three beers.

‘I used to be his size once,’ he tells Torch. 'Back when the women thought I was a fuckin’ hot-rod!’

He cackles and tries to trip me with a big old muddy boot as I pass where he's sat to get to the bar but misses by a mile. ‘Got to be faster than that, Tom!’ I tell him, laugh, and pull my wallet from the chest pocket of my lumberjack shirt. ‘You telegraphed it', Quint shouts, the bartender remains neutral.

‘Jeez, he's fast, eh!’ Tom jumps up and flops back in his seat as if gut-shot and Torch decides it's okay to laugh as I pay for the beer and plonk one in front of the logger who is pretending to be a twitching corpse. I toss one to Quint and the twitching stops, the corpse awakens, opens its beer, lights up a smoke, takes a satisfied slurp and lets go a burp. I sit, dig out my journal and begin to write about surviving another day on the rails.

Time drifts. I scribble. Quint reads. Tom shares lies and second-hand smoke with Torch for a while before falling into silence. I'm feeling ready for a nap, thinking about a bite to eat, should I call home from Prince George or wait until Prince Rupert? The monotonous *ka-cha-kacha-ka-cha-kacha* of the Skeena has me nodding off....

'Come out now sweetheart don't be shy, come to old Tom!' I'm awake now. 'Come on now. Don't be shy. Let the boys see ya!' Who's he talking to? Quint is reading and Torch is re-arranging glasses. Tom's making *cooing* noises to something in his pocket and giggling lecherously. I take a long pull at my now warm beer and sneak another glance at Quint, who stares back at me with a what the hell is going on now look on his face as Tom slides his right hand slowly from his pants pocket.

'Come meet the boys now, darlin', they're waiting for you,' he cackles, and next thing he's cooing at and kissing his hand with puckered lips. I can't tear my eyes away.

'Did you miss ol' Tom, honey, did ya?' He flutters his hand, wiggles the fingers, smiling, lost to the world, and next thing he's kissing each finger individually. Quint's eyes are like saucers in his head and Torch has run out of things to polish. I'm gauging the distance to the doorway....

'You're the only one that never said no to old Tom aren't ya sweetheart. Come to the one who loves you,' and next thing James Dean is making out with his right hand like a scene from a puppeteers porno.

Total silence except for the sound of lips kissing hand. Torch breaks the ice by whistling a rendition of Burton Cummings 'These Eyes', which brings a loud snort from me. Toms attention is diverted, he looks in my direction and he isn't pleased.

'You laughing at my sweetheart, Scottie?' he barks, top lip

curled back in a snarl, coal black eyes flashing, forehead creased, chest swelled. He looks like a demented rooster and this kicks me off laughing again. He growls, makes another fist, and I await the attack. Tom growls again and asks his sweetheart if I'm laughing at him. Oh, man, no more, so I grab the hand holding my pen and tell it to tell Tom, 'yes he fucking-well is,' and at this he explodes with laughter, jumps to his feet and struts around the carriage like Mick Jagger on speed throwing jabs at imaginary foes. Torch ducks behind the bar, laughing. Quint is trying to hide under the table, creased laughing. I'm stretched out flat on the bench seat, laughing like something that's just been invented.

'What's her name, Tom? Ask her if she's got a friend'

'Shut it, you!' Tom tells Quint and resumes his shadow boxing. I haven't laughed so hard since my mate wiped his ass with fibre-glass on a building site.

Tom freezes, takes a breath, and slides a hand into the front pocket of his jeans. We hold our breath as one as he closes his eyes, sighs, groans, grinds his hips like Elvis and pulls out a key attached to a white plastic rectangle with the number nine drawn on it in black marker and throws it at Quint.

'That's in case you ever need the services of Fat Susan, you Bluenose peckerhead,' he barks, and takes off down the corridor cackling like a possessed hen before retracing his steps to hand Quint a big fat yellow joint. 'Just in case!' he shouts, and takes off again laughing down the corridor; and that was almost that for Old Tom regards him and me.

'It was this fuckin' long for chrissakes!' I heard him tell an elderly couple on my way to the washroom. He didn't see me as I watched him spread his hands as far as they'd go and cackle. He was on about the size of a fish he'd caught in a river near Penny and the elderly couple he was telling the tale to looked as if they were about to have a coronary. At Penny, he stood by the door,

winked at me, hitched his pants, zipped up his corduroy jacket and staggered off into the cold dark wilderness carrying two large taped up cardboard boxes.

Short pause for effect!

'Excuse me, can you put that away please!' Oh no, its her!
'Ah, leave him alone, Tom gave him it for god sakes!' Torch tells Colleen, still polishing glasses.

'That doesn't make it alright. No drugs on this train!' she sniffs and adjusts her scarf. 'Next thing, he'll be telling you he's old enough to drink!'

And with that parting shot at Torch she hits me with a glare and takes off down the corridor in search of terrorists or the last poor bugger to leave the seat up in the lavatory.

And, yes, Tom got his key back.

Crescent Spur, Loos, and Dome Creek, like Penny, are left behind in our wake. This stretch of line has got to be the remotest between Jasper and Prince George. Ghost towns that once boasted lumber mills all look to be closed down. Hansard Bridge is crossed safely and we sail into Longworth, glide through Hutton and cruise by Sinclair Mills and McGregor. We're due to dock in Prince George around 8pm, which leaves plenty of time to find a place to stay. Relaxed, recovered from Jaspers excesses, I settle back in my seat and get stuck into Swing Hammer Swing, when Quint drops by to tell me Don the driver has offered us a spare room for the night at his place in Prince George, which he accepted with offers of crates of Guinness as payment. The Skeena follows the Fraser River slowly through Giscome, Shelley, to deliver us at our destination only thirty minutes late, which Quint blames on my driving skills. My book makes a beautiful arc before bouncing off his head, and at this juncture, I'll leave you with another Tom story so I can retrieve the book from the washroom Quint just dumped it in.

Tom had been into town on his monthly sojourn and had ended up a tad more 'into the spirit of things' than usual but still managed to hail the train at McBride and board with his supplies. The conductor at the time was temporary and Tom didn't know him and he didn't know Tom, so the engineer explained to the conductor that Tom was to be put off at Penny no matter what. Tom hit the bar car and it hit him back and the next thing the old logger knows the temporary conductor is helping him off the Skeena at McBride. It's a mid-winters night, pitch dark and freezing as Tom picked up his boxes and headed into the bush, sure of foot, singing as he went, unarmed except for two fists and a room key. He walked for miles following the moon, still singing, and couldn't find his cabin for love nor money and decided someone must have moved it for a prank while he was away. He told me he'd had a long walk back when it had dawned on him that he'd been let off on the wrong side of the train as the station had been under reconstruction and they'd repositioned the rails. Have boxes will travel!

PRINCE GEORGE

8:30pm. In the rain, Prince George Station reminds me of a smaller version of Lime Street Station, I tell Quint as we load up Donny's truck with backpacks, suitcases and old people. It seems the engineer is a regular taxi service and saviour of stray travelers. We leave the Skeena behind to drop off a sweet old pair of American wine lovers at their motel before hitting the Beer Store for our part of the bargain regards Don. Guinness please!

They couple offered Don a bottle of wine from the Napa Valley in exchange for the ride, but he just laughed, declined, and flung open the truck doors. Mr. Napa informed us that they've been traveling together for sixty-seven years, never had a fight, and unfortunately this trip may be their last due to unforseen circumstances. At this, he put his arm around her and gave her a kiss on the cheek, and this show of 'seniors' affection in a cramped vehicle had me staring out the window, holding in tears while trying to think of things other than distant loved ones. At their hotel, Mr. Napa has tears in his eyes as we carry their luggage into the lobby. Mrs. Napa hugs us and her husband shakes our hands and wishes us all the best, and we leave them behind, waving and blowing kisses to mask the emotion.

The remainder of the night is spent sat at Donny's kitchen table telling tales and jokes. The Guinness is good and around midnight we're interrupted by the engineer's wife, home from work and not at all surprised to find two half-drunk malingerers hid behind a mountain of beer cans. Her husband is famous for bringing home strays and she's used to it. She shakes her head, laughs and pops the cork from a bottle of white wine, as her friend finishes shaking out a soaked umbrella on the step before joining us for a drink. 'It's Friday night,' she says. 'No work in the morning!' And we agree. Good people, good times, good cheer!

7am, Saturday, November 7th. One hundred and thirteen years to the day that Donald Smith drove the last spike into the ground at Craigellachie, I'm stood not far from Dons house freezing my arse off on the banks of the roaring Fraser River. I'm in awe at the ferocity of it as it meets up with the Nechako. They greet each other violently, embrace, and roar southwest on the long journey to the Pacific; its a good thing they seem to get along so well.

I'm beginning to find Canada again, I'm thinking, and experience a *buzz-buzz* in my stomach and a feeling of falling in love again with something or someone always loved. I'll be heading towards the Pacific too as soon as Don wakes up. And just like that he appears at his front door, slams it, coffee in hand, and unlocks his truck rubbing sleep from his eyes. He's ready to drive his new pals to the Iron Horse restaurant across from Prince George station, where the breakfast is cheap and the women are easy, I was told by another engineer.

'Railway people eat there - it must be good!' He told me yesterday. My stomach crackles, groans, rumbles and moans at the thought of greasy food but my head rings clear. 'I feel good, lads!' I tell my companions in travel, as we wind our way through the empty rain-soaked streets of the city on a dark and overcast Saturday morning.

Prince George (pop: 75,000) is an industrious river city in a northern English vernacular, I announce to snorts, as I wipe down a foggy window and peer out at rain-spattered people stood in ones and twos at traffic lights that illuminate downtown streets in oranges, reds, and greens. The rain pours down and washes away Friday night, as I cram as much into my memory-bank as possible, as Quint chats away to Don about Halifax, Nova Scotia again. It's their hometown. Small world isn't it!

I learned last night that Prince George is the biggest city in northern British Columbia and boasts the University Of Northern British Columbia as source of student entertainment. Pulp and paper mills are still the main industry here, but despite that and the oil refinery, unemployment is a problem. Prince George remains a hotspot for Bikers, and like the bookstore owner said, it *can* be a tough place depending on where you get lost. I hope to explore more on the return trip next week.

Highway 16, the Trans-Canada, also known as the Yellowhead Highway, runs east/west through here on its way to Prince Rupert from Edmonton, occasionally crossing paths. Quint and I have followed this long and winding road for 737 kilometres. Highway 97 runs south from the Yukon, through Prince George, and carries on to meet the Oregon Trail on the west coast of the US of A. You can drive to anywhere on the continent from this city by car and the first humans to inhabit the place were the Carrier Sekani who traditionally carried remains of dead husbands with them for three years in a bag (Janice!) Things were pretty peaceful around here until explorer Alexander Mackenzie made his way through on his well-documented, *Crossing the Continent 1793 tour*, and just about ruined it.

Simon Fraser also stopped by in 1807, on his journey down the river that would eventually bear his name, and on this journey he set up an outpost which he named Fort George after his King, George III; the nobhead who let America break free from *The Empire* without so much as a scuffle. The Madness of King George indeed. According to the movie, the poor bugger was more interested in what was in his morning chamber pot than what lay across the Ocean, and at this point in time I know the feeling. Not again!

Meanwhile, Fort George remained as a trading post until the Grand Trunk Pacific Railway moved in around 1912, followed by The Great Pacific Eastern Railway, who stuck its nose in to take a piece of the action. Bob's your uncle - Prince George, *The Crossroads of the North*. But enough for now I have a train to catch.

7:45am aboard the Skeena: same seat, same crew, same condition. A good trip so far and a thirst to write (and drink) are being sated. I've been presented with oodles of visual and aural substance of which I hope do justice to and treat with respect. I've decided I want to be a writer. If not my paintbrushes and ladders are awaiting back home. Don booked me the use of his couch on the return journey to Toronto. He won't be driving with me today as he's on a spot of leave, which is too bad, as it would have been cool to see the look on my mate Brads face as I drove the Skeena through Terrace; he'd be well impressed.

Unfortunately, we missed breakfast at the Iron Horse due to a slow as molasses old waiter who was swamped with orders. *Breakfast in America* was playingand from a sound system that looked and sounded to have been born before the waiter. Exit two starving bastards who made do with free VIA coffee and a muffin at the station. I couldn't find a newspaper or public phone either, what can you do?

At this moment in time I intend to do nothing except entertain myself by reading Berton's description of the driving of the Last Spike at Craigellachie which is vivid and awesome to say the least. It has me dreaming of riding the train that runs through Eagle Pass to relive the experience. I should phone Orangeville tonight but it'll be too late to talk to the kids as they'll be in bed. Can't get in gear today, I'm suffering from train-lag again and the haunted camera is acting up. Next time I'll use a disposable. If this camera where mine, I'd dispose of it alright, straight out the window into the Nechako, the fast-moving river we've been following through logging towns and lumberjack scenarios since Prince George. It's the source of power for Alcan, the Aluminum smelting factory Brad works at in Kitimat. I should take a leak out the window instead to see if he gets the message.

I wonder who Baldy Hughes was as they thought enough of him or her to name a town after Baldy just south of here. I'm picturing a cartoon skinhead Elmer Fudd with crazy eyes in hobnail boots and a lumberjack shirt sucking on a big fat stogie character, as we pass through the town of Wedgewood (give us a wedgie Benn!) as a bashful sun picks this moment to peek through mist and rain that hides picturesque views of mountain peaks. Giant spruce trees guard either side of the rail line. They look as healthy as the gaggle of swans that glide to and fro in a clearing on the Nechako, as the Skeena waits patiently in a siding for a freight train to finish its passing so we can continue on our journey. A logging camp sits deserted in a clearing, the slipstream from a passing train is rocking me to sleep. It must be ten miles long, but I manage to stay awake to record a colony of beaver munching the legs from under a magnificent fir tree.

Beavers are good at their job, very industrious. They remind me of construction workers in Toronto as they go about their business. Mighty beaver all looking busy while white hatted bosses keep watch over them ready to dock pay at a moments notice. I asked Don yesterday why a line of trackside trees had been sliced to about waist height on an average bear. 'Was it a specialized train, mate?' 'You seen the size of the beaver in these parts buddy!' Yeah, its a specialised train with a big saw.

A log cabin sits to my left with a fresh bearskin nailed to it drying in the sun. A bald eagle sits tall in a treetop and surveys the river and the log cabin. Fort Fraser beckons so we stop for a minute at a former trading post built by Simon Fraser himself in 1806. Another last spike was hammered home here on April 7th, 1914, upon completion of the Grand Trunk Pacific Railway. Fraser Lake appears, followed by another Fraser Lake! Simon must have been one egotistical bastard or he smoked a lot of weed, or maybe they just had problems thinking up new names for things back then.

Fraser Lake II is famous for its molybdenum mine. Molybdenum being a metal element used for the hardening of steel and this molybdenum mine is the biggest producer of molybdenum in the world.Great name molybdenum. Sounds like an Irish drinking song. I'll wager with your money, as I wave at Endako (population 90), that Fraser was glad he jumped aboard a rickety raft to float down a river to find two lakes so that he could name them after himself. Imagine the after- party as they relaxed around a roaring camp fire, rums or bums in hand; well-pleased with themselves with all the exploring and naming as bright stars twinkled above and insects entertained.

'I say chaps. Let's call this country-Fraser!'

Deep in thought arse and head scratching....

'May I suggest it be named the Dominion of Simon!'

'Good idea, Endako, old chap. Now pass that bloody rum bottle!' Cheers of agreement from all in attendance as Fraser hops aboard a tree stump to hush them.

'Lads, I think I have an anthem!' Intakes of breath.

'Don't be shy sir, let's hear it!' Rumbles of agreement.

'O Simon Fraser, our cold and native land....' Dancing ensues.

Lakes Burns and Rose slip by, next up is Houston, named after a newspaper baron. It was called Pleasant Valley before he showed up though. A large sign welcomes us to Houston which boasts a Legion, a Rotary Club, and the world's biggest fly-fishing rod. A Tim Horton's sits surveying the scene as vehicles enter its body like ants through a rotting apple core. 'Houston we have a problem!'

'Wassup?'

'We're out of cream, sugar, and orange crullers.'

In space no one runs out of cream!

Aye, I know, it's been a long day. I'm stricken with exhaustion with it all at Houston. I can't keep my eyes open any longer....until Smithers (pop.5800) awakens me at 2.10pm Greenwich Mean Time. Thank you Sir Sanford Fleming.

On the platform at Smithers, Conductor Colleen finds and informs me, as I tried to hide in the shadow of mountains that surround, that Smithers is a service centre for forestry and mining, as passengers of all ages and description on the loose scramble about in search of free coffee or anything worth capturing on film. The old station is in midst of a re-shingle and closed up tighter than a duck's arse. No chance of coffee here unfortunatley. A now bored crowd gather beneath a peeling, tattered station sign waiting for something to happen. The Napa couple want me in on a group photo for some reason. 'Come on fella, you're in on it with us all too,' growls Mister Napa. In on what, I'm thinking and join the herd. Another couple insist I make an appearance in one of their photographs and a complete stranger hooks me for a third. I feel like Santa at the mall. A dozen 'seniors' snatch me and next thing all passengers are stood smiling beneath the flaking sign grinning, acting daft and shouting CHEESE and PIZZA at a dozen lenses. Flashes blind as we take turns shuffling back and forward to snap or pose. I'll be blinded for the rest of the day with all the flashing but I don't care, I tell them all before falling onto the track. This is one of them moments, I'm thinking as a hundred hands appear to pull me back aboard the station concourse. Someone snaps the moment using a Polaroid Land Camera and I'm laughing so hard I give myself a headache. I'll never forget Smithers. Too bad I don't have a photo. You guessed it. Argh!

On a sad note, I watched from the window of the train as a native family waved their pre-teen boy off this morning at Prince George. Don't know why but I kept an eye out for him, said hello a couple of times in passing, he seemed a nice kid. I just said goodbye to him as he made his way past us lunatics and wished him well. He replied in kind and asked me for a dollar. This annoyed me but then made me sad as I'd just been reading about the railroad that helped cut off his ancestors from their way of life and forced his relatives onto welfare, reserves and reservations, and helped take away their dignity and pride. I felt more than a little ashamed of my heritage as he walked off into downtown Smithers with his dollar. 'I'm a British subject and I'm proud of it, I carry the burden of shame,' by UB40 came to mind.

The Annex. Toronto's Annex neighborhood was in decline in the winter of '85. Trying to make up its mind whether to fall victim to neon and new money like its southern funky punky neighbour, Queen Street West, or remain the last bastion of Hippiedom in little Hungary. I lived in a bachelor apartment on Walmer Road, and would pop into a local pizza joint for a take-out on Thursday evenings after work and read the NOW, or EYE magazine, while waiting for my order. Sometimes I'd slip in a quick Black Label lager while waiting. I liked the place. It was owned by a friendly Asian family and the ambience was quiet and homey, just how I liked it.

I was in there one wintery Thursday, when the door flew open and in blew fresh snow and four native guys who looked like they'd been on the street for a while. The place was empty apart from me and they made their way silently to the front counter, stopped in a damp huddle, and waited for a tall, well-mannered young man with long black hair in a ponytail to speak. He smiled and ordered four beers from a suddenly nervous server, who called out to the owner, might have been her father, bringing him from the store room or kitchen, spatula in hand. He took one look at his customers, sucked in his belly, and yelled '*NO BEER, NO SERVE!*' Banged on the counter with his spatula and pointed at the front door. I watched in amazement and disbelief as all four turned on their heels and traipsed out into the swirling snow and neon lights like scolded children. The door slammed in its frame, shutting out the sound of traffic and a Salvation Army band. More than a little confused, I confronted the owner who stood alone behind the counter. He smiled at me. 'Why didn't you serve them?' I asked him, as he placed my pizza on the countertop.

'All Indians drunks!' He said quietly, and made his way to the till to take my money. 'They were here long before you and me mate.'

'Still drunks!'

I told him where to shove his pizza and walked out wishing I had belted him. I could hear him yelling as I made my way down the street to a Hungarian joint called The Castle in the bowels of a dark, dank building decorated with peeling medieval coats of arms and rusted iron railings, where the goulash was cheap, the draft cold, and the racism generally non-existent.

Memories play tag as The Skeena passes Moricetown, a vital fishing site for 5,000 years, and traverses roller-coaster-like trestle bridges at Boulder Creek, before snaking through three tunnels (one 630 metres in length) at Bulkley Canyon, to arrive somewhat breathless at New Hazleton. Which sits amidst a spectacular panorama view of rivers Skeena and Bulkley that clash in a mish-mash of color and murderous rapids at the base of a mountain named *Stegyawden* by the Gitksan people thousands of years ago. Nineteenth century miners renamed it *Rocher Deboule,* but it doesn't look like a box of chocolates to me.

In a small house in Paris all covered in vines,
lived two little girls in two straight lines.
- Ludwig Bemelman

I make conversation with an easily amused, elderly lady, as she attempts to marshal a small boy away from death by steep stairs as he charges from one window to another laughing himself silly. My Grandad fed me sugar 'butty' sandwiches at this kid's age but I never had such energy. She tells me it's his first train trip and has just finished eating a chocolate bar. She's familiar with the distance I've traveled to watch her stop her grandson from falling down said stairs as she's just bought two horses from a stud farm on the outskirts of Orangeville. I ask her how she intends to get them all the way back here. '*By Rail of course*!' she shouts, and is gone, last seen chasing her grandson around a car park at Kitwanga station. The Skeena kicks into gear and slowly gathers momentum-and while laughing at grandma's attempts to strap the lad into a car seat, I'm buzzed in the belly by a thousand bees of memories that surface as raindrops spatter glass: Retiring to bed after a few drinks watching the Ken Loach film, Riff-Raff, with an old pal, and leaving my sleeping daughter in her pram in the hall after bidding him goodnight from the front stoop, to wake up at 2am remembering where she was. I was mortified!

Vacuuming the living room carpet as my son choked on in the kitchen. I couldn't hear him coughing despite being in the next room with the door open. I took a look and his face was blue. In a frozenpanic I yanked him from his highchair, straps and all, to back-slap an unchewed apple slice that pinged off the fridge door like a dart from a blowpipe and just missed George the cat.

A sleeping Madeline ejected from her red plastic wagon as I bounced it up and over a high kerb on the main drag. Not noticing how much lighter the wagon was I kept on whistling and walking until an out of breath old-timer caught up to alert me that she was lying on the sidewalk still asleep.

We had a pet squirrel named Sammy, he showed up one day with a sibling and we let them bunk in the garden shed at the bottom of the garden, where they would frolic and perform acrobatics in tree's and allow us to feed them birdseed and fruit. The sibling went missing and Sammy got closer and decided he liked hanging out inside a padded sweater I wore. It had a hole in the armpit which he used to climb in, for a nap at first, but then he sort of moved in. One day we went to the grocery store and while unloading groceries at the checkout Sammy came alive and the cashier asked me what was moving about inside my sweater. I told her and she didn't believe me so I raised my right arm to the ceiling and Sammy popped his head out, which didn't go down well. She screamed and we had to leave without the groceries. Sammy moved house to a birdbox hung in a tree on the patio and would made frequent appearances throughout what remained of the summer and then he was gone. I think I still have the sweater somewhere and Leaders let us back in eventually.

William looking up at me with admiration as I told a neighbour about being attacked by a family of raccoons that had been using his paddling pool to bathe in during the night and how they had surrounded me grunting, hissing, and cursing, as I chased them off with a three-bristled broom wearing only boxer shorts.

We always had cats around our first house in Orangeville. One winter morning I got a call from a Chiropractor whose business was on a busy corner of a main street. 'We have your cat, can you come pick it up please?' Good thing we had the collar engraved, I told the kids and went off to retrieve the runaway. 'I've come for the cat, thanks for letting me know. Sorry if he was a nuisance!' The receptionist alerted the boss, who appeared from a back room carrying a black garbage bag which he handed to me, full of apologies. 'What's this?' I opened the bag and there was our cat, frozen and flattened into a wafer about two feet long with its tongue hanging out. 'Jesus! What happened to him?' The receptionist found him first thing that morning. He'd been run over and flipped onto the snowbank covering the lawn. He had a tire mark the length of his....'Sir, can you put him back in the bag please, patients are passing out!' I apologised, re-bagged the cat, thanked everyone in the waiting room for being so kind and took off home with the bad news, again. We never had much luck with cats.

Madeline bouncing on our bed, falling off and breaking her arm and upon arrival at the hospital telling staff that her mom did it. She was mortified!

William having a seizure as I carried him into a cold shower fully-clothed, as police, fire, and ambulance screamed to a halt on the front lawn. I'd miscalculated the amount of medication to give him for an ear infection. They had him sorted in to time but it would be best to take him to Sick Kids just in case, and boy did they get a laugh waiting for me in the ambulance as I changed clothes twice before leaving the house. Shock, they told me, but my son was fine.

Madeline grabbing a much older bully by the throat and chasing him up the street after he'd attacked her brother with a hockey stick, and...I have to stop with the memories, the replays, take a deep breath, photos from my wallet, heart pumping away in the front seat of a roller-coaster as the Specials play that tune again to an empty hall. What *am* I doing here?

I'm reminded of another cat, George. He had wobbly eyes like George Bell the ball player when I got him as a kitten. Crazy cat. Thought he was a dog. Nutso, but I loved him. At the table during dinner one evening he insisted on parading around showing us his bum. 'What's up mate, what's wrong?' He looked unhappy so I bent down to take a closer look. Something black was peeking out so I took hold with finger and thumb and pulled as he walked away slowly, swaying from side to side as the thing got longer, and tighter, and longer, and he kept walking. Thwack! the slimy black thing pinged and hit me on the hand. Never saw such a happy cat. He'd been in the clothes hamper, ripped up my favourite pair of underpants and swallowed the elastic.

Changing the tune a bit, I join Quint downstairs in the Park Car, and in no time at all we have the 'been confined too long again brain storms', during which he suggests I should have taken a photo of every washroom I've used on this trip for the coffee-table version of 'Shitting across Canada'. I agree and suggest it be oversized like his head. We envision crap reviews from constipated critics as he performs an arse-wiping mime as we pass through another ghost town named Cedervale, or 'Dumpville' according to the degenerate I shared a hotel room with in Jasper. He's got a point, Cedervale looks to be a scary place from here, no sign of life, abandoned shacks and the rusting remains of a Volkswagen Beetle placed strategically close to the track. 'Fuck off whites' is sprayed on one side in orange Day-Glo paint. And we do, as fast as The Skeena can carry us. For a short while all are silent.

The mountain to our left resembles a luscious breast, and according to local legend the mountain range this mountain belongs to is 'The Seven Sisters Peaks'. I make a note to find out if the sisters were famous in these parts for ample bosoms. I read this to Quint who laughs and copies the quote to his journal. Talk of getting the giggles in church while in charge of my sisters whilst waiting for a white-gloved hand to tap me on the side of the head followed by the whispered threat of imminent death if I didn't behave. Now we're safe to giggle all we want now and Quint suggests I jump off at Penny on the way back and pay Tom a surprise visit. We discuss how close to his cabin I would get before he'd stroll outside guns blazing like the outlaw Josie Wales, and as I lay dying in the snow the last thing I would see in this life would be Tom gazing lovingly at his right hand, *Nice shootin' sweetheart, come back up here to 'ol Tom!*

At 5pm the engineer gives five rings of the bell as the town of Doreen appears from out of the fog like a John Carpenter novel; another apparition in a series of lonesome town sightings. I overhear Colleen tell a passenger that Doreen was founded by a trapper named Old John who lived here with his six wives in the fur trading days. Seven Sisters, six wives, five bells, ding -dong old timer!

Quint reckons they must have all ran off and left him as the place looks like a female hand hasn't taken a broom to it for years. At this I take aim and hit him on the side of the head with the mouldering remains of a sandwich crust found in an ashtray in the arm of my seat, as Terrace, my eventual destination, comes into view. I get the urge to suddenly alight (flame on, Torch!) and end the journey here, but decide at the last minute to stay the course, I'd never forgive myself. I can't bail out now, besides Prince Rupert can't be too far off. Another freight train screams by in the dark and rocks us in its wake. The last three hours have taken forever. We've spent most of it sat meekly in the trenches, a victim of the pecking order in the western rail world - bottom of the food chain, stuck on the rails forever, whatever, and as I peer through yet another fogged up window I spot a bar called The Skeena – and have thoughts about nipping in there to call Brad. If he turns up we can wave from the departing Skeena as we disappear around a bend laughing into the night. Nah, better not, I need somewhere to stay, but it would tickle his carpenters funny bone.

The last two hours on the Skeena are spent in the company of Theresa from Dublin, as she sits holding court sipping at a large plastic cup filled with what she says, is gin but smells like gasoline.

'It's only Tonic water, son.' she assures me, sat balanced on the arm of the seat in front attacking all within hearing distance with tales of the 'owl' country, and most are in stitches. I join in and we swap well-honed lies and share the devils lemon brew from the same cup. An elderly, grey-haired gent joins in with his stories; he's been listening to us for miles, he tells us. 'I couldn't help but overhear just how much fun you guys were having.... mind if I join in?'

'Nahhh, that's alright my love, just plonk your lovely self here!' Theresa cackles, and pats an empty seat arm.

The gent had been a Tail Gunner in the Royal Canadian Air Force and flown twenty-four missions over Germany. He wanted to tell us all about it, and we listened attentively as he told us about the night his plane was hit by 'ack-ack' and ended up in the drink and how he and his crew were captured by the Germans and locked up for the rest of the war and how upon arrival home in 1946, the government had refused him a pension because he'd been presumed dead and not a prisoner of war. We commiserated and called those in charge of such things all the names under the sun and more, and at this he got quite emotional. Fifty years later he still hasn't received any compensation from Ottawa and has long since given up trying. Theresa poured him a drink, gave him a hug, and invited him to dance. I offered to get my gob iron out and Quint volunteered to sing

'Whiskey You're the Devil' if he would, and this got him laughing. The look on his face was as memorable as his wife's when she made an appearance to rescue her beaming husband and whisk him to safety. She told us she didn't think he'd had that much fun since he leapt from his burning plane.

Theresa is short, dark-haired, middle-aged, dressed for cold climates and has the knack for making anyone laugh. 'Eh! Are you from Liverpool?' She inquired loudly in the cozy confines of the Mural Lounge not long after Tom had departed the Skeena. 'Yeah, don't tell anyone!' I'd replied, stood at the bar waiting for Torch to crack the code and remove plastic-wrap from a sandwich he'd been selling to me for miles.

'A Scouser! Eh, Scouser, get your arse over here now!' And that was me finished regards any peace and quiet for the duration of the trip. We sat and entertained ourselves about all things 'over der' convinced nobody could possibly decipher our accents, but to our amazement the crowd grew larger as the tales grew longer, the accents thicker, and Theresa's laugh louder as the ate up the track.

Time spent with her reminded me of long ago trips on a charrabang (coach) to Blackpool or Southport on stag nights or birthday parties with friends and family. Singing and cavorting, telling jokes, suit jackets off, sleeves rolled up, ready for anything as routine was left behind in exhaust fumes.

Saturday night in Blackpool. 'Get the ale in, Mally.'

'It's your Paul's round!'

'Is it shite I got the last one in! '

'Wahayyy!'

'Sound!'

We disembark into more drizzle at an ocean-side platform at Prince Rupert station. Thoughts of what family and friends might think of me making it this far west flash through my transmogrified head. I'm reminded of something I read this morning in Berton's book, written by another immigrant covering the Riel Rebellion in 1885:

Until the coming of the railway, all of the North West had been like a great desert with scattered oases of population, each sufficient unto itself. Now, the cross-fertilization process had begun. A new kind of Canadian, the 'Westerner' was making his first impact on the men from the sober east. He belonged to a more open-handed and less rigid society; over the century that followed he would help to change the country.

One war correspondent's description of a prairie town mirrored the astonishment of an Ontario city man on first coming up against western life:

"Here is where the man who has a turn that way can study the human face divine, and the human dress astonishing. Men well dressed, fully dressed, commonly dressed; awfully dressed, shabbily dressed, partly dressed; Men sober, nearly sober, half drunk, nearly drunk, quite drunk, frightfully drunk, howling drunk, dead drunk; Men from Canada, the States, the United Kingdom and from almost every state in Europe; men enormously rich and frightfully poor, but all have a free and easy manner which is highly refreshing to a man fresh from the east who is accustomed to the anxious expressions of men in our silent streets at home."

PRINCE RUPERT

8:30pm, Saturday, November 7th. Quint and I take turns to lob stones into the Pacific Ocean, 4,730 kilometres from Toronto, an equal distance between Hogtown and the city of Liverpool, England, I believe. I'm a bit disoriented, brain going a mile-a-minute, amazed to be here as I bid fond farewells to fellow travelers. Theresa is subdued upon sight of her husband, which surprises me, she seemed to just switch off. The Napa's and friends are tired but excited. The veteran looks to be disoriented. We find a pay phone and free hot coffee inside a warm station and I take a moment to compose myself as Quint talks to his mum in Nova Scotia.

I'm feeling rather pleased by completing the first leg of the journey, I tell Janice, as passengers within hearing distance listen in. I try to explain a feeling of accomplishment as a First Nations elder sits rocking in a chair waiting patiently for a taxi. She smiles a toothless smile from across the waiting room and I smile back. I think she knows exactly what I'm thinking and the situation I find myself in. Janice tells me she's excited for me and has a girlfriend over for a beer so we don't get too mushy, which is good as Quint is stood in front of me sipping on a coffee with a grin plastered all over his newspaper-ink-smudged face, laughing at me now as I had at him during his conversation with his mom.

I tell Janice I'll call back in the morning to talk to the kids, as they're in bed again, I'm off for a walk into town to find a warm doorway to curl up in and hang up to the sound of her laughter. The feeling of what its like to be stood here at the doorway to the other side of the world I had tried to explain but couldn't find the words. If we were to commandeer one of numerous fishing boats tethered here and set sailwould we end up in Japan? I know one thing for sure, it wouldn't be the Isle of Man. Ramsay, Douglas, dirty postcards and Manx kippers are as far, far away, as the Budokan but its sure smells the same.

Prince Rupert (pop: 17,000), named after the cousin of Charles II, is the halibut capital of the world, the fishing capital of the northwest coast, the terminus of the Yellowhead Highway, the City of Rainbows, over-shadowed by Mount Oldfield (cue Tubular Bells and the theme from The Exorcist).

That's quite the resume. I'd love to stand here for a while longer gazing out to sea poetically but we have to find a room for the night with a tub, as I'm in need of a hot bath and a change of clothes again, my smalls have taken on a life of their own. My backpack filled with un-needed items is bloody heavy as we trudge up steep Bill Murray Drive. Groundhog Day wasn't that good was it?Groundhog Day wasn't that good was it?

We moan and groan our way in the general direction of downtown. A man stood staring out to sea having a conversation with his dog points the way as a convoy of taxi's leave us behind like wayward turtles. To prove the point we almost fall in the inky black ocean in while following bright city lights.

'Wonder why they never called this John Candy Avenue?'

'Because Canadian Bacon was shite, I reply, and advise him to stop staring through tinted windows of muscle cars occupied by large local men sporting flat-top haircuts or mullets, and fortunately for us, he does, as some occupants look ornery and bad, man, but we manage to survive the trek and have no problem finding a room at The Rupert Hotel, which is as deserted as the waterfront.

It's off-season, I remind Quint, as we fork over thirty dollars apiece to a smirking, stoned desk clerk with a bad bleach job and assorted metal things inserted in both spud filled ears. It's Quint's turn to fill in registry forms so I take a gander about the lobby the closed restaurant. While liberating a handful of tourist leaflets from a display on the lobby wall I overhear the desk clerk ask Quint if he wants separate beds, which gets a laugh from me and the 'dancer' stood beside me amidst a cloud of Obsession perfume. Quint laughs too. '*Whattayouthink*?'

'Just asking,' Blondie replies nonchalantly which draws more laughs. With a wink to the lady in the high-heels and tight-mini, I tell Quint to book a single if its cheaper, which brings more laughter from her. He takes the double and we make our way to the elevatorwhere a potted plant skulks waiting to attack but we scare it off.

The room is neat and clean with requested beds and the bathroom comes equipped with a large bath, loads of fluffy towels, and oodles of Aloe Cream products, ha, all mine!

A surprise awaits upon opening heavy drapes that fill a large bay window as a grandstand view of what appears to be Prince Rupert's entertainment district unfolds. I'm sat here watching drunks get arrested by nasty looking coppers on the main street as I wolf down a burger and fries and swig on a bottle of Sam

Smiths.

The view is worth the expense, as are the supplies we picked up at Al's, a Happy Days-style burger joint situated on the lakeshore across from the Liquor Store (open late seven days a week!) where I spent half an hour talking to a Greek owner who told me that Prince Rupert is losing its young people fast and furious due to a lack of jobs. 'Nothing for them to do here anymore, the place is dying on its feet!' he sang to an empty room. He warned me to stay away from certain downtown bars, but I forgot to ask which.

Its been seven long years, but I love you just the same.

Anticipating an early night with the television, I dialled Brad's number from a public phone outside the hotel being too cheap to call from the room. I wanted to let him know where I was staying how much I was looking forward to setting eyes on him, Tanya, and the kids in the morning, let him know how good it was to be in town and great it was going to be to grab a hot bubbly bath and hit the big comfortable bed early.

'Ha-ha, no way Paulie, he's on his way to find you!' laughed Tanya. She told me Brad was on his way as he'd hardly been able to sleep for days and that he'd booked off work early. This was all a surprise to me, I told her. He should have been there hours ago, she said. 'Ah, he's probably stopped off at church on the way so he doesn't have to go in the morning,' I offered, and bade her a goodnight until tomorrow.

Back in the room, a bit puzzled regards the phone call, I stuffed myself with junk food, knocked back a couple of beers and fell asleep on the bed spilling half a beer over myself in the process.

Quint's large loud laugh brings me back from the dead. He's tucked up in bed watching LA Confidential, the only free movie in the hotel system, and by sound of things well worth price it. I peel beery clothes from my body with a Swiss Army knife and fill the tub full of hot water and soapy things - looking forward to a good night cuddled up in clean cotton sheets - and after forcing my wrinkly but clean forty year old body from that tub full of hot soapy water, I'm engulfed in big fluffy towels, drying myself off, ready for bed, when the phone on the dresser goes '*Ring-ring*! and stupidly, I answered it.

'Paul?'

'Yeah!'

'Where are you?'

'You phoned me, you should know!'

'I did and it's me!'

'Sorry, you've got the wrong number.' I can't resist.

'It's me, what are you doing?'

'You can hang up now Blondie,' I tell the desk clerk and a feint click tells me he has. 'That you Brad?'

'Yeah, its me you (sound of breaking glass) you...who's Blondie?'

'Just an admirer mate. How are you where are you?' A male voice yells '*Show us the pelt baby*!' in the background as Axle Rose wails about patience, more yelling followed by a scream.

'I'm in a bar, Paul.'

'Sounds like jail. Which one mate?'

'I don't know.' Which draws a big laugh from both of us. I pick at the plastic that keeps the lamp-shade clean and tell him I'm in bed knackered, as Quint snores tucked up in his bed.

'With the blonde?'

'Yeah, he's blonde,' I laugh, knowing what's coming next.

'Well, get your clothes on coz I'm coming to get you!'

'Brad.'

'Yeah?' Smashing glass, more yelling, cheering, I'm not looking forward to this.

'Hang on. Gotta get me a pen... HEY BUDDIE! YEAH YOU! YOU GOTTA PEN? WHAT? YOU ...OH YEAH!' The *clank* of the reciever bouncing off something hard.

'Paul! You still there?'

'Yeah!'

'Give me the name of the place....'

I oblige and shuffle into a clean pair of jeans. Quint is awake and laughing, remote in hand, as I tell Brad the name of the hotel, slam down the phone, and pull on a clean teeshirt.

'Told you he was a nutter, didn't I?'

'You're not going out are you? It's late!' He looks amazed. 'I am!' I tell him, sliding cuffed jeans over boots. 'I'll see you later. Be good and don't let Blondie in!'

Waiting for the elevator I think I hear Quint laughing but it may be just the wind. I get the feeling I'm headed for trouble.

Brad's waiting for me in the lobby sporting a big grin. Still got the skinny sideburns, short hair, tall and handsome, built like a wiry short-stop, he'd still look good in Yankee pinstripes. He always had a sense of style; distressed brown leather jacket, Wrangler jeans and work-boots, the hillbilly from the big city look. We hug, play fight, and hug again. He's drunk. 'If you knew which hotel to call how come I had to give you the name of the place?'

'Cold calls.'

'Ah, clever arse!' We saunter outside and into the backseat of a waiting cab, where we resume fighting. The driver ignores us, drives about two hundred yards and stops in front of a bar.

'This it guys?'

'Yeah, thanks,' Brad tells him and hands over three one dollar bills. The driver is not amused. He wants to know why we didn't walk. I take the three back and hand him a five, tell him to keep the change, which he does, and we vacate the rusting vehicle into pouring rain.

'Does it ever stop raining here?' I ask Brad, and retrace steps to pull him from a lake in the sidewalk.

'Nope, not in this shithole, and don't cross the street on a red, man. Look at this it's worse than Toronto,' he spits, and pulls a jay walking ticket from his coat pocket.

'Where did you get that?'

'Crossing the street to get in that cab.'

'Expensive trip!' We enter the bar like gunslingers. where I immediately regret not wearing a hard hat. A dancer is doing her bit on a tiny stage at the foot of a mountain-range of inebriated locals, one of whom is wearing a raccoon hat. We cut through a dark room to the bar and something flies past my head.

'What the hell was that? I ask, as Brad orders beer.

'Looked like a platform shoe to me,' he replies, as Stray Cat Strut reverbrates from unsafe overhead speakers.

He points stage left and we make our way over to a table occupied by two friends of his. I'm introduced, bottles are *clinked,* hands shook, and Brad and I attempt to catch up over questions from his stoned pals and the roar of the crowd, which roars anew as a fresh meat is introduced to the arena. She's tough and articulate and has the animals in the palm of her hand in seconds. Brad's pals whoop and holler, the crowd joins in, the dancer smiles our way, I look to the ceiling and take a long pull on my beer. What am I doing...? Brad gives me the thumbs-up so I settle in, luckily for the short haul, because just like that, the bar is closed, shutters are up, and the sidewalk is full of drunks, most of who are heading towards a nearby dance club where Brad's pals want to go. My warning system is on red alert and I talk my pal into coming back to my room for a beer instead, besides the place looks like a whorehouse.

Relieved to find his car where he left it, we liberate a box of beer from the trunk via the backseat as the key won't open it, and slip through the chaos and commotion of late night Prince Rupert to the safety of the hotel; where Blondie's not at his post and the potted plants have escaped.

The wee hours are spent catching-up and sipping beer by the light from behind a half-closed washroom door as Quint sleeps. Brad asks if I have any shoe polish or a magic marker and I tell him to behave. Quint's not waking up with a make-over. What a reunion. It really couldn't have happened any other way.

Sunday, November 8th, 9:00am. The sun finally shines on Prince Rupert as I share a farewell breakfast with Quint jammed into a corner table next to the kitchen door by a none-too-friendly hotel restaurant waitress. Brad sleeps it off in my bed, dead to the world after his big day out.

This is the end of the road for Quint and I. Boswell and Johnson we aren't, yet, but we've had a laugh and it's time to part ways, separate destinations await. He's headed to the Charlotte Islands and I'm off to Terrace as soon as soft lad upstairs wakes up. Quint's been great company, an avid listener, a good friend and I'll miss him, I tell him. I hope hanging with me for a few days instilled some wild abandon into his university addled head, and he tells me it has. I tell him next time he books a room he best have a woman on his arm, and he promises he will. We finish breakfast surrounded by post-church, First Nations families breaking bread, and I go in search of a phone as Quint heads back to the room to pack and shower.

Next thing I'm stood on the sidewalk, phone in hand, talking to my kids as Sunday morning folk stroll by enjoying a glorious fall day on the ocean. Bobbing boats glint and wink in the harbour as I'm told how much I'm missed, that everything is fine back home and moms applied for a new job. There's been a major drug bust in Orangeville and it's all over the national news. Swimming lessons are going well, Madeline has a new tooth coming through and William had his milk tokens stolen at school; and it's snowing – a lot! I miss them both big-time, I tell them, say my goodbyes and replace the phone back in its cradle pretending not to notice fresh blood splattered all over the brick wall the phone-booth is anchored to. I compose myself, take a deep breath, and stroll across an empty mall parking-lot in search of film, batteries and postcards.

Some scoop on 'Prince Rupe' from a hotel tourist booklet to keep you busy while I'm shopping:

The Northwest Coast has fed the human spirit for thousands of years. The creatures of sea, land and sky, the lush coastal rain-forest and the moody seascapes are the sources of inspiration - first, for the indigenous people, and then for the non-native settlers. It's no wonder that artists are bred here and that visitor's to this coast are so taken by its beauty and its spirit that they often return.

Ayup, here's the drugstore. Nice mall this, reallyclean.

The land and sea has generously supported a vast First Nations population for nearly 100 centuries. Long before European contact, Prince Rupert's inner harbour was the most densely populated area north of Mexico. The sophisticated and prosperous First Nations culture bred a unique, stylized art-form, which is acclaimed throughout the world today.

Wonder what batteries I need for this bleedin' camera?

Prince Rupert is a crossroads. Travelers are served by ship, rail, road and air. Newcomers find themselves surrounded by some of the world's most spectacular scenery and scarcely touched wilderness, warmed by the Japanese current. The town site sits at the foot of two peaks on Kaien Island and overlooks a deep fjord, sheltered by a rim of protective outer islands.'

Double A's should do it, great, thanks, now for postcards.

During the height of railway building at the turn of the century, the visionary Melville Hays (who had that much vision he died on the Titanic. A last letter of his is displayed in the Maritime Museum in Halifax, Nova Scotia). Hays *chose Kaien Island to be the terminus for Canada's second transcontinental railway. As the president of the Grand Trunk Pacific Railway he intended to create a city that would be an elegant showpiece for his ventures. With Hay's death in 1912 and the end of the railway era, the city's fortunes turned to fishing, attracting more people from around the world. The salmon fishery thrived near the mouth of the Skeena River and the Halibut fishery exploded in 1919 just before the Herring fishery came into its own.*

During the war years, the city served both Canada and the USA as a strategic gateway for equipment to build the Alaskan Highway and for freight and personnel destined for theatres of war in the Pacific and an estimated 150,000 troops passed through.

What you mean you don't sell stamps, missus?

Prince Rupert benefits from a moderate marine climate. Winter temperatures hover around the freezing mark, summer temperatures in the mid-60s. Rainfall is abundant, usually reaching 90-100 inches a year and the sun often shines when it's raining. These moist and moderate conditions give the coast around Prince Rupert unspoiled ecosystems and abundant wildlife unique in the world.

I know all about the wildlife after last night. You can catch a ferry to Alaska, Port Hardy or the Queen Charlotte Islands any time of the year from here and next time I'm up this way I'm going to check-out The Charlottes, bet they sell stamps over there.

On the road again, in Cow Bay this time, two minutes from downtown Rupert where Brad pulls the car over for me to have a look around and calm down a bit more after recent events while taking in the sights. Its high noon, which may be appropriate, because after returning to the hotel to gather belongings and say farewell to Quint, I found the bathroom afloat from an overflowing toilet blocked courtesy of stomach contents fired into it via the big mouth of one of Brads friends, who having found the hotel this morning had Blondie call our room and soft-arse Brad answered and let them in to get cleaned up and use the amenities. The bathroom was a disaster and I was not amused. Quint wasn't either as his name was on the bill and I felt responsible. What a mess what a farewell scene. I could have murdered Brad for letting them in.

'What am I gonna do, Paul?'

'Sorry Quint!'

'I'll have to pay for this!'

'No you won't, if you do send me a copy of the bill.'

'I will if you send me a copy of your book.'

'It's a deal, take care mate...and tread carefully!'

'I will. Take care, b'y!'

'You too my friend, sorry it had to end this way.' And we both laughed as I sneaked off to find Brad about to bounce his pals head off the elevator door. 'You want to do it, Paul?'

'Nah, let's go. Leave them here.'

'I can't pal. I have to work with them...', and here I am in Cow Bay, stuck with 'them'.

When you wake up in the morning and you can't remember much about the night before. A small reminder of the state you were in are all the tattered clothes across the floor. Your head still keeps singin', your phone still keeps ringin'. Remember just exactly where you've been, 'cos there ain't no doubt about it there's no better things to see than what you've seen. - Slade

I used to love that song! Anyways, Cow Bay is named after a Swiss dairy farmer christened Nehring who used to let his cows swim to shore from his boat. That's it, all I have on the place. It reminds me of the coast of Wales. I'm stood here smiling about the cows, the air has that seaside tangy taste and burns my nostrils. I inhale deeply. Get this, there's a Wales Island just north of here at the mouth of Portland Inlet. Ha, small planet we inhabit. I'm scanning the bay for seals but they don't want to play today. Must be the company I'm in. The staff at Cowpuccino's Restaurant won't let us in, won't open the door and I don't blame them one bit.

On the tip of the lip of the ocean and I'm in a sour mood. 'We should have booked a room at the Eagle Bluff to watch the sun set and the eagles soar instead.' I tell Brad, as we amble up a steep grassy hill.

'It's probably a good thing you didn't considering the wrecking crew I brought with me!'

'They still following us?'

'Yep, they think we're gonna leave them here.'

'We should, come on lets do it for Quint.' I want to belt one of them but something tells me I don't know the full story.

'I can't leave them, Paul!' I just laugh and boot a rock into touch. Brad winces - he's hurting.

One hundred and forty three kilometres to Terrace, the sign tells us as we pull to a halt at the Pacific Mariners Memorial Park where the sun glints from a wall adorned with names of lost seafarers. Strolling about with the camera I'm drawn to a bronze statue of an ancient mariner stood proud and tall facing the harbour,. He's pointing to the horizon with a right hand covered in bird shit, his left fastened for all time to a ship's wheel. He draws me close with intense eyes. I get the feeling this is a place full of ghosts. From a distance he looked regal, but upon closer inspection his face has been painted in a macabre, tragi-comic death mask and his weathered green trunk covered in magic-marker anti-white obscenities.

'Who's that?' I ask, but Brad can't answer as he's away in the bushes throwing up.

'That's Prince Rupert,' pipes up the pukers mate.

'Is that right?" I ask while reading the inscription on the base of the statue.

'Yeah, man - he discovered Prince Rupert.'

'Who told you that?'

'Common knowledge!' he replies, all serious as we read and admire the graffitee.

'Do you know who Prince Rupert was?'

'A sailor. Him!' he says, nodding at the vandalised Captain Ahab.

'Read that,' I tell him, and point to the inscription that says, *'WE ARE OUT THERE. We know you care. And pray to God. We are out there. In the care of God.'*

He's reading it aloud slowly as Brad rejoins us, face the colour of the statue.

'He reckons this is Prince Rupert.'

'Looks like a dead sailor to me, Paul.' He suggests we make tracks as he's not feeling too hot.

'Its a dead sailor, lads.' My faith in Canadian history taught in Canadian schools takes another beating as puker skulks off with his pal and yells over his shoulder, 'No it's not, its Prince Rupert!'

I look at Brad and we laugh. Rupert was a royal land baron. The monument in question was erected by the people of Owase, Japan, and the residents of Prince Rupert in recognition of mariners lost at sea from both cities and I'm not going to let the subject die as far as I'm concerned, with two party animals storming off in direction of the car, heads down, hands in pockets kicking grass, heads together obviously conspiring.

'He did look a bit like Prince Rupert!' I shout, above the roar of the wind, as we bomb along Highway 16, leaving Seal Cove, Sourdough Bay, and Butze Rapids in our wake. Nobody laughs, as we cross the Wainwright Basin by bridge, exit Kaien Island and hit the mainland at a fair clip, bombing along the Yellowhead Highway at a hundred clicks an hour. Brad is in one hell of a hurry to get home and I'm having fun on behalf of Quint. I won't let passengers sleep, especially the driver, by roaring out questions and making a general racket. They hate me and I love it. Road, rail-line and river look to be copulating as they intertwine and snake-like through spectacular mountain ranges and scenery as the setting sun winks from behind tall trees, tunnels, and mountain peaks. Yeah, man, I'm here, I've been let-loose in the wild, wild, west at last.

Somewhere along the Skeena Valley among the Coast Mountains at Kwinitsa, a lone shoeless man makes figure eights on a ten-speed bike in the middle of the highway. At a blast from the car horn he looks up and glares at us in mid-pedal as if we are invading his space before slowly taking to the hard shoulder so we can pass. 'EH! THAT'S PRINCE RUPERT! Did you see him?' I shout. No answer. 'No, seriously, that was Bernie Howgate, an author from Toronto who rode his ten-speed bike around the world and wrote about it. Took him nine years.'

'Who? Nine years to write the book, or...?' Brad manages.

'Never mind, I'll tell you later! and stick my head out the window to drown in fresh air and almost get decapitated by a rock jutting from a tunnel wall.

'What the!...you see that?'

'Carwash Rock buddy. Washes your car for free, yeehahhhhh!' Shouts Brad, who looks to be recovering, and we both give it the loud laughs.

Eagles soar and glide in slow motion around lush, green Mount Kenney and next thing we're roaring into dusty downtown Terrace on a wing and a prayer. We dump unwanted company on a deserted main street and speed off in direction of the Pretty Homestead. 'WATCH OUR FOR PRINCE RUPERT ON THE WAY HOME LADS!'

Ha, fuck off!

TERRACE

In the land of the rare Kermode Bear, Tanya waits in the driveway with the kids as we pull in. Slim with the new skinhead haircut she still laughs a lot. Colton, the first born, is eight now, still shy still looks like his mom, still has the stuffed-dog toy we gave him for his first birthday. Brad asks me if I remember taking the boys to Toronto's Queen Street West for haircuts and I do. Two strollers, two proud dads, once upon a time in another world. Sydney the youngest and Montana in the middle are both amusing and cute chatterboxes and have me roped in as constant audience in minutes. Tanya takes off in the car to the store for booze and a bit of peace and quiet as I unload my backpack onto the living room couch, my bed for the duration. I like couches as mentioned and this monster is a very comfortable couch.

Brad's dogs are big and mean looking. Two of them running about the back forty snarling and barking at the scent of bear, and me, but after a few head rubs turn out to be quite playful. I wouldn't want to get cornered by them after breaking in without wearing a suit of armour though. *'He came in through the bathroom window...argh!'*

Dogs are a necessity here to keep bears away, Brad tells me, especially if you have kids who like to play in the woods at the bottom of long, wild gardens. He reckons each household in the neighborhood has at least two dogs and I'm imagining the feeding and picking up after.

Night falls and it gets cold fast outside so we head in for a scrumptious meal of fresh salmon bought from Brad's indigenous neighbour for a bargain. After a gallon of red wine over dinner, we kick back, catch-up and fall asleep in front of a daft science fiction movie rented from Blockbuster where I got into conversation with a bunch of native lads who insisted on leaning on our car while we were inside choosing. 'Be careful pal, they're looking for trouble.'

'Everything alright lads?'

'Yeah, you talk funny.'

'Have a nice night!'

'Yeah, you too!'

It's good to be with old friends and their offspring. I wonder what Quint's up to and raise a glass before turning in for the night.

Monday, November 9th. Not much of a chance to write today as I've been kept busy listening to the life story of the Pretty family and explaining my tattoos, jewellery, and where I'm from over and over again. Argh! These kids can talk.

I've had to sneak away to the corner store for some peace and quiet, make journal entries and mail postcards under the guise of buying a newspaper. I'm sat here on a buffer log in a car-park, sun on my face, with an unobstructed view of a mountain range known as Sleeping Beauty. I'm scribbling happily away until a grinning chappy wearing a cowboy hat pulls up in a big black exhaust spewing truck, parks inches from the toes of my boots and blocks out the sun.

Engine rumbling, stereo blasting, gun rack in the back window, he climbs down, hitches his jeans and spits. 'Nice day, man!' he shouts over his shoulder, laughs, flicks a cigarette butt into the road and strolls into the store I'm sat in front of, all full of himself.

'It was, man.' I reply quietly, and spit like pa taught me too.

'Nice hat,' he counters when he comes clumping back in Cuban-heeled cowboy boots, still smiling, carrying a box of shells, a carton of Players Light and a newspaper. He tells me I can have my sun back, to take care, and hops back into his tank and roars off, Shania Twain yodeling on number ten from an open window.

I smile, keep my mouth shut, my fingers to myself and resume my scribbling. Life is good, don't want to ruin it, maybe someday I'll write a country song regards this moment.

Over lunch, I tell Brad and family how lucky they are to be living at the foot of such awe-inspiring mountains, a continent away from the west-end 'hood still haunted by drug dealers, pimps and gangs. They agree, and next thing I'm on a twenty kilometre trip in the car down Highway 37 to Lakelse Lake where Ponderosa, lodge pole, pine, spruce, and Douglas fir tower above lush foliage. Six foot tall Devil's Club plants covered in evil looking spikes skulk amongst tropical florae before a lake that magnifies the sun and obliterates my eyeballs.

Bird song, damp misty jungle, no squirrels, black bear warning signs, so far no encounters. Green-brown strands of moss hang from trees like Rasta dreads or strings of snot. Swampy smells clogs nostrils. Bugs must be huge here when it warms up. The damp air reminds of northern England, foliage resembles the Amazon, not that I've been there but I peruse magazines on a regular basis. The winding road that led us in to and through this British Columbian Shangri-la was deserted. Not a soul about.

My neck is stiff from staring up at treetops, the size of these tree's! my arms are sore from measuring their girth. The view back along a trail we follow is of evergreens enveloped in thick mist,where five year old Sydney reminds me to make lots of noise to scare away the bears as we navigate the terrain, singing. I tell her I would faint dead away if a bear popped up to ask if it was me who ate all the porridge. She laughs and tells me I'm silly and points out bear prints in sand on a beach close to the waters edge. She kneels and places her hand in a paw imprint so I can take a photo. Her print is tiny compared.

'Don't be scared, Paul,' she tells me, smiling, one lens of her glasses taped to correct her vision. Brad tries to wind me up by telling tales of local folk eaten by bears as we throw rocks at a log floating in the lake, the *splooshes* creating waves that obliterate all prints in the sand.

A huge mansion sits empty across the lake and we muse on when it was built and by who. Who owns it now, is it haunted? Two large dogs swim and run the beach as happy-couple owners cuddle and kiss in the mist and watch over them lovingly. The sun breaks through to help paint a brilliant rainbow in the sky, which causes us three to 'ooh!' and 'ahhh!' and as we count the colors Sydney names them all.

On the walk back to the car we investigate empty campsites and I wish it was still camping season. to spend a night here would be fantastic. All this wilderness and rainforest make campsites we frequent on Lake Huron seem pretty tame. I find myself falling in love with the place and the bear threat makes it all the more thrilling, but we have to leave as Sydney is tired and the light is fading, so we stroll noisily back through the jungle with me taking photos as we go. My favourite being father and daughter walking hand in hand along a misty deserted road dwarfed by vegetation as the sun sends blades of golden light through treetops.

When camping in British Columbia, be very patient if a black bear attempts to share your tent or sleeping bag. Stay calm; eventually he will leave. – Tourist pamphlet

Things learned about Terrace over a few bottles of red wine: Terrace is 55 Degrees North Latitude and sits at the crossroads of highway 37, which heads north from Kitimat to Stewart and the Alaskan border. Terrace doesn't boast a *World's Biggest* anything except maybe hangovers.

I found it hard to dig up anything historical about the place at first, but thanks to a quick stop at an online museum while sharing bottle number two, I learned that locals are extremely proud of their heritage and localis. Terrace once had the largest population of Indigenous people on the West Pacific Coast; among them the Nisga's, Haida and Tsimshian; Gitsan, Tahltan and Tlinglit. Ol' Alexander Mackenzie and his explorer mates helped put paid to that on their travels in search for the fabled Northwest Passage, or the route to the Pacific Ocean. Indigenous peoples decimated by disease and murder in quest for fame, riches and religious superiority, well-documented by better qualified than I, of course.

The city of Terrace (pop around 13,000) is laid out in a square on a flat plain surrounded by ancient villages and archaeological sites, huddled amongst mountains and waterways. It's been known to rain year-round here and snowfalls are legend. The place leaves me with an image of a carved stone bowl left out in the rain. The shy and mysterious Kermode 'spirit bear' is both official British Columbia mascot and well protected, its image everywhere on signs and advertisements and like most I have yet to encounter one.

After falling asleep thinking about encountering spirit bears, I awake disoriented from a dream in which I have the ability to leap over tall trees, logging towns and mountain tops. I mid-leap I lose my powers and overcome with great sadness fall slowly back to earth as a pleasant voice whispers, *every t'ing gonna be alright* in my ear. Sweating, I open one eye and focus on a cat lapping at an upended wine glass beneath a flashing green light from the VCR sat under the television in the corner and slide into a thick dreamless sleep.

Nature is careless of the individual, but careful of the species. - R. D. Lawrence

Tuesday, November 10th 6:30am. After a cup of tea and a giggle about the night before we exit a sleeping household to enter into quite the winter scene, the car is thick with frost and its freezing. I snap a few photos of Sleeping Beauty mountain from the driveway as Brad scrapes ice from glass with a plastic implement, before piling into the car, and after several splutters the old banger coughs itself into life. Alaska, here we come!

Fresh snow on the mountains is luminous against a blue-grey backdrop of sky, seen from a gas station courtyard. Brad fills up, does driver things, as I sit in the front seat and watch the sun slide up and over the mountaintops bringing shadows to Terrace. It dawns on me, no pun intended, that daylight is held up a bit longer here as the sun scales mountains to make a complete appearance and bathe the city in its warmth.

Gassed up and on the road I spot bald patches on mountainsides which indicate loggers are still at work, or were until recently. Government signs planted roadside announce what's happening regards these man-made razorings of ancient landscapes. The government looks to be intent on putting an end to clear-cutting despite the job market being on a downward spiral. Brad tells me it has been for a while. Local towns are hurting. To cut or not to cut? A quandary.

We discuss this as we head down a foggy highway 34 with the Skeena River raging strong, true and grey alongside. Conversation regards explorers and loggers braving such rivers on flimsy rafts brings a shudder to my hungry frame as we pull into the parking lot of a greasy spoon in Kitwanga, where a window-full of truck drivers shake their heads in disgust as Brad and I fool about with the camera in front of a big log sign that proclaims: **North to Alaska, Stewart 237km, Hyder Ak. 240km, Bear Glac. 201km**

It's Hyder we're after, so after a few more photo's we hop in the car feeling a lot better for the BLT and coffee, to resume our endemic road run, or 'Carry On Up The Khyber Part II' as we have christened it.

Brad wants to show me a reserve (rez?) where I can snap some pics of totem poles and that, but I decline due to my hatred of the whole 'us' and 'them' thing, which is prolific here I'm discovering. Besides, reserves and segregation bring to mind apartheid and the old divide and conquer tricks by those once in charge of the British Empire. Kitwancool and Mount Weber flash by as we bomb down the highway in our Junker 98, taking in the sights and yapping a mile a minute to match the speedometer. Brad has me in stitches with stories and I reciprocate when I can get a word in. He was recently working in the land of the rising sun constructing a house, and I wager that due to the amount of Saki drank during the course of construction the house has fallen over already or is leaning at an acute angle.

We haven't seen another car for over an hour. It's just us two and the lava beds of Kitwanga, frost on the trees and flocks of birds.

I've developed a sore throat from laughing and a sore bum from sitting as we reminisce. Last night was hilarious, all six of us squished on the couch watching a black bear amble down Terrace's main street via the news on television.

'Are the sales on?' I asked the kids.

'Noooooooooo!'

'Is this Bearwatch?'

'Noooooooooo!'

'Yeah, the bears looking for a new red swimsuit.'

'Nooooooooo!' From all in unison again as I acted out a bear running down the beach in slow motion scaring the crap out of the cats.

'That's just down the road, eh,' said Brad'

'You're kiddin', said I.

'Nope.'

'Arghhh, lock the doors the windows the fridge!' I warned, before disappearing under a pile-on of laughing dogs, cats and kids. The thought of a black bear walking down Yonge Street had us laughing again. The visuals! Would the mayor call in the army like when it snows?

Back on the road a truck is overturned in a ditch to our left so we slow down to take a long look like they do in Ontario. It's empty of bodies so we speed up again. 'Why didn't you stop? Somebody could have been in that.' Brad looks at me all-knowingly, 'Could be a trap, Paul,' and laughs the laugh of the demented local.

Just past Cranberry Junction, on Highway 37, the driver takes his foot off the gas so I can eyeball a single lane bridge that spans a gurgling, fast-moving Nass River. Two lane highway one lane bridge. Hmm, we have to cross but like in the war movies it's too quiet. So we stop to take a leak in some roadside bushes. I have no idea why as the landscape is deserted - when from out of nowhere a big exhaust-spewing truck pulling two dancing trailers comes barrelling down the hill toward us from the opposite side.

'What's the odds on that, man? We haven't seen a truck all day.' I hide and take another photo from the safety of the bushes.

'You wanna play chicken, Paulie?' Brad shouts, as he runs towards the car, laughing and kicking stones.

I tell him to take a hike, wave, and give the driver the universal sign to toot the horn, which he does as he roars across the bridge and sails up the hill that we just came down. Both of us jump up and down in the slipstream, hands over ears, as the truck and trailers disappear over the horizon like a hot-rod dinosaur. What a laugh. Chicken, my arse.

Back in the car waiting for our hearing to return, the map on my lap tells me that if we were to carry on up Highway 37 we would split Mount Edziza to the west and Spatsisi Plateau to the east on our way to the Cassia Mountains and eventually end up in the Yukon, the birthplace of Pierre Berton.

'Want to give it a shot Brad. We got the time?'

'Nah, too far, someday we'll come back and see the Yukon,' he promises, as we head north-west on highway 37a, where a yellow road sign pock-marked with bullet holes warns us not to stop for at least two miles as we are in an Avalanche Area. So we don't, not even for the ptarmigan in the middle of the road that looks like its headed somewhere important.

'Looks like he missed his bus.'

'Stupid birds. The local's call them road chickens.'

'Road chickens?'

'Yeah, they taste like chicken. Throw your coat over it and hit it with a bat then grab its head with both hands. Put a boot on each wing and pull. Instant chicken breast.'

'Are they easy to catch like?'

'Slow as molasses.'

He coughs and sinks back in his seat, eyes on the road ahead like Clint Eastwood. 'Tasty too!'

'What a waste,' I tell him after taking a look in the wing mirror at the blood and feathers spread over the road behind.

'Yep, stupid alright!' And the highway rolls on as we swap stories of love won and lost before retiring into silence for a few miles, lost in clichés as Bear Glacier appears on the horizon.

Very dangerous!
Don't stop!

Don't get out of the car!

Black on yellow signs warn of impending doom but we pay them no heed. Even under threat of death by avalanche, sometimes you just have to take a leak.

The glacier we sprinkle upon is a remnant from the last ice age, the Fourth Ice Age in terms of ice ages. Glaciers once covered most of Canada, Alaska and parts of the United States and some of the biggest in the world are just up the road from us in Kluane National Park. Go see them before it's too late, they are melting fast.

I'm reading about the First Ice Age that happened sixty million years ago, followed by a last big meltdown of four that occurred ten thousand years ago, which formed huge pre-historic lakes like Lake Agassiz which was bigger than the Great Lakes as we know them put together. Then Boom! A heat-wave caused Lake Algonquin to melt and flow all the way down to the Mississippi and beyond and that was that.

'Some meltdown that, eh mate'

'Yeah, but not as big as the one Greg Norman had at the Masters.'

'Ha, true. Fore!'

The glacier drew rock-mantled shoulders north, like a great rasp, gouging out lakes, faceting rock, leaving mounds & moraines, fluted drumlins in drumlin fields, leaving scraps & terraces, eskers, erratics & rat tails leaving the Cambrian hills. -Esta Spaulding

I whistle a rendition of *Amazing Glacier* and zip my fly out of respect for the glacier that looms before us. The temperature seems to have dropped about ten degrees and its bloody freezing all of a sudden. We take turns throwing rocks that may have been lying around here waiting for us to throw them into a deep black pool at the foot of the glacier for eons, and we can tell it's deep by the long splooshes after rocks smash through ice leaving bubbles in their wake.

'Take the plunge, man!' The glacier is within swimming distance but we'd be ice-cubes in minutes. A microdot plane splits a pale blue sky leaving a white Etch-A-Sketch jet-stream behind. 'Way too cold to be falling in there, mate!'

Total silence reigns as we take in were we are, ruined by a fart, and we laugh like schoolboys and throw more rocks at a glacier that looks styrofoam and is actually moving. Missiles fall short and take a dive into inky water that comes between us and the ice-age. Black and white episodes of Doctor Who and the Daleks invade my brain. 'Exterminate!'

'What are you on about?'

'Ha, the BBC tried to replicate what we see before us in the late sixties. They did a good job too despite the visible strings and wobbly sets.'

'Right. Before my time buddy.'

My pal wants to take a photo with the glacier all blue-white behind me, so I squat down in the old classic footballer pose, remove my hat, and manouvre as close to the edge of certain death as I dare. I smile, he clicks, nods, and hands back the camera.

'Did I have hat hair?'

'No, you looked good,' he lies.

Bear Glacier was big enough to rub shoulders with the highway we took to get here until about the seventies but has suffered fifty yards of melt since due to global warming. Cars, trucks, 8-track stereos and sub-woofers rumbling by look to have took its toll. Earth Wind & Fire, Donna Summer, Hot Chocolate, Jason & The Scorchers, the Red Hot Chili Peppers blasting away. Elvis and the Sun sessions started the melt though. Daft thoughts take a back seat because I can hear rocks and stones trickling from somewhere above and behind. They sound like rain as they scurry down the rock face and bounce across the highway.

I get Brad's attention and point at the big wall of sound. '*I know. Get in the car and don't slam the door!'*

We speed-walk nonchalantly making sure not to look up in case we jinx ourselves. Passenger doors are sneaked open carefully and we slip inside holding our breath. Brad turns the the key and instead of the usual coughing and spluttering the engine turns over in one go and purrs like a jack-hammer. I take a look behind, as Brad hits the gas. A rock bounces across the movie-set and takes a dive into the pool, followed by few more. SPLOOSH! SPLOOSH-SPLOOSH! SPLOOSH!

'Holy shit! Lemmings.'

'Ah, they missed us.'

'Why are we laughing?'

'Fasten your seatbelt!'

At Argyle Creek, a swathe of trees about two hundred feet wide have been flattened. 'High winds?'

'Sasquatch?'

'Windigo.' My driver toots the horn to chase an eagle from its eyrie in a tall branchless tree. It swoops down out of sight and comes up with a great flopping fish in its beak before returning to base for a feast. I'm informed by the same driver that this part of the country is a popular fishing spot for bear, man and eagle, as we cross Bear River into a suddenly blinding sun that could have caused premature entry into Wards Pass Cemetery, where tombstones lay partly hidden among long swaying grass like rotted teeth and we vow to stop on the way back to do some charcoal rubbings. Stewart is too near to stop now and we've developed a terrible thirst from the excitement.

STEWART. Busy beaver ponds skirt Dyke Road and we enter Stewart through a gap through snow-capped mountains. *Welcome to Canada's Most Northerly Ice-Free Port,* says a sign that lets us know us that the usual institutions found in most Canadian towns and cities await, plus a total of nine churches, I'm praying that there will be a friendly bar.

Homesteads old and new capped with slanted, metal roofs are scattered in an orderly fashion on the edge of town. Brad tells me that slanted roof's are needed for the amount of snow that falls every year here, twelve feet being a regular occurrence, and that eighty-two feet fell during the winter of1970.

'Imagine shovelling that lot?'

'Not even with your spade.'

Real estate signs are everwhere, it seems that everything is for sale on the banks of the Portland Canal. Downtown is lined on both sides with closed or boarded up stores. Sea birds are prolific, especially above the marshland to the west of the city. The absence of vehicles and pedestrians makes it all mysterious, the place is deserted. My guide tells me this is a product of the closure of the Westin Gold Mine, and we stare in silence at the sadness of it all. The *rat-a-tat-tat* of the engine disturbs a flock of seagulls in the road and they fly screaming. A row of faded, peeling store signs boasts a *Bonnie & Clyde Hair-styling & Gifts,* where antiques and solar nails can be purchased and lashes tinted.

'That's the place for me.'

We roll from our bucket seats, stamp dead feet on cracked sidewalk, and don't bother feeding the meter because Stewart appears to be Sunday seven days a week.

Strolling about in the silence we check out a Wanted poster taped up in the window of *Hub's Pharmacy*. The face of a man wanted for the murder of three teenagers in Kitimat stares back at us amidst faded ad copy for corn pads, toothpaste and Kodak film. Brad tells me the teens had been making fun of him and hassling him for being a loner. They wrecked his antique car so he shot them dead and took off into the bush, where he's still on the loose with his dog.

We spot a place across the street that appears to be open, so we mosey on over, spurs jangling, as the sun winks off a wall of glass and temporarily blinds us. Tumbleweed blows on through as if auditioning for a John Huston movie. We take care not to fall into deep potholes as we'd need someone with a long rope to haul us out. I'm whistling the theme from, *The Good, The Bad and the Ugly*, as we stroll towards the log building that backs onto the Portland Canal. Somewhere a dog barks once, twice, and sends those seagulls flying again. I reach for a door handle and pull hard, and the '*brinnggg*' of a bell above our heads welcomes us into the Canada Tourism building.

The joint is picked clean of free tourist leaflets to a background sound of my guide chatting up a young lady dressed in Welcome Wagon garb. She's bored. There's nothing to do in Stewart, she tells us. I tell her not to worry as things will surely pick up once we leave, and sign the guest-book, *Paul Henry Sutton - Liverpool, England*, for some strange reason. She wants us to stay longer but we have a border to cross.

The car waits precariously on the lip of a pothole like a needy old dog, but is soon fired up and rumbling along a dusty road that comes to a dramatic halt on the doorstep of the United States of America like a black unrolled carpet.

ALASKA

High-Noon in Hyder, Alaska, where a Canada Customs agent return's my wave from Canada as I stand in America taking photographs of the old town jail. I smile at her. She smiles back, picks up the phone and dials. Why am I nervous?

Ahhhh, America, finally. My first time here. I can't help but think of the scene in West Side Story when the Puerto Rican chick sings '*Viva ra viva ramereecahh!*' before the Jets and Sharks meet in the parking lot, as I stroll about taking photos of everything and anything Americano. *Last Exit to Brooklyn*? Green and white signs attached to hydro poles remind us where we are and how fast to drive. The speed limit is 20 and Brad pushes the limit, laughing at my expression as I gawk from the open passenger door window trying to take it all in at once. I feel like I've landed at Ellis Island. America has the same trees as Canada but they look different which is hard to explain. Red, white and blue bunting is strung high across a gravel road.

'They're expecting us.'

Lush, green mountainside appears to block our path but it's only an illusion as the road suddenly veers right into the shady outskirts of downtown Hyder.

'You wanna get Hyderized, Paulie?'

'Where, how, and why?'

'The Sealaska bar, it's supposed to be a laugh.'

'What do we have to do like?'

'Drink a draft beer with a toe floating in it without swallowing the toe.'

'Nah, I don't feel like a toe. Maybe on the way back.'

'You sure...look at those shacks.' Old wooden shacks lean-to on either side of the road that look to be hiding dark secrets behind rotting shutters.

'This is right out of the movie with the banjo player...look at that one!'

We creep slowly past a half-collapsed shack with a big old rusty bear trap with jaws wide-open in a front garden of mud, a broken front door that leans and creaks when the wind catches it.

'Think his wife set that trap last night?'

'Don't be giving Tanya ideas!'

'Reminds me of a place we moved to in '72,' I tell my driver, wiping away windshield crud with a paper napkin, the statement loud in the stillness.

'Where was that?' Brad wants to know, eyes locked on a pockmarked gravel road that curves sharply, leading us to who knows where.

'Ah, they built concrete estates in fields surrounded by....' I'm stopped in mid-sentence by the sight of a big baldy guy in sweats washing a truck while pretending not to notice us as we bounce past smiling at him.

'Wouldn't want to fight him!'

'Did they have bears on those estates?'

'No, plenty of sheep though.' I'm cut off again as we disappear into a pothole in the road. History forgotten about as we search beneath seats for a flashlight or matches as it's gone very dark in here...no matter, the engine roars and the car pulls us up and us out the other side and putters along suffering no injury.

The Friendliest Ghost Town In Alaska, boasts a sign and I'm keen to find out if it speaks the truth as we crawl past a Museum and two tiny houses of worship. 'Fuckin midgets!'

'Aye, I know a little bar on the edge of town where you can really set 'em up and knock 'em down.'

St. Paul's Orthodox Church rubs shoulders with St. Paul's Fellowship Hall, a close neighbour of The Trading Post and Café, all no bigger than your standard garden shed. We bump and grind our way through a strange hamlet lined and dotted with shacks and stores of all description. The US Post Office is a trailer protected from the elements by a wooden canopy. It's parked next to a Public Library, between a couple of rundown bars, a store that advertises fireworks, public washrooms and a Border Bandit trading store covered in lightbulbs that brings to mind a miniature Honest Ed's.

The Brookside Baptist Church is the last building standing as we exit Hyder, whooping, laughing, and drumming on steering wheel, thighs or dashboard. Viva America, indeed.

'By the looks of things,' I shout, as we roar down a dirt road that takes us into the bush, 'that place can't have changed much over the years. ' I'm trying to be serious as my ribs can't take much more rumbling. Brad's reply is almost lost in the roar from the engine, but I manage to make out that officers of the law are very few and far between here and the nearest jail is in Juneau, hundreds of miles away.

Great stuff, I'm thinking, as talk has become futile. I finally make it to the Frontier and there's no law about.

'*Where's the bank, then*?' I shout, and both of us mime the shooting of six-guns.

Food for thought: Why is the second building you see upon entering Alaska (the first being the empty jail) the *U.S. Army Storehouse Number 4*, where are the other three, and what's stored in them?

The sun fights, wins a split decision, and makes an appearance from behind thick white clouds, blinding us with bursts of golden sunshine as we leave Hyder behind in the dust in search of trouble. A slight bend is rounded to find a wooden sign with ***Bear View*** painted on it nailed to a fence post set in the middle of a small car park sat beside what turns out to be the Salmon River. We find a parking space, ha, the place is deserted, and head on foot in the direction a painted arrow on the same sign points us in. To find a clearing and a slow moving river that glints in the sun as it winds its way towards bigger waters via a hole bored beneath the road that led us here. But it wasn't that simple, it never is with Brad.

'What's this then?' I asked him as we pulled up and he switched off the engine.

'A bear watching spot, man. C'mon, lets go find you one.' And he took off on a mission towards the river, nose stuck in the air like a retriever, leaving me behind in the ticking car.

'*Shall I leave the door open, just in case*?' I shouted after him.

'*Yeah, if you want to find a bear sat in your seat later,*' he yelled back and disappeared down an incline in the river bank.

I stayed and enjoyed the silence for a few more engine ticks before following him at great speed.

BEARS, SALMON, EAGLES: *Three miles north on the Granduc Road, one will find the Fish Creek Wildlife Observation Site operated by the Tongass National Forest. There on the banks of Fish Creek throughout July and August, the visitor will have a chance to observe not only the annual migration of spawning salmon, but as well the co-dependent cycle of bears coming to feed on them. Grizzly bears and black bears, at the height of the season sometimes virtually line up along the banks taking turns to dine al fresco on nature's bounty.*

With luck or patience one might also view an eagle enjoying his share of the banquet by snatching a fish directly out of the creek or the Salmon River nearby.

The renown of this natural phenomenon has brought with it considerable pressure on this habitat. Please practice safe and sensible viewing and respect the attendant wildlife. 'Drive Safely!'- A Leaflet from the tourist centre

I don't want to be anythings '*Alfresco*' I thought, as I climbed from the car on tingling feet, and as I did I heard a rustling in tree's close by that had me whistling a breathy rendition of *Born Free,* a husky *Born to be Wild,* and a high key *Born to Run* as I chased after Brad on wobbly legs.

That '*Here piggy, piggy*' scene is sent '*soooweeeing*' from my overactive mind as I make my way through tall grass that sways in the wind along the lip of the river to stumble across the remains of a burned out homestead, fireplace and chimney still standing in testament to long gone pioneers.

Sliding down the riverbank I encounter half-submerged jagged rocks and smooth boulders that make for a treacherous path across the river, which I'm wobbling across like a high-wire walker on hot coals when I hear more rustling.

Thoughts of a young English painter running down a muddy path brandishing a roller pole in Algonquin Park come to mind (see the return journey) only to be chased away by a '*HEY, PAUL,*' from up ahead.

'*HANG ON,*' I shout, and instead of retracing my steps like a cowardly John Inman, I forge ahead to find Brad all smiles and as cocky as you like, kneeling in a secluded break overhung with branches and hidden by tall grass, tickling black salmon that swim sluggishly and as thick as thieves in the river.

'Still life salmon! They look like rocks waiting for a bus,' and submerge a hand in cold, clear water, to tickle a salmon belly as its pals try to swim away as if drugged. 'They're dying, this is the end of the road,' Brad tells me.

'No wonder the bears like it here,' I reply, sadly, as he plucks a limp fish from shallow water that wiggles suddenly and splops back to join the queue for the bus. I can't believe it, free fish and not a plastic bag in sight.

A shadow passes overhead, I stare into the sun andspot an eagle hovering.

'Watch it doesn't shit on you.'

'Did you bring the umbrella?'...and we're laughing, dodging imaginary shit bombs at the river's edge. A big old tree downstream overshadows what remains of a smaller one that's been beheaded and is missing most of its bark.

'Wonder what happened to that?'

'Bears.'

'What? That's it, I'm off!'

'Don't be scared, it looks like they've been sharpening their claws before they eat and that one tree looks like it's been killed by a grizzly.'

I spy with a terrified eye a wooden platform just across from the slaughtered tree with a sign attached that says, **Bear Feeding Area - Danger!**

'You wanna check it out. Grizzlies?'

'Yeah, c'mon, let's take a look,' and off he goes with me in tow, thinking, *'If he put his finger in the fire, would you, soft lad,'* as I give chase, after possibly a last glance at the salmon in the water.

The Bear Café is simply a flimsy looking wooden structure that looks likely to topple over with one swipe from a paw or claw, but I still follow my guide up river to a place where birds of many colours zip about and sing in tall dry grass that bows to us in a dusty wind. Two by fours have been nailed to four by four posts that have been hammered into the river bank or attached to a creaking tree. A rickety handrail loaded with splinters is what we lean shoulder to shoulder to spit in the river. Not a word is said or needed at this moment in time but you know us.

'How tall is your average black bear?'

'About seven feet standing, why?'

'Because we could lean over and scratch its head from here,'

I answer wisely, and spit in the direction of an imaginary bear fishing for its supper.

'Yep.'

A floating leaf is used as a target for pebbles as I digest this and the wind raises another miniature dust storm and the sun hides behind a fast-moving black cloud.

'I'd rather put my hand up your arse than scratch a live bears head,' I tell him, as I photograph a tiny red bird as it takes a dust bath at my feet. The click of the camera, the splooshing of pebbles, more rustling in tree's behind are the only sounds to be heard besides that of laughter.

'What's Hyderized, again?' I ask my guide who leans back on the rail and offers his face to the sun.

'It's a tradition at the Sealaska or the Glacier Bar, you'll love it.'

'What do they do?'

'You'll see.'

'Was that you?'

'What?'

'You throwing pebbles when I'm not looking?'

'That's not me, it's you!'

'Its not me mate. I'm aiming mine at the same log as you.'

'Probably a beaver.'

'I hope so. There it is again!'

I'm fumbling my camera back into its case as the sound of an animal rustling our way becomes one of branches being snapped. I throw whats left of a handful of pebbles that hit water like bullets from a machine-gun and speed-walk back in the direction of the car.

'Don't be daft it was me!' Brad shouts, as I make my retreat and break into a jog.

'*IT WAS ME!*' He yells.

'*FUCK OFF!*'

'CHICKEN!'

'I KNOW!'

The car is as empty as when we left it. No hairy going through the glove box in search of a snack. Nothing chewing the steering wheek or asleep in the back seat. The bastard turns the key again and we roar off towards a steep incline known as The Granduc Road. The air in the car is filled with talk of copper mines, glaciers and grizzly bears.

A bald eagle sits proudly at the top of a tall tree at the base of a mountain. It appears to be sleeping. Brad hits the brake and leans on the horn and the bird doesn't fly or blink an eye. *BEEEEEEEEEEEEEEEEEEEEEEEEEEEEEEEEPPPP!* Nothing.

'What's wrong with it?'

'Must be deaf.'

'A deaf eagle?'

'Or dead!'

'You'll be dead if I catch you throwing anymore rocks.'

'Ha!'

The Granduc Road

'Courtesy of past mining operations, this 30-mile road provides access to some of North America's most spectacular and daunting scenery. The road snakes along the Salmon River through Alaska before returning to British Columbia and the site of the old Premier mine site. Thereafter, prepare yourselves for the awesome vistas of the Salmon Glacier, Summit Lake and Tide Lake beyond. Summit Lake provides a rare natural phenomenon when mid-summer, the entire 5-mile lake drains under the Salmon Glacier, leaving behind an iceberg littered lake-bottom and scattering million-year old ice down to the Portland Canal. Near the end of the road, remnants of the Granduc mine defy scale in the glacier-dropped heart of the coastal mountains, and looking east, you will see Tide Lake. Take the time to explore the alpine meadows inhabited by rugged, yet fragile wildflowers determined to survive during the 2 months of exposure in this snowbound country.

Scenery, wildlife and the roots of our historic mining heritage,

the 'road' is a journey of truly grand proportions.
'Drive Safely!' - a leaflet

Logs, dead trees and silver-grey driftwood appear to be playing dead along the nearly dried up river bed. What was once a roaring Salmon River is littered with rocks and boulders. The smell of dead fish is cloying. Remnants of wild, boreal feasts lay scattered about in stinking piles of skin and bone. Everything is bathed in a coppery glow. Mountains opposite boast avalanche scars gouged as if from a painter's palette. The air in the shade is cold and damp like my trousers as we creep slowly up The Granduc Road, parts of which are missing or covered with rocks and stones. The mountain-top is hidden by thick mist its base crumbly and craggy.

'It's a *lonnnggg* way down,' sings Brad, in a deep baritone, as he navigates the road, sometimes steering that close to the edge the wheels seem to spin in the air like in a *Roadrunner* cartoon. Potholes are scattered like land mines that result in tremors, via battered shock absorbers, enough to dislodge fillings as we rattle along. Fresh water trickles down a sheer rock face on to freeze on contact with the road. I'm close enough to reach from an open window and snap off two long icicles and hand one to my driver. Its thirsty work this driving and navigating. Brad pokes his head out of his open window and whistles straight down to the river bed below as we pass a sign nailed to a wooden post that tells us, **Avalanche Warning for 3 miles**.

We look at each other and laugh as two eagles decide to dive-bomb us and fly off down into the chasm. I swear I hear them laughing as they go. The vibrations make it hard to scribble this down but with patience I manage a half-intelligible scrawl. We pass an 'Exploration Camp' perched precariously on the left side of the road. Its just a small hut resembling an outhouse sat waiting to be claimed by the drop. Why it hasn't fallen to its doom yet is a mystery. It should be in the next *Outhouses of Canada* calendar, the first of which was given to me by my mother-in-law

Mrs. M. It would look good next to her favourite from Egmont Bay, Prince Edward island. 'Good spot to stop, eh.'

'You gotta go?' Brad is using peripheral vision when he's talking to me now as he's afraid to take his eyes off the edge of road.

'Nah, I'd have to be fast if I decided to use that one.'

'You want me to stop, Paul?'

'No thanks mate, I'm alright, but I can't imagine anyone taking anything in there to read.'

I swear, and loudly, that this stage of The Granduc 'road' is only eight feet wide at most but we keep on truckin'. Up and around and around we go. It's like going up the down staircase or a kids slide at times, scary and exciting. We stop at a flat grey moon-like plateau that looks to have been a popular spot for truck drivers to hang out at going by the extra-wide tire tracks that spaghetti the surface. A junction of unmarked roads lead nowhere but the plateau has enough wide-open, wind-swept space to get lost in, so I take off for a wander and find a good spot to sit and ponder. There is so much to capture on film up here, besides me sat grinning, and I wish I'd thought to bring a video camera. It's breathtaking. The wind picks up, dies down, sneaks back, dies down and picks up again to scatter black dirt as if Sahara sand.

I make do with single shots of the valley below and toddle off in search of souvenirs and find a handful granite rocks and chunks of copper, or fool's gold as it's known, and a piece of driftwood that resembles a bonsai tree. A wee jog is in order to stretch the legs and next thing I'm stood at the lip of a precipice filling my lungs full of fresh air.

'Don't do it buddy, she's not worth it!'

'Ha, check this out!'

'They get some snowfalls up here too you know,' Brad tells me, smiling away, jacket puffed out in the wind. Next thing we're doing the lean out into the wind thing, the view is enough to silence Hilda Ogden. The drop is endless, beautiful, and terrifying. The wind picks up again and almost takes my hat. 'Stood on the Lords step we are,' but he can't hear me. Brad that is. The sun lights up purple clouds to recreate one of them God and angels paintings that fascinated me as a kid on visits to The Walker Art Gallery in Liverpool. The painting in front of us is all oranges and reds with streaks of purple and flecks of gold amidst swirls of wispy white clouds, and take a few steps away from the edge in awe, it's exhilarating and overwhelming.

'Is this a vision from the lord, Paul?'

'Is Moses about to appear, Brad?'

'I hope so buddy as I'm all out of tablets.'

I'm suddenly back in the Walker stood among musty memories of pale pink half-naked rotund women of all ages and description relaxing in poses on lush-green banks of idyllic calm blue lakes in company of pipe smoking sombre and pale bewhiskered men bedecked in funereal suits, stovepipe hats, and silly shoes; but my reverie (or vision) is interrupted, the religious experience ruined, by Brad as he unzips and takes an obviously much-needed leak over the side and bursts into spontaneous songbustion. '*This is our mountainnnn - give us a beeyerrrrrrrr!*'

'Watch out for the back splash there young feller. *One, two, three, all together, THIS WAS OUR COUNTREEE AND YANKS ARE ALL QUEEYERRRRRR!*'

It's one of them moments and it feels marvelous to be acting daft halfway up a mountain in Alaska. God must be laughing too.

Brad thinks he's letting me down gently by telling me the gold I found is only copper, and tries to pocket it as we head back to the car, refreshed, revived, relieved, revitalized and ready to resume our attack on the summit of this abandoned copper mine. Heads resume bouncing off the car roof, skeletons shake, teeth rattle and stomachs roll as we hit the road again.

'I gotta see a dentist when I get home.'

'A shrink.'

'A hooker.'

'A man about a dog.' My ears hum and the car groans and squeaks as it inches us along onwards and upwards towards a sign screwed to a tree trunk, **Danger! Rock-slide Area!**

'Hey there driver.'

'Don't bother me!'

'Don't want to ruin your concentration but how wide do you reckon this stretch of road is?'

'Twelve, maybe fifteen feet at most, why?'

'What do we do if a truck comes barrelling towards us like at that bridge over the Nass River?'

Silence, so I fasten my seatbelt and rub my fool's gold for luck. Without further incident we make it to an outcrop of rock, bush, and tree that overhangs the river now miles below. The outcrop looks to have been a spot for vehicles on the way up to cower from those on the way down. We climb from the car slowly as if from a tin can chrysalis that appears to take a tired breath as it ticks and hisses in the sun like a grumpy old beetle.

Stretching, grumbling and yawning, joints popping in humming silence, we stroll carefully to the crumbling edge of the outcrop to be rooted to the spot, frozen by another beautiful vision of a view. I wish I had a cigarette on me. It's the perfect time to light one up and admire the scenery. Instead, I make do with a healthy, succulent blade of long grass pulled from the edge of the world, on which I suckle and chew like a sheep in lumberjack's clothing.

We get a perfect view of the Salmon River as it runs miles below us like a mattress of ice. Rocks tossed overboard take twelve Mississippi's to hit the river bed that winds like a dried out snake-skin along the valley floor. The tundra on this captured vantage point is a mix of tall grass, loose rock and shale and small bushy trees that hang out to dry among thick foliage that hides trapdoors to the devil below. Spruce trees grow long and lean, anchored to the mountainside by spider-like roots. Evergreens lean into thin air like darts tossed by giants. A minute's silence for James Cagney is observed as the wind whips up and lies down in respect. Top of the world, ma!

While posing for the camera with wild kingdomheaven for a backdrop, I'm wondering what William and Madeline will think when they see this photo.

'Probably, look at that daft Nelly!'

Brad taps the camera and tells me he thinks it might have run out of film. 'Don't worry mate its haunted, throw it over the side,' I tell him.

'*Take dat ya dirty rat!*'

I'm a gnome in God's garden, I tell Brad, which has him raising eyebrows and laughing, so I write it down, warmed by the sun and the fact that I really am a daft Nelly, as he toddles off to check out the road ahead, see how much snow there is covering it. It doesn't look good from here, so, I put on my sunglasses and 'observe in awe and try to take it all in silence total silence the valley lit up by the sun. Summit Lake is incredible. I'm here I wish you were too.'

'Hey driver!'
'What now young feller?'
'I've just composed a pretentious poem.'
'Oh yeah, let's hear it then!' he hollers from the road,'...but we ain't going any further it's too dangerous, too much ice,' he shouts, and slips on his arse.
'You okay?'
'Yeah, but I've soaked my jeans...' He's out of sight below the outcrop now and I can hear him laughing.
'*Let's hear it then!*' he commands.
'You'll laugh. Ah, sod it here it goes...'Suffering Christ on a bicycle, suffering Christ in a car, suffering Christ, I knew I could do it, I knew I could get this far.'
At that I'm splattered with a big wet snowball and I don't

blame the thrower for throwing it.

Down, down, deeper & down. - Status Quo

It's getting colder and a bit late in the day to be hanging around soaking up panoramic views, so we toss a few more rocks and kick one last boulder over the side and climb into the still ticking car. We're not going any higher, its downhill all the way baby, which should be a lot easier on gas, nerves, fillings and friendships. Lucky me, I'm on the outside this time and get the not so thrilling anymore long drop view to the riverbed below. I'm glad I thought to bring my shades as the sun has turned the windshield into a kaleidoscopic Grateful Dead poster, making it tougher for Brad to navigate the still rock-strewn road. He has to poke his head out the window again as he goes and he refuses to wear his sunglasses, the crazy stubborn shitheel, and I can make out black ice hidden beneath dustings of snow.

'Put your shades on.'

'Don't need them.'

'Don't be daft.'

'I'm okay.'

'You may be but that's a long way down mate.'

'Its all good.'

'Here, pull over I'll drive!" This has him smiling, then laughing at the thought of me driving.

BANG!

'What was that?'

A tire blows causing the car to lurch left, but Brad coaxes the steering wheel expertly to avoid confrontation with a wall of rock or worse, disaster is averted for now.

'Jesus Christ! A fucking flat!' he shouts, and slaps the steering wheel. I stare at him saucer-eyed as the engine cuts out and we come to a shuddering halt.

Tick, tick, tick goes the car as air hisses from the burst tire... tick, tick, tick...hissssssssss, 'Are you sure it's a flat?' I'm trying for a laugh but he's sat there ashen faced, shaking his head and I think I'm in shock.

'We have a spare, right?' I ask the roof of the car in my best John Lennon accent which usually means I'm shitting myself, angry, or annoyed.

Brad looks at me and gives me a small nod. I want big nods, lots of big nods, but he won't oblige. I notice my reflection in the wing mirror and I'm as ashen as him.

'There's a spare in the trunk but I'm not sure if we have a jack,' he mumbles, wrenches the door handle, and escapes leaving me to stare at a flapping door creaking in the wind on rusty hinges.

Squeak, squeak, squeak...I sit there for a minute playing thought cards while staring at a hole where a screw once resided in a door panel. The raised trunk has blacked out the rear window and I'm thinking that I don't want to die at forty and one week and why am I sat here doing nothing while he's out there looking for a spare wheel and a jack while I'm sat here acting like his bloody wife, which has me laughing for some reason.

Twenty six men were killed working this Granduc Mine, when one of the worst avalanches in Canadian history hit at 10:16 AM, February 18, 1965. The survivors remembered that it happened silently, with no warning. The mine was closed for good in the mid-eighties. - another leaflet

All is quiet as I climb from the car except for the usual *tic-tic-tic* from beneath the hood. A bird trills close by, hidden below the edge of doom that we would have gone over if the wheels had jammed left instead of right, or vise-versa, I'm not quite sure. I leave the passenger door creaking in the wind like its opposite number and survey the damage. The left front tire looks to have been bitten by something strong and sharp and it hisses disapprovingly at its fate. Brad is hidden behind the trunk lid as he searches for jacks and tires. Feeling numb and kind of dumb

I step back a few paces, taking care not to get too close to the edge. The car appears to have been dropped by a crane causing its doors to pop open and sounds like its dying. It hits me that we might be in serious trouble. While Brad is immersed in his trunk muttering away, throwing stuff about, I glide towards the rock face seemingly inches off the ground and snap off a few icicles to suck on as my mouth is cottonwool dry. That bird trills again, must be a nest, might be the same one. I whistle a reply as Brad pops up like Lazarus from the dead, cradling an oily blue jack to his chest like a firstborn, looking everywhere but in my direction.

'Found it, we're in luck, man, grab rocks for the wheels!'

'Aye, aye, cap'n!' I reply, and follow orders. My belly is buzzing. He's spaced. I've a thirst the size of Ireland so I snap off another icicle and start rooting through a pile of rocks of all sizes a short way down the sloping road, where there looks to have been a bit of a rock slide since we passed by earlier. A fine trail of sand streams down the rock face like an egg-timer to join the rock pile that I plunder from. It starts about two hundred feet up at a brittle looking overhang that appears to want to fall any at any minute. I pick out a couple of fair-sized rocks and head to the car. On my return, the trail of sand is being joined by tiny stones that appear to greet and nuzzle each other when they come to a halt.

'You find that spare yet, mate?' I ask Brad quietly. The riff from *Brown Sugar* buzzes in my head as I wedge a rock under a back wheel. I'm at the '*you kept me up all night*' bit when Brad pops up from the trunk again holding a miniature wheel above his head like the Stanley Cup. 'Found it!'

'What's that?'

'A doughnut. The spare wheel.' I stare at it. We both laugh before I shush him while pointing at the trickling rocks and sand. 'Whoah, I see that!'

'Yeah, shhhh! Watch you don't drop that doughnut on your toe.' I saw it happening, saw it bouncing over the edge as we scrambled after it.

'You can't put *that* on the car Brad, it'll tip over,' I warn and wedge another rock under the undamaged front tire.

'Only one we got, man. It'll get us down.' He tells me, slides the oily jack beneath the front chassis and cranks the handle. I wedge a big rock under the bumper as we are on a downward grade and one slip of that...nah. Lug nuts are unscrewed with a rusty tire iron as I take stock of the situation. 'Need a hand? I used to be a diesel fitter...these'll fit me mam, these'll fit me dad and that.'

'Nah, I'm fine Paul, jjust make sure nothing slides.' So I go about the business of burying the car beneath a rock cairn and wedge myself against it just in case.

It's getting colder and the sun is taking a slow dive. Neither of us wears a watch but we know its getting late.

'You reckon there's grizzly up here?'

'Oh yeah, mountain lions too.'

'You're full of shite!"

'Take another look at that pamphlet.'

'I can't, I'm holding the car up.'

'Don't drop it!'

'Nice up here isn't it.'

'Lovely view!'

'If you think I'm walking down there in the dark....'

'What?'

'Just singing mate.'

I'm lost in thoughts of wild beasts hiding and whispering to each other if the wheel doesn't work.

'Mmm, it's the one with the accent, he looks juicy.'

'I claim his buttocks!'

'Mines the leg.'

'Lots of meat on him, plenty to go round.'

'Good. I love foreign food!'

Back in the land of reality, the wheel is changed and damaged goods and tools are stashed in the trunk in record time, which is strange as everything seems to be happening in slow motion, especially when we put the rocks back. After piling the last one against the rock face I noticed sand and bigger stones shimmying a bit faster from beneath that overhang, and one big stone hit the road and bounced past us to swan dive over the edge.

We watch rocks commit suicide as the engine turns over like a cat puking and the car grinds into gear, doors are closed gently and seatbelts fastened tightly.

'What's the sense?' I flick mine open. I want to be able to perform a swan dive if we go over.

'Hold on tight.' Brad whispers, laughs quietly, and slowly lets out the clutch as we roll forward on three wheels a doughnut and a prayer. I stick my head out the window and spit to measure how long its going to take to hit the bottom and it blows right back in my face.

'Mountain Dew!'

'Fresh as a mountain spring.'

I pull my toque and gloves tight, jam a foot against the dash, grab hold of the door handle with my right hand, the back of the driver's seat with my left, and hold my breath.

'What's with the hat and gloves?'

'I'm not freezing to death caught in a tree or bush sticking out if we go over!"

'We're not going over.'

'Sure you don't want me to drive?'

'You were good with them rocks back there.'

'I know.'

'Did you see how fast I changed that wheel!'

'Yeah, give us a kiss, besides I was too busy holding the car up.' I check the camera and its working again, not run out of film, and snap away at the sky, the valley, my feet, the gurning driver, the rictus grin on my face looking back at me in the wing mirror, because it feels good to be doing something other than shit myself.

'After you pointed out that mini-rock slide I was scared to fart, man.'

'Same here.'

'Was that you?'

'Scary, eh!'

'You need cleaning out, you!'

And on it went, daft banter all the way to the bottom.

Humans are most reluctant to think of themselves as being expendable. I am no exception in this regard. - RD Lawrence

Upon arrival back in Hyder, safe and unsound, happy to be alive but weighed down by thoughts of death and dying, the car sputters to a halt at Honest Ed's mentioned earlier, where I intend to purchase postcards, which proves that I must still be in shock. Postcards? It's quiet, too quiet, as we stagger from the car, nerves shot, on numb legs and feet. I chase Brad around the car, fist cocked, for a laugh, to get the circulation moving. He stops running long enough to pose for a photo, one hand patting the hood of his noble steed, foot on the bumper, face set in an it'll take a lot more than that to kill me, grin. A long walk is discussed but we don't want to end up in a Peckinpah film. Across the way a shadowy figure watches us from behind a dirty cracked pane of glass. The shack leans at an acute angle and has un-tethered horses corraled in a front yard, stood in oozing mud blowing steam clouds from flared nostrils. It's colder, damper and well eerier in Hyder than it was up that mountain, I decide, as we climb creaky wooden stairs in search of bloody postcards. *BrinnGGGgg*, goes another bell above another door and drives away thoughts of murder.

'*Come in, don't be shy!*' A strong odour of cigars, damp wood and wet fur engulfs us. I want to retreat but we are too far inside for that. '*Can I sell you gentlemen anything or are you just wasting my time,*' a tobacco smoking bullfrog croaks but we can't make out from where.

'Just lookin!' Brad sings, in the direction of the question and finds himself a hiding place behind a rack of furs in a corner, laughing quietly as he browses. It's hot in the store and I'm sweating as I find and confront ol' hillbilly deluxe himself stood leaning on a long glass counter with both hands. That and a battered old wooden cabinet filled with weapons of all description stands between me and him, and he's grinning, or smiling, it's hard to tell behind all that hair.

'Hello there! Nice store you have here - do you sell postcards?'

'Yep, ya passed them on the way in!' He growls and points. He sounds like that fellow in Slingblade the movie. I retrace my steps to where a rack of postcards stands in full view next to the door. You can't miss them! The postcards are mostly old, some have images of Richard Nixon and the Apollo Moon Landing on but I manage to find five with wilderness scenes and the front of this store on them. The owner of which studies me from his lair and puffs on a big turd-like cigar while scratching away at a well-nicotined beard.

He coughs and swallows loudly and I'm not hungry anymore. I hear Brad chuckling from behind a sheepskin fort waiting for me to be fleeced. 'How much do you want for these?' I ask the man with the cigar, loudly, full of English cheer, and spread five postcards on his chipped glass countertop like a busted flush. Rows of knives, daggers and knuckle-dusters are displayed beneath us in the glass case. A long serrated bayonet hangs in a leather sheath hooked to a leather belt around his waist, which I ignore, and pretend to study handguns and long guns in a padlocked, meshed glass cabinet behind him, second-hand army surplus gear is piled on the floor beside it.

'Looks like an armoury in here.'

'How many ya got there?' he rasps, not smiling anymore.

'Erm, f-f-five.' Suddenly I'm Hugh Grant. I can hear Brad laughing, the shitheel bastard.

'Let me see nowww...five cards at fifty cents each like it says on the sign above where you got them, cough, comes to the grand total of, cough-cough, three bucks even. Will that be cash or credit?' He croaks, and hits me with a fake smile and a blast of cigar smoke,

but I refuse to flinch despite this man being as wild as a rabid dog in August. Instead, I ask him if Canadian money is good in these parts.

'Huh! Monopoly monies all's ya got I guess it'll have to do. That'll be six bucks.' I catch a glimpse of myself reflected in a chrome paraffin heater on the floor behind the counter as I count out six Canadian dollars in as small change as possible. Goddamn it, sir, I am forty years old and I have no idea why I am buying postcards from you, I think, and not say because he has guns and a big knife and I have Brad. *'Anything else I can do you for you British gentlemen?'*

'No thanks mate. Just the postcards!' I'm wandering why I said mate when Brad shows up all serious faced. 'Ready to go, Paul?' I'm about to reply when a door in the floor opens behind the counter and an apparition wearing a green ball cap atop a shaggy grey head attached to a dirty lumpy body appears.

'Howdo!' It grunts, wipes its hands with a filthy rag, smiles, and exits through a rear door whistling.

I look at Brad, he looks at me, 'Let's go,' he advises, and we head to the front door, stifling a laugh after wishing the owner good luck and a good evening.

'Have a nice evening yourself now fellers. Take care and good luck with the tire....'

Outside, down the steps and heading towards the car.

'Let's get out of here.'

'You see the shotgun!'

'Where!'

'Under the counter, reflected in the floor heater.'

'Jesus!'

'He'd have used it too.'

'Jesus.'

'I think he thought we were gonna rob him.'

'Get out!'

'Serious.'

'Fuck him, let's go for a pint.'

'After we leave the wheel at a garage.'

'Fancy getting shot buying postcards!'
'He thought you were a limey fag.'
'I am.'
'I know.'
'Brad.'
'What.'
'How did he know about the tire?'

Oh ho! It's Murphy. Tell me, why are you wearing dat terrible lookin' trilby? We sold de hat stand, an' dere's no place ter hang it.' - Puckoon, Spike Milligan

'So much for America!' I tell the not-so-friendly-anymore Customs lady as she asks us questions while searching the car. 'You don't mind if I take a photograph of you searching the car do you?' I ask, politely.

'I do if you don't mind!' She snaps.

'Oh, okay, sorry,' I reply, as she searches under the seats, door panels, the glove box, and when finishedcomes over and sniffs the air around me like a female bear.

'You guy's been to the Yukon?'

'This car doesn't go that fast! I tell her, stumped by the question.

'No. It's us. We were just through here.' Brad reminds her and we strike poses to jog her memory.

She squints, 'Oh, sorry. Thought I recognise you - did you get Hyderized?'

'Not this time.' Brad shows her the burst tire.

'Oh my God! What happened,' and off he went wasting precious drinking time spinning tales of woe and misfortune, which she laps up. I'm wondering how many men dressed like us, one with a scouse accent, have passed through here in the last few hours.

'Hyderized? We could have ended up winterized.' I tell her. She thinks I'm funny. I ask her if she's heard of Pierre Berton. She hasn't. She's never heard of Orangeville either, but wishes us a safe journey home as we drive off waving, horn squawking.

'She was impressed with our story, eh.'

'I think she would have been impressed with the weather forecast, mate!'

'True.'

The beer is cold in *Casey's Place* situated in the bowels of the King Edward Hotel, so I order two more and bother a drinker at the next table for the correct time. He tells us its 3:48pm in Stewart, which we can't comprehend, as it feels like we've been gone for days.

All stools at the bar were occupied when we strode in so we grabbed a table and ordered. The bar has the feel of a good place to relax in, have a good drink and meet the locals, then again most places are. We look the part and are full of tales but it's a three hour drive to Terrace and Brad doesn't want to stay here overnight and I can't blame him. Who wants to hang out in a bar full of old miners, trappers, loners, murderers and mountain men? Me, I do! It reminds me of a pub I used to drink in, even shares the same name. I could sit here all night. A native guy with a big bucknife on his belt, sat at the bar, smiles and gives me the nod as we drink up and leave.

'Seemed like a nice feller.'

'Cut your throat for a buck.'

'Here we go!'

'Don't start, Paul...' So I don't, though I should and he may be right but I need a ride.

The mechanic at the downtown garage told us he would need about an hour to fix the flat and that hour is up. I don't phone home from the lobby like I said I would on the way down as I don't want to worry them with tales of burst tires. Well, I wanted adventure! I have to catch a train to Prince George in the morning, at least I'll have something to write about.

Like, stood on the outskirts of town surrounded by mountains that slowly fade to black as the night draws in, except for one that wears an ice overcoat lit up by a setting sun. I'm waiting for Brad to come back from the garage as he dropped me off here on route to the garage to take in more sights. This is what I've been searching for, for so long. Canadian wilderness shows without the Lorne Greene voice-overs. Giant snowflakes flutter about my head as I marvel at a blue-green glacier that glows like a blow-fly and looks to be giving me the royal send-off. What a day. *Honk-Honkkkkkkk!* Clouds heavy with snow look as if they're about to drop a load any minute. A big snowfall is on the cards, warned the bartender at Casey's. Memories of a young lad spellbound by Canadian tales told by a Scouse uncle come to mind, and I have to dam a tear with the sleeve of my scratchy lumberjack shirt. *Honk-Honkkkkkkkk!* I don't want to leave right now and if Brad doesn't stop with that friggin horn I'm going to poke him in the eye with my pen.

Two of us buying postcards, on our way back home. -Beatles.

Back in the car, he tells me a big rusty nail caused the damage to the tire. The mechanic had asked him if he wanted it and he told him to bin it. 'Ah, that would have made a great souvenir,' I whine, as he drives like a bat out of hell and tells me to keep an eye out for moose as we don't want a high-speed encounter on the highway. Moose signs are everywhere, I suggest he slow down, but he's not listening. Turns out he can't get a signal on his phone and Tanya and the kids are expecting us for dinner. Who knew! To kill time and keep the driver awake we revert back to form and think up a name for the band we're going to put together if we survive the night. *Flaccid, Soft and Moist* is the winner and has absolutely nothing to do with age and performance.

Ears popping, bellies rumbling, we stop at Bear Glacier to empty bladders bursting from the beer and the familiar film-set fades to grey before our eyes. I take a look around and try to take it all in as you do on the last day of vacation. 'Takes a while for night to settle in out here, eh.'

'That's why I've got the foot down buddy.'

I'm thinking the opposite as I pee into ink-black water. 'Don't fall in!' I'm lost in thought and good fortune beneath glistening stars when the soft clunk of a car door closing bounces off a rock face and Brad breathes life into his car again with the twist of a key, and takes off slowly down the highway.

'Daydreamer!'

'Eh! Come back.' He lets me run behind for a minute before stopping, 'bastard!' and in no time at all we sneak up on a frozen over Surprise Creek, as the still sinking sun hits it with a last orange flash as a bright half-moon comes into play.

We follow a line of cats eyes and roar into darkness as Brad tries to reach Tanya on his cell phone again but still can't find a signal. A reminder of the shit we'd be in if we were stuck up that mountain or a tire were to give up the ghost again out here, something we don't want to talk about for long.

At Mezidian Junction the lake glows orange before being extinguished like a naked flame. Twilight of the Gods. Hanna South Creek is covered with a dusting of sherbet frost, as yellow lines and cats eyes and bright stars lead us on home in silence, both too exhausted, hungry, and tired of each other to discuss daft excursions into the wild without a life jacket.

The diner in Cedervale is owned by a friend of Brad's so we pull in for a bite to eat and hopefully a deal on the tab. Burgers, fries, coffee and water do the trick as I relay events of the day to our waitress, the owner unfortunately has the night off.

'You always have that effect on waitresses. It's your accent.'

'Don't be jealous, they feel sorry for me.'

The fight over the bill is a feeble one. I win and grab a handfull of mints on the way out after handing over the cash and stop to wave to the staff.

'Look at her smiling!'

'I know, it's the vampire in me.'

We arrive home too late to go out for dinner, to the disappointment of the kids, so we entertain them and their mom with tales of our adventure-filled day, to their great and sleepy amusement. I swap thanks, chuckles and books with Brad before we retire for the night, and he gets The Wasp Factory and I end up with Don Quixote, before I shower and pack, make ready for an early start. I've another journey ahead, hopefully filled with further laughs and adventure. A last glass of wine and a scribble and I'm fast asleep before something to do with a head and a pillow.

I've seen the mornings in the mountains of Alaska, I've seen the sun set in the east and in the west...and I'm far, far away, with my head up in the clouds. - Slade

'Paul, I hope you have made it back safely from Alaska. I want to hear all about your adventures after we parted ways. Write a letter, I will as well. I hope the wife and kids are well. I want to thank you for all your help and company. The journey just wasn't the same after you left. Your advice has helped me greatly and I think of you as a true friend. Stay in touch.

PS: I sent a card to Terry & Eric as well. I bet you 20 bucks Terry doesn't make it back for Christmas.

Your traveling friend,
Quint'

The Return

Having been told by a fellow factory worker in the spring of 1980 that I would be back within a month with my tail between my legs; I'm sat here on the Canadian wondering if he's left home yet. - Notebooks of Paul Henry Sutton

Wednesday, November 11th: Remembrance Day, a public holiday in British Columbia. I'm solo on the Skeena again after a farewell breakfast at a cozy Terrace restaurant, which was great, a fitting end to a fine stay. The girls were honest and cried and I tried not to be as I hugged them and their mother and father on the platform afterwards. I insisted that they didn't hang around too long as it was too emotional, so Brad drove off one last time in a cloud of dust, leaving me behind at a deserted Terrace train station on a cold and frosty morning.

I had no time to dwell on emotions because as soon as they were out of sight I had to hightail it to a nearby hotel as the station was sealed as tight as a jar of oven-roasted peanuts. After receiving permission and directions from an amused and efficient hotel receptionist I found myself sat keeping an eye on my backpack sat alone out there on the bathroom floor. The stall was too small for it to fit and the latch on the door was broken. Barry Manilow wrote his songs from a speaker behind ceiling tiles above my head and I whistled along in tune with him. Blueberry pancakes, maple syrup and black coffee was a silly thing to do to myself on such a cold morning. Not again!

To be 'matter of fact' about the world is to blunder into fantasy – and dull fantasy at that, as the real world is strange and wonderful. - Notebooks of Lazarus Long

Train-I-ride. I find myself surrounded by obnoxious middle-aged women who carry on as if at a bingo emporium in this cosy compact train carriage. It was funny for a few miles listening to them refer to the men in their lives like alien beings from another planet but, enough is enough, my heads pounding and I'm wishing that they would shut the hell up. Come back Barry Manilow, all is forgiven.

'Wonder if THE MEN have figured out how to open the food containers yet?'

'WHAT! Before they finish the beer you mean, ha, haaaa-aaaaaaaa, snort!' Another one yells and shoots her hands above her head like she's won the jackpot.

'Did you leave INSTRUCTIONS?' roars a third, and they machine gun each other with ear-splitting laughter as high-fives are cracked.

Four of them sit facing each other across a pull-out table and play speed Bridge and babble as they demolish a family size bag of Lays chips and knit at the same time. One woman's ears move as fast as she can chew and looks to be winning the game.

I don't want this it's too much of a change from my last trip on the Skeena. I want peace and quiet. Is that too much to ask for a fool such as I?

No way the train wasn't stopping at Terrace with this lot waiting on the platform surrounded by husbands, parents, friends and various-sized offspring. No way it was sneaking past, no need for a red triangular STOP sign I was told by Colleen Jones that I'd need to use to halt the Skeena at Terrace station. For the engineers who drive this train are decent men so they stopped, and the men that the Bingo Babes own breathed a combined sigh of relief that they did. A sigh powerful enough to dislodge hats from heads as train brakes squealed in protest and I was ping-ponged to the back of the queue in the mad rush of women to be first aboard, and I sit here bruised and battered trying to read Swing Hammer Swing, write something earth shattering, and get my shit together after a hectic three days. But the only thing earth shattering is coming from the mouths of them that resemble a World Wrestling Federation traveling circus on wheels. I watch them in search of something to eat as they unpack bags and boxes of food and swap waking-up on time stories, sandwiches and seats; some wander the aisles like hungry caged felines of all size and description.

But upon reflection - and what a pissed off one it is staring back at me from my window - it's cool to be the lonesome traveler again. I'm going to miss the Wild West, I hope it's not another seven years till I get to revisit it. I never thought I would become so attached. Scribbling in my journal has my eyes watering this morning and I vow to wear my glasses more often as a sandwich flies over my head and lands in the aisle, a casualty of the Food Wars of '98: The Sweat Offensive.

'You missed!'

'Sorry!'

I still can't believe I didn't think to take a photo of Brad changing the wheel up that mountain. I guess the camera was the last thing on my mind at the time. I wouldn't have missed it for all the tea in China though. It was not our turn to die. An image of this lot up there with us has me laughing out loud. At least we wouldn't have starved to death.

An old-timer dressed like Wild Bill Hickock stood at the station earlier wielding a brass tipped cane guarding a large cardboard box wrapped in yards of Scotch tape. I made the mistake of getting too close and he warned me off with a glower and a slight waving of the cane. His face was a picture when these women showed up, but they paid him no heed either and carried on regardless. I thought he was going to wipe them all out with that cane but common sense prevailed and he warned them off with his eyes. 'We're outnumbered, man.' I offered with a smile. He glowered. I winked. He growled. I moved on.

The women must to belong to a club of some kind, or a rugby team on tour, maybe heading a pie-eating contest. They have enough luggage for a month in Texas. A traveling pot-luck-dinner brigade, or battalion, are the Bingo Babes, as they keep on keeping on in a blaze of laughter, hairspray, perfume, sweat and nicotine.

'RIGHT LADEEE'S LET'S EAT!' roars the square one with the red hair.

'Sounds good, Wanda!' squeaks the mousy one with the nervous tic.

'WELL, WHATTA WE WAITING FOR - LET'S DO ITTTT-TTT!' orders Wanda, who reminds me of Sergeant Fury.

'Who's got the potato salad,' enquires a matronly card player as she swaps inedible cards for a plastic plate.

'Over here! Where's the knives and forks,' squeaks Mousy, standing on her seat.

'Mavis has them, Mavis has them. Where's Mavisss,' comes a cry from a rear seat.

'DON'T TELL ME SHE'S IN THE WASHROOM AGAIN!' roars Wanda, loud enough to rattle windows.

'I am and the white plastic one's are with the cabbage rolls!' comes a muffled shout from the washroom door.

'Got them right here...two packets. Who has the wine?' Oh, nice, a cigarette and alcohol drawl from up front and I make a note to find out who owns it.

'Dolly's got the red. DOLLEEEEE!'

Suffering Jesus!

'SHE MUST BE IN THE DOME. DOLLEEE!'

The Dome is only two cars away.

'Alrighty already, I'm right here. Whoops, why do I always do that with the mayo?'

'WHAT'S SHE DONE NOW, remember when she....'

'The damned mustard is all over the napkins. Awwwww!'

'Always the same with that woman, remember when she...'

'*Who* left the mustard open? Don't worry about napkins we'll wipe our hands on our clothes like the men do!' And they all cackle as one, even her still in the washroom.

I pull the peak of my ballcap over my eyes, sink lower in my seat and hide behind my book, use it as a shield to ward off mass cackles loud enough to scare birds from track-side trees. I could be in a mental institution. Maybe I am. Imagine living with them. Argh!

Luckily for me they vote to feast in the lounge car where they devour the lot according to one inmate. *'Not a nibble left,'* he whispered, as we compared notes at a water fountain. I tell him to be careful, take no chances, lay low until they stagger from the train. I tap the side of my nose twice and blend in with the scenery. He heads back to the Dome carrying a cross, a rolled up umbrella, and silver bullet for protection.

Later on, back at the water fountain, my spy informed me that conductor Babe (a ringer for the farmer in the movie) entertained, brown-nosed and tickled them allwith compliments and tales of his profession as they fattened him up for the slaughter in Prince George as that's where they're headed to do some shopping apparently. While up there pretending to be asleep, he heard them talking about a guy who went missing in the bush recently, an experienced hunter who knew what he was doing, found minus his guts. Black bear, they said, he must have scared it, they said.

Another hunter from Terrace shot a moose last week, they said, and had to stand there and soil himself when a grizzly appeared on the scene and stole his kill. He must have known he was safe as he didn't shoot the bear, they said, as after dinner knitting needles clicked and clacked in rhythm with the train as they discussed a story about a killer and his dog still on the loose somewhere between Prince George and Hyder. He's managed to avoid the Mounties since July. Shot four teenagers in Kitimat, they said.

Clickety-clack goes the Skeena, as it slows to a halt in the middle of nowhere to allow the old-timer with the cane to disembark with his taped up box. I watch him limp towards a cabin nestled and half-hidden amongst tall trees and dense bush about a hundred yards from the track. I follow his top hat as he makes his way down a path made invisible to onlookers by snow-covered hedges, obviously comfortable in his surroundings. Does he become a happy man when surrounded by what he knows and loves, free from the burden of the big city, safe at home, no tag, no slide. I follow the hat til it disappears behind a chubby spruce and wonder if he needs a key for his front door and does anyone await his arrival sat in front of a spitting woodstove.

I want to know what it takes to live out here. I need

to talk to him now. I grab books, pens and camera and begin stuffing them in my pack. Another train will be by in two days, I'll be all right. I'll rap on his door and he'll welcome me in and we'll sit around the stove and talk about what I need to know and I'll write it all down. I'm zipping zippers on my pack as a neighbour nursing a baby slips me a worried look.

She pulls the baby closer to her breast as the strange man in the lumberjack shirt leaves his seat, hefts his pack, and pulls the peak of his cap tight over his eyes and heads for the exit door.

I'm gonna do it, I'm getting off the train. I haven't a clue where I am and it's snowing hard out there but I don't give a shit, I'm gone mate!

What does she think of me: a passenger in a panic or a lunatic? Her child lets out a sharp cry and the train begins to move, engines hum louder, lights flicker and trees speed up, snowflakes strike glass hard before melting. The baby breaks into a full-on hungry scream and breaks the spell. I'm just a confused Englishman stood in the aisle with nowhere to go. Like I said, a lunatic. I sink back into my seat and unpack as the mother soothes her child beneath a white blanket. I smile, she smiles back. I apologise if I scared her, she tells me I didn't, asks if I'm okay. I tell her I'm fine, probably just need some sleep, maybe a moment of travel fever. She agrees, and I lay my head against the window and watch the great white north pass by.

It's passed now, the madness, whatever it was. I notice that local hunters mark trails with orange ribbon-like material tied to tree's and fences. One such trail comes to an end at a collapsed and dilapidated wooden shack like broken dreams, which for some reason has me thinking about drinking cold water from a stream overlooking Salmon Glacier yesterday, which leads me to a school camping trip in the Lake District in the early seventies.

Three cold and rainy days on the shoulder of the lake where the speed-freak Donald Campbell breathed his last, an energetic teacher who owned and drove an antique Bentley decided to take us Fell Walking. So, we packed sandwiches, donned non-waterproof clothing, tightened laces on Doc Marten boots, hid cigarettes about our person and went Fell Walking. We would have preferred hanging out with the girls from the inner-city school that shared the trip with us but Fell Walking it was, and off we went up a barren hill in teeming rain.

In a losing quest to spark up a cigarette and keep his box of matches dry one of the lads fell down a deep crevice and had to be rescued by two hung-over teachers with a rope as we all stood laughing and pointing. A steep hill developed into a mountain and we were warned about hypothermia, broken limbs, the dark, hunger, thirst, dying and death if we were to wander off alone and get lost. The happy teacher warned us not to drink from streams no matter how thirsty we were, despite us not carrying any water, but no sooner had he said it and took off at speed over a crag with a teacher from the girls school, all gobs were submerged in a stream as if guzzling life itself. After more Fell Walking we reached the summit to find the decomposing body of a sheep half submerged in the water supply. 'Yis didn't did yis?' Warned the energetic teacher to a chorus of vomiting which we were told could be heard back in Liverpool, but all survived after a brisk Fell Walk back down the mountain for a cup of tea and a chocolate biscuit. I haven't been back to the Lake District since, but sat here, can recall it all, especially the chapped lips, blue balls, and the girl with the cool sunglasses and long curly hair who lived in an afghan coat that smelled like a wet dog.

Kitwanga, which means people of the place of the rabbits, a favourite sketching site for Emily Carr the Group of Seven artist. A totem pole stands alone and the Seven Sisters Mountains peer through swirling mist in the distance behind it. I'm looking down upon the same road that we used to find Alaska. Blowing snow reminds that we were right to get out of Stewart when we did or we'd be still drinking beer at the bar waiting for ploughs to rescue us. Ice covered lakes and streams we passed yesterday look somehow more colder and desolate from the train. Trees appear to wait with snow-bowed heads for the next Samurai sword slash of winter. Mist-covered mountains pipe the Skeena River past as it pursues its mad dash journey to ocean adulthood from pre-pubescent trickle.

Smithers, historic ghost towns, totem poles and Chinese graves can be found in the centre of the Bulkley Valley, surrounded by Hazleton, Babine, Omineca and Telkwa mountain ranges. Grizzly, moose, and mountain goat that roam the Interior Plateau are hunted here. The time is 1:20pm and it's snowing heavily, I love it. The mother and child are fast asleep in their seat. A bald eagle follows alongside before swooping skyward as The Skeena slows and comes to a halt at Smithers, a familiar place. The old station is still closed. and wood-chippers sit idle next to trucks filled with lumber destined for the big city, and I'm off for a walk outside to clear cobwebs from my train-addled head.

The frontier bar in Prince Rupert reminded me of past excursions to Toronto bars on pay-day Fridays in company of work mates from all over the world. Another lesson in a city nailed tight to the Golden Horseshoe after another gruelling week painting sealed up Victorian mansions in Toronto's affluent Rosedale district with a paint fume damaged crew of painters. After one week on the brush I let myself be steered into the warmth and sounds of a Yonge Street strip bar by a workmate from South America. We should have nipped into the Duke of Gloucester instead but found a seat, ordered beers, and made ourselves comfortable. Beer arrived eventually, carried high on a tray by a waitress acompanied by a dancer who introduced herself and asked if we wanted her to dance. I told her just one song as I had to be on my way home soon. Two songs later she was still sat charming us with tales of motorcycle gangs in Montreal and she loved our accents. I ordered another beer as Bob Seger finished running against the wind and a DJ told drinkers to give it up for Candy, which I didn't feel like doing. Gathering gloves, scarf and coat, I thanked the dancer and handed her a five. 'You're joking honey, make that forty!' she sang. 'Six songs, one dance, forty bucks, pay up,' she told us and slapped a hand on the table. My work-mate told her she was full of it, we gave her another five each and after using the washroom, headed for the exit where a well-fed, tattooed troglodyte sat half-cocked on a high stool wearing a tuxedo teeshirt, jeans and motorcycle boots.

'You owe her forty bucks, buddy,' he grunted in my ear and pointed back over his shoulder with a thumb the size of a chicken leg at the dancer now 'dancing' for someone else. I shook his hand from my elbow, told him to take a hike and handed a ticket to a gum-snapper working the coat-check, who popped a pink bubble and went in search of my tool-bag which I'd been required to hand over upon entering.

'Forty bucks buddy, best pay up!'

'No chance, pal, she's on the fuckin scam. We gave her fifteen for one dance.'

I had to shout as a long-dead Australian singer sang about his big balls. 'Pay up buddy or I'll have to call the cops,' he grunted at my pal and made a move to grab my arm, but something behind us caught his attention as I sidestepped rather quickly. Ahem.

I grabbed my bag and we were outside among pedestrian throngs navigating Yonge Street. Nobody gave chase. 'Total scam, mate, last time we go there!' My pal agreed, laughed, and went in search of a streetcar as I went north to the subway. My family were sleeping, the house quiet when I arrived home. I crept into the shower like a two-bit thief in the night and vowed to stay away from strip-joints.

I woke to the smell of coffee and the silence of an empty house. A note on the kitchen table told me I was on my own for the day, they were Christmas shopping and would be home for dinner. The neon Elvis clock with the swinging leg on the wall told me it was almost noon. I stuffed work whites into the washing machine, making sure to be liberal with the bleach, put the kettle on and made some lunch.

The bag in the back porch wasn't mine. I knew it as soon as I spotted it from the kitchen. It contained shrink-wrapped copies of *Butts*, *Juggs* and *Spank* magazine, a Walkman disc player still in its packaging, a price-tagged multi-colored scarf, a new pair of leather gloves, a six-pack of batteries and a large chocolate chip cookie.

It was a bit of a chore but I got my bag back, tools all accounted for, the gum-snapper had a good laugh about it and Meathead wasn't there.

A bullethole spotted in a waiting room window at Terrace Station has me pondering life as well as who pulled the trigger. Judging by the amount of dead foliage scattered either side of rail lines, beaver have no idea which way victims are going to fall as they continue their mission to wipe out the tree population of British Columbia, CN property, fences and power lines.

Shrieks of machine-gun laughter have me sat up straight in my seat at Broman Lake but I'm not complaining as I might have missed the sight of a valley filled with beautiful yellow flowers. High up on a hill sits a tiny house, smoke pouring from a single chimney, posing, as if waiting for an artist to happen by. Its metal roof winks once, twice in the sun as if to draw attention. Who owns it? I could never own something as beautiful as that as it wouldn't be mine.

Burns Lake flashes by, the gateway to Tweedsmuir Park, the centre of the lakes, home to bald eagles, prime fishing spots and millionaires. Entrance point to the biggest wilderness park in British Columbia, accessible only by train, floater-plane or boat. We don't stop, but instead cross the Endako River back and forth numerous times in an orderly fashion. The navvys who laid this section of line must have been on the whisky as it's like a sideways rollercoaster.

I don my invisible man cloak as the Bingo Babes stream in from the dining car to inform anyone that gives a hoot that *'it's minus twelve in Prince George,'* which means, *'it's time for the long-johns, ladies!'*

Those who find ugly meanings in beautiful things are corrupt without being charming. This is a fault. Those who find beautiful meanings in beautiful things are the cultivated. For these there is hope! - Oscar Wilde

Prince George.*Thursday, November12th.* I awaken disoriented but well rested at 7am on the nose. Wind howls and blows causing branches to scratch at rooves and windows as I lay here warm and comfortable beneath a big fluffy comforter in a king-size bed in train driver Don's spare bedroom. I'm camped in the back of his split-level house on the banks of the Fraser River. It's still dark and it sounds rough out there. I can't imagine steering a raft down the Fraser in these conditions, man. Some explorer me, I would need a cup of tea first. Dons still sleeping. I heard his wife take their son to school earlier and thoughts of my own offspring starting the day in similar fashion has me missing them even more.

We had a lot of fun here last night as we sat around the fire recounting tales and lies of things done and seen since my last visit which felt like months ago.

True to his word, Don was waiting for me, patiently as always, at Prince George station as the Skeena pulled in over an hour late and off we went for a pint at a downtown Pub, where I hammered him with tales of Alaska, Stewart, supposedly abandoned mines, flat tires, overflowing toilets, and the train ride from hell to get here. Don just shook his head, smiled, laughed, asked more questions, and ordered us another Guinness.

The kettle on the kitchen stove boils bringing forth a gargled whistle from a frothing spout. My train leaves for Jasper at 8:30am. For now I have only a ticking clock on the wall for company as I think of home and the long journey ahead to reach it. An alarm goes off somewhere in the bowels of the house and

startles me into dropping a steaming tea-bag onto the tiled kitchen floor via my bare foot. Don's awake. It's time to go.
Free coffee awaits us hidden in a corner of the waiting room at Prince George station. We say our goodbyes again and wish each other well and I stroll off, deep in thought, towards the Skeena, boots crunching prints into fresh crisp snow. A smiling face appears from behind a movie-camera in an open train doorway and the owner proceeds to record me for posterity. For posterity's sake I dance a wee jig, smile back, and sing a 'Good mornin' how's it goin,' and climb aboard to be told by Smiley that we're in for more snow and it's going to get much colder. I tell her I hope it heaves snow just for the hell of it and sure as shit it does. Giant white flakes kiss glass as we head off in the direction of Jasper. I forgot to take a picture of the Iron Horse restaurant again. Oh well, I'll be back someday. I tell a hung-over again Conductor Babe how much my head still aches from the pounding it took from him and the Bingo Babes yesterday. He gives me the old 'Ohh now, we were just having some fun, what life's all about,' and moves on gingerly. I laugh as I unpack and he becomes even more stand-offish. Things would be different if I had a first class ticket, I tell Smiley and her camcorder as she films me acting daft again and fills me in on her English heritage and Canadian experiences. She's Australian and obviously under the watchful eye of Conductor Babe as he wobbles about giving me the stink eye and checking tickets. I think he's jealous. Nice one!

Giscome (Est.1863) glides into view on the edge of the McGregor Plateau and once boasted the biggest sawmill in British Columbia. It's situated at the lowest point of the great Arctic Divide, a fitting place to steal a newspaper from the food car to find out that Everton Football Club lost again, this time to Sunderland in the Worthington Cup, but the big story in these parts is the settlement the Nisga have won from the Crown after much arguing back and forth for decades. They've been granted two thousand square kilometers of their own land back and I envision about six thousand native people giving it the thumbs-up on the Charlotte Islands as I send two fingers in direction of Everton Football Club.

All of a sudden it's Christmas in Penny (pop. 32), as we stop to deliver mail to a party of snow covered locals. Snow whirls around the top of the biggest living Christmas tree I ever did see. It must be a hundred feet tall. It dwarfs us, this evergreen Eiffel tower, stood proudly yards from the track close to where the Bowron River almost meets up with the Fraser. Where families of grizzly and osprey raid salmon spawning grounds during the summer months and sub-alpine forests and fields of wildflowers are home to munching moose and hustling bustling beaver. I like that! We're not too far from McBride either (yes, that one) and just like that snow turns to rain and wipes out a winter wonderland. Everything turns cloudy, foggy and grey. Last time I rode this stretch of track I was driving the train. Wolves scatter up and over a grass embankment and disappear into thick bush to escape the intruding yellow and blue anaconda as I chow down on a roast beef sandwich and a bowl of soup made last night by a steward who will be known as 'Soupy' from now on, I tell him. He's a likable dude and I dismiss my planned attempt at being miserable with no traveling companions on the homeward journey.

As we chat a man dressed in combat gear asks me suspiciously if I thought Prince Rupert was rough. 'Not as rough as Alaska but he *was* drunk,' I tell him in my no fear of dangerous places voice accompanied by loud sniff, shoulder twitch and bob of the head, which does the trick as he takes off to the Dome never to bother me again.

An abandoned Maclean's magazine with a smiling Paul and Linda McCartney on the cover has me feeling all emotional as Canada flashes by through clear glass. Shots of Linda riding a horse weeks before her death is too heavy and I sit sad and quiet until loud laughter coming from the Dome awakens me from whatever malady engulfed and I go in search of the source.

Dried river beds and mountains greet us at McBride and the source of the laughter is a middle-aged rail buff in his cups who tells me the time is one 'o clock and that McBride was known as Siding 39 before they re-named it after a Premier Richard McBride who once ran the joint and that was that but at least I was smiling again.

Upon alighting at the premiers old hangout I find myself surrounded by the Cariboo Mountains to my left and the Rocky Mountains to my right. I decide to take respite from a biting wind by moulding in with a circa-1919 station house in process of being re-facedwith cedar shingles that smell absolutely marvellous.

Taking in the scenery, I observe Smiley, now known as Aussie Girl, being courted by various male VIA staff who cajole her into climbing aboard the baggage car, by way of a step-ladder, to have her photo taken by a photographer who works for a local newspaper. Babe fusses over her like a randy old matron and films her with her video camera as she plays the helpless tourist part to the hilt, which has me in stitches. To wipe the smile from Babes face I wander over to ask him if I have time for a quick beer at the bar up the street.

'NO, we don't stop here long enough!' he growls, followed by a nasty sniff. He's not amused at all. I watch him slaver over Aussie Girl's arse as she climbs carefully from the baggage car and retrieves her camera. She spots me making silly faces behind the backs of her admirers and points the camera my way. Babe thinks she's fiming him which has the daft get chewing on his teeth when he takes a look behind him.

'Is that gonna be on aussie telly,' I ask her and boot a large stone that bounces off a wheel bogey and into touch as she heads my way laughing. 'For sure, mate,' she tells me, clicks the off button, and informs me in a husky whisper that McBride is a close community of seven-hundred and twenty isolated souls and was established in 1913. She didn't like, but it sounded better coming from her.

Later on, while sat scribbling messages on Alaskan postcards bound for family members in England, feet up on a nostalgic steel ashtray in my favourite spot in the Park Car, she popped her head in and invited me to join her for a beer, which I did. Passengers slept or sat peering through snow-spattered windows as we laughed and told tales in the lounge car and talked of tall cedar, silver birch and hemlock that stood guard over salmon hatcheries and a log cabin surrounded by dogs and kennels and deep sticky mud as The Skeena snuck up on *Tete Jaune Cache* (Pop, 41) and I pledged to forget about anymore thoughts regards solitary and miserable.

'Competition between the Northwest Company (Nor'westers) and the Hudson's Bay Company increased as the H.B.C. pushed further and further into the trading territory previously held by the Northwest Company. In February of 1819 John Clarke, of the H.B.C.'s St. Mary's post on the Smoky-Peace River confluence, chose Jose Gaubin to lead an expedition with a band of Iroquois to cross the mountains into New Caledonia to see if the natives could be induced to trade with the Hudson's Bay Company. In December of 1819, Ignace Giasson began another H.B.C. push up the Smoky. Colin Robertson (after whom Mt. Robson is possibly named) man-in-charge of the Hudson's Bay Company's operations in the area, prepared written instructions specifying that the group be accompanied by the yellow-haired Iroquois guide: Pierre Hastination or Tete Jaune as he came to be called. The group was to ascend to the Grand Forks of the Smoky where they were to meet another group of Iroquois, wait until Spring, and then cross the mountains (via Robson Pass) to make friends with the Shuswap Indians of the upper reaches of the Fraser. On June 10, 1820, James McDougal recorded in the Northwest Company's journal at Ft. St. James that he had heard "a report of there being at the Forks of Fraser's River one of the H.B.'s Co's clerks and three men".

Due to the inability of the Northwest Company and the Hudson's Bay Company to withstand intense competition they amalgamated under the name of the Hudson's Bay Company. George Simpson took over from Colin Robertson as man-in-charge of the area. Since the time Tete Jaune had guided for the Hudson's Bay Company, he had been hunting and trapping in the area between the Smoky River Post, Jasper and Fort George and had established a fur cache on the Grand Fork of the Fraser (somewhere in the vicinity of the present day viewpoint).

By 1822 Simpson had been appointed Governor of the Northern Department. As he had reports that the area "between the headwaters of the Smoky and those of Canoe and Fraser's Rivers... abounds with beaver" he suggested the building of a Hudson's Bay Company outpost at Tete Jaune's cache. J. La Roque, with a reputation of being a good quality trader, was dispatched by Simpson to establish this outpost on the Grand Fork of the Fraser. However, after considering organizational and transportation problems, Simpson decided against his own idea and set out with his expert Iroquois canoe men to overtake La Roque. Simpson decided to discontinue fur trading in the Jasper area and transferred La Roque to eastern Canada.

Later, however, Simpson was to change his mind once more, and in 1825 he sent James MacMillan guided by Tete Jaune to survey the Yellowhead Pass area. One year later he ordered the "requisition of 500 Dressed Moose and Deer Hides be provided and forwarded by the Saskatchewan District to Tete Jaune Cache on or before the close of September proxo".

"Arrived at Tete Jaune Cache after encountering very hard travel. Three men were nearly exhausted, and one of them died of a vile disease. Tete Jaune Cache is a place where one Iroquois Indian half breed who was fair-haired, had made a fur cache, or a place to store his catch of furs and was known as Tete Jaune or Yellowhead. It is near the meeting of the Grand River - which flows from the base of Mt. Robinson - and the Fraser River."

- George McDougal, April 25, 1827

Tete Jaune continued trapping and trading in the area and by 1827 had relocated his cache from the Grand Fork of the Fraser to the vicinity of the Shuswap salmon fishing camp on the Fraser

River where the town of Tete Jaune Cache stands today. The relocation was made to facilitate trading with Fort George. Unfortunately, Tete Jaune was not allowed to continue trapping. Sometime in 1828, near the headwaters of the Smoky River, he, his brother, their wives and children were murdered by the Beaver Indians for revenge on the Iroquois for their earlier encroachment into the Beaver's hunting territory.

-Jeff Waugh, local historian, November 1998

3:00pm. Winter blooms at Red Lake as I sit scribbling undisturbed in the Park car, feet up on the same ashtray, sipping on a hot cup of tea watching the wilderness do its thing as two bald eagles fish from a tree at the foot of Mount Robson all shrouded in thick white cloud from ample belly to mysterious head, Moose Lake still sat at his feet reflecting her lover, driving snow flecking her face. It's just gone five bells and there to meet me in Jasper is a herd of elk. I ask them if they missed me as much as I missed them but they just ignore me and carry on shitting and grazing.

It's finally cold enough to wear my winter coat for the first time, I tell Soupy, as I bid him farewell and ignore Babe who returns the favour. It's good to be back in Jasper. Old Man Mountain still watches over as travellers meet and greet on a platform festooned with plumes of breath and steam from human and machine. I take a gulp of cold mountain air and enter the overheated station to use the phone. No answer at home, so I hit the sidewalk in search of a place to stay.

I have a place in mind. Quint pointed it out to me last week.A quaint white house on the corner of Cedar and Patricia where the landlord offers me a single room for $25 a night. I tell him I'll take a look around first and traipse around town for ten minutes pretending to look for somewhere cheaper and on return the landlord tells me the rent is still the same, which has us laughing. He hands over the key and shows me how to lock the front door before giving me a short tour of the house, and here I am in a small clean room with a single bed and sink with clean towels, a plastic chair, and wooden table with cheap lamp placed next to a window with a view. The house is empty apart from me and Bruno who tells me I can pay the rent in the morning and that Jasper is quite isolated in case I decide to renage. He's a funny guy! The bathroom and fridge in the hall are all mine as well, he tells me.

Around 6pm I'm stood yapping with the family on a public phone close to rail lines as trains clank past and that same herd of elk manicure a grass verge close-by while eyeing me hungrily. Janice doesn't believe me when I tell her how close trains and elk are. It's been a while since we last spoke. All are still alive and healthy and miss me and my postcards have started arriving and its cold and snowing in Orangeville as well. I'm told to watch my spending until I get to the West Edmonton Mall where I can go nuts with the credit card to buy them pressies. The kids leap from the receiver and I'm stood there feeling like a lost boy wondering what possessed me to leave them for such a long time. Next thing I'm yelling 'good-byes' to the amusement of a couple of passing dog walkers. I smile back and head off down a deserted road in search of something substantial to eat. A sandwich seller in an empty fast food emporium gives me the impression he thinks I'm about to hold him up but I surprise him by paying for the roast beef sub. A liquor store is empty except for a friendly owner who points to where beer is kept in a glass walled walk-in enclosure in a corner. He encourages me to navigate loaded shelves filled with expensive wines and sherry's on the way there. I spot myself on a security monitor situated above a large glass door which I can't figure out how to open until it dawns on me I'm trying to open a fixed window. The door I need has ENTER written in bright red letters on a piece of paper stuck to it. I give myself a smile on the monitor and look back at the amused booze seller and point at the sign and he smiles back and makes a pulling motion with both hands and I find myself stood in ice-cold beer nirvana, as shoppers wander in to browse and observe me floundering from brand to brand like a scouse goldfish.

After a few laps I exit the store with a six-pack of Black Label cans after handing over cash to a highly amused owner who pretends not to notice my recently developed facial tic.

On the short walk back to Bruno's I can't shake the feeling that I've lost something. I slip into an all-night grocery store in search of junk food and a newspaper and spend ten minutes walking the length and breadth of small compact aisles before deciding upon a large bag of Lays Barbeque. Concern is drawn all over the face of a dear old lady stood behind the counter with one hand on the phone. I can't help it, I want to tell her, I'm stuck in a one man play and can't get the curtain to close. I smile and she smiles back as I pay for the chips and yesterday's news and escape clutching my brown-bagged haul to scurry Quasimodo-like across a slushy main road and up icy stairs to the safety of my warm room, to find the sub cold, the beer warm, and the chips stale.

The headline on the front page of the Edmonton Sun roars about a recent rash of murders in the city as The Kinks sing 'paranoia deep destroyer' in my head. I bin the paper and curl up naked beneath clean sheets and fall into a deep sleep in which I dream of hot chicken fajitas, cold Mexican beer and Juliette Binoche.

Friday November 13th. I awake at 6:30am from a dead sleep thinking about my Nin, Lizzy Mac, who dreaded Friday's falling on the 13th in any month in any year in her lifetime. Black Irish, she read tea leaves in cups and coals in fireplaces and when Gypsies came -a-knocking selling clothes pegs, wild flowers, dogs or children, she would put the kettle on and refuse to answer the door in case they laid a curse on her for not needing any of the above. Pro another logue on the fire....

It's not the leaving of Liverpool that grieves me it's my darling when I think of thee. - The Dubliners

History mystery. I was born in Liverpool not down by the docks or the son of a sailor a sailor's son, just the offspring of a handsome Catholic builder from one side of the tracks and a beautiful Protestant mother from a much more interesting and entertaining other. Brought into the world in Broadgreen Hospital when Teddy boys were ripping up picture houses to the sound and vision of the likes of Little Richard, Bill Haley, Gene Vincent and Eddie Cochran; as two teenagers practiced songs, harmonies and the guitar in Jim McCartney's kitchen as he played the piano in the living room. 1958. The Empress of Canada was shuttling former devotees of a shriveling Empire from the Mersey to the St. Lawrence in droves, and Liverpool where stuck in the depths of the second division, Everton Football Club above them by a million miles and smiles.

One of my earliest memories is of me sporting a kiss curl aboard the grand old Empress as my Uncle John and Auntie Betty and Cousin John ascended a gangplank as massive funnels grazed rain heavy clouds as the ship waited patiently for passengers and cargo to board. I was given the chance to explore her decks before she departed as families bade happy and sad farewells. I remember the smells of the dirty old river and the sounds of leavers and stayers yelling, laughing and crying, before being drowned out by klaxon horns. I remember waving like mad as the Empress, freed from thick restraining ropes, nuzzled big black tires strung along the wooden docks of the Pier Head and sailed off to another world. I remember how much I wanted to be aboard.

Uncle John failed to settle down 'over der', unfortunately, and returned home somewhat sheepishly in 1968 by plane accompanied by wife and mystified son. My mum, now separated from my father, needed help to pay the rent on a flat in a big old Edwardian house and they took her up on the offer to share flat, rent, mould and leaky roof. And beneath that leaky roof sat a house divided into four homes. Ours consisted of two large bedrooms and a living room complete with working fireplaces, a bathroom, and a long hallway leading from a huge front door, a door fit for kings. Coal was the only source of heat apart from speed-walking on the spot or running to the shops for change for the electricity metre. We had a tiny kitchen too, minus a fridge which we didn't need as jellies and trifles would set in the front bedroom, powdered milk never went off and margarine lasted as long as the bread and jam did.

That long cold hall served as lifeline from that large front door and dark nooks and crannies would hide ghosts of former owners and tenants. Off the hall to the right was a mildew battered bathroom complete with rusting ancient claw-foot tub and a pull-chain toilet which in winter would freeze solid and surprise us all in. Ever pee or worse on ice? Saturday nights held world records for the quickest baths by a family of seven with Uncle John last one in wearing his flat cap to keep warm, and barnacle tide marks took ages to scrub off with Ajax once the cold water drained.

The landlord of this gregarious money-pit was a salacious character by the name of Bobby Fagan who would have given his movie namesake a run for his money. Beneath all of this Edwardian charm was a dank Edwardian cellar, the bane of my existence, where coal was stored. Smelly coal emptied from sacks by big coal-blackened 'coal men' through an exterior 'coal hole' covered by a rusted iron grill to make sure we didn't follow the coal into the hole. Sometimes this rusted iron grill had a mysterious habit of dislodging itself in the dark leading to misfortune for those attempting to steal washing from the line in the back yard if they chose that route.

My main job around the house was to fill a bucket with coal every morning and make and light a fire in the living room fireplace, praying that a fuse wouldn't blow in mid-shovel as tendrils of iced- fog swirled about my feet. Don't scream, panic, or drop the shovel, find the stairs and pray that someone hasn't locked the door for a laugh. After leaving school I was offered a well-paying job down a local coal mine and was laid flat by a sudden mysterious illness until the position was taken by someone lucky enough to have had central heating or a servant as a child.

This grand olde Edwardian mansion came complete with my secret garden where I hid out in or played football with my cousin John in all weathers with burst plastic footballs for hours on end. In summer it was a magic garden filled with withered apple and pear trees sagging beneath the weight of belly-aching fruit, which without fail would draw neighbourhood thieves like flies to boiled shite. There was plenty for everyone according to my mum when we first moved in, she was a kind woman until a gang of midnight marauders, sweaters bulging with pilfered fruit, stole our tent and what remained of her goodwill and that was the end of that as far as she was concerned, they could all starve, as it was raining cats and dogs at the time and my mate and I were fast asleep in the tent.

Ah, rubber groundsheets, smelly old blankets, library books, flasks, and cheese sandwiche. Camping out in a leaky old army tent in our garden during the summer holidays was all the rage and the freedom to burp, fart, swear and giggle with mates all night was unbeatable.

I wondered if all Edwardian homes smelled of fresh air in a can and fly paper, did they all have wallpaper that smelled of cheese, as I found a warm bit in the bed and made up songs to entertain my sisters pretending to be asleep in the bed they shared with my mum. The big front room we slept in was divided into two bedrooms by my new wardrobe, dressing table and chest of drawers for privacy. 'The house is alive with the smell of mildew,' I would sing which would have them laughing and our mum running. On with the light, 'What's going on, who's laughing?'

'No-one mum it's our Paul!' they'd answer in unison, and I'd lay there pretending to be dead with my eyes open as she stood there shivering in a housecoat, nightie, two pairs of socks, curlers and a knitted wool hat. 'Who's laughing, I said?' And that would be the signal for us all to laugh.

'I thought you were dead!'

'I am mum.' And off we'd go again, laughing, it was great.

It must have been murder for her to laugh at all as the family was rank with the smell of divorce, but she still managed to make us laugh at the daftest things. She had to be strong as apart from keeping us from starvation or death from apple robbers and mildew, she was 'the divorced one' to neighbours, workmates, bosses and shopkeepers. A single mother in male-dominated Northern England raising three kids without assistance from government or master builder ex-husband. After she was granted the divorce on grounds of cruelty, he never paid a penny in alimony and disappeared.

So, instead of dining out with him and his secretary we had powdered milk over corn-flakes and toast buttered straight from the coal fire, fried eggs and chips with peas, tomato soup, corned beef hash and beans and banana and custard with the skin on and more tomato soup; and we learned how to roast chestnuts over a spitting fire while singing and telling stories as flames licked up the blackened chimney and shadows danced on living room walls. I never owned nylon or polyester shirt, socks or pyjamas without burn holes in them. The power people and those in power would go on strike and send televisions, homes, neighborhood and entire counties and country into darkness, the sounds of empty streets and bolts slamming home could be deafening.

'What's that you've got there?'

'Nothing mum.'

Just a prized turtle shell slipped it into my mouth like

a forbidden sweet at dinnertime, and while doing my Henry Cooper boxer imitation burped the shell into a bowl of soup causing my sisters to scream.

'Dirty little swine, where did you get that from?'

'Dug it up this morning mum.'

'From your pet graveyard?'

'Yes mum.' Good Catholics never lied.

'Just you wait!'....The chase was on, rat-a-tat-tat with dishcloth, spoon or tea towel as I fumbled with the door latch in effort to escape as my sisters laughed in the background. We are all in this together and we will laugh and ignore the fleas brought home from school.

Saturday nights were spent taking turns entertaining around the roaring fire. Uncle John would imitate Al Jolson dressed in a British Legion jacket with soot-blackened face and white-gloved hands which he waved about in imitation of his idol. 'Swanneee, how a luv ya, how a luv ya,' to the vinyl record spinning on the portable record player hidden behind the couch that his audience sat on in various states of shock or catatonia as he mimed away into the broom handle. He was a master mimicker of the great white minstrel was uncle John and I still associate Saturday nights with Jolson and the smell of burning coal, cigarette smoke, brown-ale fumes, and, 'When the red red robber goes rob, rob, robbin' along...'

Sunday mornings were reserved for cleaning the house with hung-over adults accompanied by Engelbert Humperdick and Tom Jones. We all warbled as we polished until chores were finished which would lead to tales from 'Over der', and its avalanches and ten mile wide freeways and boat-sized cars and massacres of priests in Kwebeck by Indians and the tales got taller as winter turned to summer. 'The snow was so deep you had to climb down the chimney to get in the house, lad, good thing we lived on a steep hill.'

'Thirty cars wide the road was and if you missed your turnoff you were knackered as it would take a week to get home, right Betty?' '

'Should've seen the blood lad! Gallons of it running down the steps like red floor paint. Who's changing the friggin records?'

Pleeeeeezzz releeese meee, let me gooooo....

'He's great him with the carpet on his chest isn't he!' Come two o'clock they'd all be back in bed snoring, leaving us to put the records away, stoke the fire and play with my turtles. Uncle John hoovered my newt up one Sunday morning in a cleaning frenzy and denied it but I knew it was him when I found the body in the bin covered in dust. He broke the head off a shepherd in the Crib one Christmas and glued it back on with brown glue. It stood on the mantle-piece with a wobbly-head til new year waiting for the glue to dry. 'The fire'll dry it lad.'

Saturday afternoons, when we weren't playing football in the Somme-like mud, him Peter Thompson me Gordon Banks, my cousin and I would be sat in front of the same roaring fire sipping tea and reading 'Yankee' comics or playing Table Soccer while listening to the football results as they came crackling over the radio in a plummy, we still rule the world, the rain in Spain regulation British Broadcasting Company accent.

'Forfar, Five...East Fife, Four,'....crackle, hiss, whine....Hamilton Academicals, nil... Queen of the South, nil,' *whistle, croak, hum, screech, hum.'*

We never won anything because of a 'boorgewah' plot to keep us in the shit according to Uncle John sat at the table scribbling or jabbing the air with a chewed nub of a pencil while flipping a well-worn slipper with an angry foot.

'Wait till the revolution lad. If we win the pools him on

that radio will be first against the friggin wall.'

Saturday also brought the hair-washing with the special shampoo and torture with the steel comb after the bath olympics, after which we'd be sat on the floor in front of the rented black and white television in cold nylon pyjamas, sucking quietly on our sweets and burping fried bread, eggs, bacon, mushrooms, tinned tomatoes, black pudding, sweet tea and warm lemonade residue. Competitions to see who could make the sweets last the longest was always won by sister Maria as Batman and Robin Kerpowed the Penguin and Joker into cartoon catharsis.

The latest news on Vietnam or Northern Ireland or Ted Heath and Harold Wilson failed to ruin the mood, and we'd sit there waiting for a glimpse of John and Yoko Ono Lennon which would bring forth sage wisdom from concerned elders. 'Oh eh, he's not well him that Lennon.'

'Look at the head on her!'

'It's the drugs lad. See what happens when you take that cannabis!'

'He was alright till he met that chinee, wasn't he Sally?' and my mum would go along with it as the, 'friggin' weird Beatle', alienated himself from the world between stark footage of blanketed bodies in Belfast streets and napalmed girls running naked down Asian roads. 'Yeah, yeah, yeah!' Dr. Who and The Monkees would make an appearance before it was 'Night, night, sleep tight, watch the bed-bugs don't bite!'

On the downside, the Football Pools man never knocked on our front door clutching a suit case full of pound notes, which I blamed on us living in that big house with the fruit tree's, which from the main road made us look well off, plus the actor Rex Harrison was rumoured to have lived there at one point. In reality, the Addams Family had nothing on us.

'You must be loaded living in a house like that,' a lad from school told me despite the fact that I wore the same 'Bobby washable' jeans as he did.

I was 'Massambula of the Big House 'I decided one morning sat on the front step watching the rain wash my bike for free. I would tell my rabbit's I wouldn't let them end up in the pot as I fed them carrot-tops and potato peels. Hiding up a tree one morning I overhead Auntie Betty tell Uncle John, 'We're skint, but we have each other,' and he told her, 'Yer not poor as long as you can laugh girl,' and this made me laugh that much I nearly revealed my hidey-spot.

I wish I'd carved, 'An uneventful childhood is a wasted childhood' into the bark of one of those fruit tree's but my mum would have battered me and school beckoned with a long scary finger.

Yeah, Canadian seeds planted in the fertile mind of a young lad in late sixties Liverpool. I like to think it was the constant rain that helped bring them to fruition, but it was more explorer nutrition courtesy of Uncle John. At school we were learning about the countries of the Commonwealth but they didn't know yet that the Empire was long gone as they still used a map with all the pink bits that used to be red till they faded. After Australia and the smaller countries that started with a 'B' came Canada, and somehow my teacher had been informed of my Canadian relatives and no sooner than I could say 'Kwebeck' a note was dispatched to Uncle John and after some words of encouragement and cajoling along the lines of, 'Get up there yer big Jessie, what's wrong with you have nothing else to do,' he was at the door in his just ironed Legion suit, shirt and tie, shoes and hair spit-shined in preparation for a one-hour presentation on the colony of Canada.

I'd never seen him look so clean as when he walked into the classroom after giving me a wave from the skinny window in the door. Politely ushered in by a fawning teacher and after whispered instructions in her ear, at least I think that's what it was, he commandeered her desk with his arse and off he went.

Fabulous stuff, all of which I knew off by heart. The snow, the bears, the freeways, the blood, the Indians, the priests, Expo '67, ice- hockey, all enhanced even more for the occasion. He was a star and I was proud of him as class members stood to applaud. I swore I did see him blush, which he blamed on the temperature of the classroom, 'the heat in there Sally, you could have fried an egg on my forehead!'

He'd had to nip in the Huyton Park on the way home for a quick pint to cool him down, he told us all later.

I remember the girls giggling and the boys laughing when he'd raised his trouser leg to demonstrate how high winter boots went to on your average Canadian and the look my fellow milk monitor gave me, she was impressed. Nevertheless, the attention wore off and things reverted to football and bullies at school and football and pets at home. Sally married Frank and the union brought brothers John and Francis into the mix and the Lee's moved on, next door actually, but that's another story, and we moved into a nice mildew-free council house just down the road and I got my own bedroom. Life moved on, but I never forgot about 'Over der'.

Yeah, two younger brothers and I was back in charge as the eldest but I never took either to a Pet Show or church. I did take a five year old Francis to the pub once, folk thought he was mine at the time because of the age difference, and he never smoked or played Dominoes again. John would have been at home watching television, which he loved, with thoughts of joining the army, which he eventually did. Seven of us in a new council house on a new estate built in a field and the locals talked funny.

'Paul, do you want Nin's ticket? The doctor said she's not well enough to go to Canada.'

I wipe moisture from a window pane and leaky eye with my sleeve to find Jasper deep in slushy snow. A solitary figure wearing a toque and snowshoes loiters in an alleyway below, before darting up a driveway and out of sight. This small bright room, or pension as they say in continental Europe, is quiet and safe and I have no need to pack belongings or dash to catch a train or make conversation with strangers. I think I'll stay here another night to rest and think and write. I'm tired, hungry and in need of a bath. I am forty and twelve days and this is the first time I have felt my age, 'and that's better than feeling nothing', said the bishop to the actress.' Thinking back on sights seen so far, Lakelse Lake stands out. Chin on hands, I press my nose against the windowpane to watch snowflakes fall slowly as little Sydney appears showing me bear prints in the sand. Tree's tower above swampy campsites, mountains, a mist covered lake, and if I don't get cleaned up soon Bruno will be in with the fumigator.

A hot bath truly is a wonderful thing, as is a double shave and a triple tooth-brushing, but a Grand Slam breakfast at the Miss Italia Restaurant around the corner beats all that hands down. Delicious eggs, smoky bacon and sausage, buttered pancakes, toast and a hot cup of sweet tea. A window seat affords me a perfect view of downtown Jasper and the mountains that surround. I eat alone, it's the slow season, I hope. The place is all mine as Mario Lanza and Frank Sinatra compete with a wheezy squeeze-box and take turns wafting from a speaker above the bar. A waitress from Quebec smiles and glides across the red carpet in a white shirt and black pedal-pushers to top up a porcelain teapot sat on the table before me. I read in a tourist leaflet, as Melanie pours, that Jasper National Park is the largest park in the Canadian Rockies, all 10,878 square kilometres of it. And the Columbia Icefields is a rarity because it can be accessed by road and that road can be accessed by foot from here, ayup! Jasper was established in 1907 and the original site was founded much in 1811 opposite the present site at Henry House, a fort that David Thompson of the North West Company had built for fur traders and adventurers like me.

Melanie wants to talk history and travel and I'm in the mood. She recently departed Quebec for Alberta in search of work, and after swapping travel tales she brings more hot water for the teapot and hands me the bill, insists I relax and stay longer, which I do, until the ambiance is ruined as the place starts to fill up with hungry locals.

As I stand to receive my coat, I tell her that I have to find a post office to mail postcards to my family back in Ontario and she insists that I come back soon. As the bill comes to only five dollars and change, I tell her I most definitely will and wave to the owner polishing glasses behind the bar as I take my leave. Melanie walks me to the door and waves me off with a big smile. I wave back feeling like I'm in one of those International films with subtitles and find a secluded spot on a wrap-around balcony to take stock and a deep breath. I can see for miles from this vantage point so I take time to watch the town awaken as citizens venture out into the sunlight in search of sustenance and exercise.

It's already 10:30am and the newspapers are just now being delivered because of that sudden dumping of snow yesterday. All roads are in bad shape but the trains run on time. I can see them running from here, they never end. I decide not to do anything too strenuous or risky today because of the date and head off to mail my postcards.

The post office is ancient and friendly and the people in it are friendly and ancient, especially the tall, smiling woman with the blue-rinse who sells me a book of stamps and asks cheerily what part of Scotland am I from. 'Liverpool,' I reply, smiling.

'That's not in Scotland,' she tells, flashing a bigger smile.

'Oh, yes it is!' I state, bigger smile, trying to compete.

'Oh, no its not, it's in England,' she insists, smile as wide as the Mersey now. I can't see her ears for the top of her head.

'But you just told me it's in Scotland,' I counter,feeling a severe case of lockjaw coming on with all the smiling.

My lips are beginning to crack and bleed from it all and she resembles an inside-out head now with all her smiling, and my head is pounding like a hammer on an anvil with happiness and I can see her tonsils quivering in her throat as she smiles one last time before exploding as I take my leave with REM sing *Shiny Happy People* somewhere from above.

A solid wooden door slowly creaks closed behind me as dust-mote leaden beams of golden light pour from overhead skylights in the mailroom. Coloured lead-glass windows afford me a wonky view of Jasper House across the road and I'm slightly lost in thought, scribbling this to notebook, stood leaning on a battered wooden desk placed strategically below those elaborate windows when suddenly a gang of old-timers barrel in to check for mail. They all smile and beam hello and I'm thinking 'sod this for a game of soldiers' and take off outside into a mini-blizzard to give my face muscles a rest. Snow-flakes the size of old English pennies kiss my eyelashes as I make my way across the town green towards Jasper House. I decide that Jasper has to be one of the most, if not *the* friendliest place on earth and I hate it. What stress-free, peaceful lives they must lead here all stoned on weed.

A granite monument to 'The Overlanders' stands solid and proud in front of Jasper House in its latest guise as a government-owned tourist information center. '*The Overlanders of 1862 used the Yellowhead Pass to get to Jasper, the passage from here to Tete Jaune Cache was apparently one of the most dangerous ever encountered by anybody-fur trader or adventurer.*'

Local historian Jeff Waugh has this to say on the subject, *'It wasn't until the early 1860's that the Yellowhead Pass again began to be frequently utilised. In the Fall of 1861 H.J. Moberly quit his post as H.B.C. Factor at Jasper and made his way (to Ft. George) through the Yellowhead with the aid of a young Iroquois guide.*

In 1862, a group of 115 men and 1 woman began to ascend upon the Yellowhead Pass. They had left Ontario some months earl-

ier and were heading to the British Columbia Cariboo in search of gold. While in Fort Edmonton they discussed the merits of this pass with a party of miners returning from the Cariboo and decided to travel this route to reach their destination.

They abandoned the last of their carts at Lac St. Anne and struggled onward (spread along the trail for over 300 kilometres) with pack oxen and horses and with packs on their backs. After crossing the height of land at the summit of the Yellowhead Pass the first of the Overlanders camped at Cow Dung or Yellowhead Lake. As their provisions were running frighteningly low, some horses and oxen were killed and the meat dried. Others hunted and ate squirrels, small birds, a porcupine and even a skunk. They continued on and camped at Moose River, Red Pass, and at the original's Tete Jaune's Cache.

On August 27th the first of the Overlanders reached the Shuswap salmon-fishing camp at the new Tete Jaune Cache. Here they traded ammunition, clothing, needles and thread, etc. for salmon, huckleberries, saskatoons and pemmican. On September 7 another party of Overlanders passed by Yellowhead Lake. They became trapped on an island by rising flood waters and were at the point of starvation before being rescued by later arrivals."Still no sign of the company. We are all beginning to feel very weak. If they don't come up soon it will be very serious work for us. Took our last meal this morning, hardly, a tea cup full of thin soup made with a bit of beef about the size of your hand, a thin piece of cake about the same size. Leader is very bad. We lie about the fire and smoke nearly all day, passing the pipe from one to the other, and, strange to say, I find the talk among men nearly starving is what they would like if they were at home..." - Alexander, September 10, 1862

The last of the Overlanders reached Tete Jaune Cache on September 16:At Tete Jaune their trails diverged. One group decided to float down the Fraser to Fort George and from there head south to Quesnel. Canoes were made from dug-out cottonwood logs and from oxen hides. Most of the men chose to build rafts on which they tethered the oxen (or stored their meat) for the journey. For the first 5 or 6 days of travel down the river no serious obstacles were encountered. It wasn't until the Grand Canyon of the Fraser was reached that disaster struck. Canoes were overturned and rafts torn apart. Four men died from drowning or hypothermia."Onward they sped like an arrow. They seemed to be rushing into the very jaws of death. Before them on the right rose a rocky reef against which the furious flood was lashing itself into foam, threatening instant and unavoidable destruction, and on the other side a seething and eddying whirlpool was ready to engulf in its greedy vortex any mortal who might venture within its reach. With fearful velocity they were hurried along directly towards the fatal rock, their ruin seemed inevitable. It was a moment of painful suspense. Not a word was spoken except the necessary orders of the pilot, which were distinctly heard on shore above the din and tumult of the scene. Now was the critical moment. Everyone bent manfully to his oar. The raft shot closely past the rock, tearing away the stern rowlock, and glided safely down into the eddy below. The agony was over. The gauntlet had been run..." - McMickings Diary

On October 8, the main group of Overlanders reached Fort George. The other group of Overlanders left Tete Jaune Cache and travelled overland up the McLennan River with over 100 head of cattle and horses. About sixty miles from Tete Jaune Cache their guide, Andre Cardinal, turned back to Jasper. The Overlanders slaughtered their cattle, turned most of their horses loose, and began constructing rafts for their journey down the Thompson River to Kamloops. During the run through Murchison rapids and Hells Gate two men died. On arrival in Fort Kamloops October 13, 1862, Catherine Schubert, the only woman amongst the Overlanders, gave birth to a baby girl. From this point and from Fort George the Overlanders would make their way to the Cariboo gold!

12 Bells, Noon from an open window in my room, the Jasper Lutheran Church is framed by snow-covered spruce and the Pyramid Mountains are hidden from view by a swirling mist. Bruno shovels wet snow from the fire escape as excited kids play noisily in a fenced-in yard in front of the Activity Center across the way.

'Hey Bruno, you need a hand?'

'What?'

'Ya wanna hand.'

'No, is alright. Loverly day!'

'Nice day for a walk in the mountains.'

'Snorra that nice, ha!'

'Sure it is. Wanna come with me?'

'Sano thanks, you watch out forra da bears, huh.'

'Will do. See you later!'

'Okay, maybe.'

'I'm gonna stay one more night by the way.'

'That's a good, everything ok?'

I nod and tell him it is. 'Good!' he shouts, and takes off up the front path with his shovel. He still hasn't asked me for the rent money. Who doesn't take rent money up front fromstrangers? Jasper really must be secluded and hard to escape from. 'He won't get far on that old bike, the wheels aren't waxed'

Hey, according to today's Edmonton Sun the Leafs are the best team in hockey after they whupped the Blackhawks 10-3 last night. The Oilers are second best and Edmonton will be hosting the Grey Cup semi-final between the Eskimos and Blue Bombers while I'm there. Big rodeo on the cards too, but for now I'm off on a hike into mountains I've been babbling on about all morning.

Wilderness tips take a walk on the wild-side keep the wild in wildlife, and in order to do so I take the scenic route to the train station by foot to photograph trains at work and play. Leisure time shots before heading up Pyramid Avenue in search of lakes and adventure. Ambling and rambling through packing snow, I find a spot to stop at as clouds part and the sun beams through to reveal the full glory of majestic Old Man Mountain, guardian of the Valley of the Wicked River, commonly known as Maligne Canyon, just down the road from Medicine Lake. I'm leaning against a supple sapling basking in that big old sun, when just like that dark clouds move in to wipe the Old Man from view. Engines pulling long lines of box cars into position. Melting snow caps drip and splash from flat roofs onto long lines of curving rust coloured rail tracks. One bright green car has been tagged by FLOW. Train tagging looks to have made a comeback by looks of eye-catching art on the move. One boxcar in Winnipeg had a black and white painting of a gremlin by OTHER and was very cool. Wonder if taggers ride the rails or just hop a fence to find a canvas. I could be tempted to do a Stompin Tom all the way home from here if I was a hundred years younger. Some elk tagging for you:

'Urban Elk - Their Story: In park town sites, you may see elk peacefully mowing someone's front lawn or pruning the back yard shrubbery. They look pretty tame, but they're not. They are wild animals that have learned to survive in a place that's full of people. "Urban' elk have the same needs as other wild animals: they need to feed, rest, mate, and bear young - undisturbed. If these needs are not met, survival is threatened.

And whenever a wild animal perceives a threat - say someone approaching too closely - it is likely to attack. The only other option is to run away, but in populated areas there just aren't many places for an animal to run. Instead we're the ones who must "back off". Bull elk are particularly dangerous during mating season. Elk are dangerous - no matter when or where you see them. Give elk the right of way and stay at least 100ft away.

Report all conflicts with elk to park staff.'

I'm thinking about what mating season must be like around here as I eyeball road signs that point the way to Lake Patricia. I scale a man-made stone embankment and find a narrow path, hurdle felled trees, and take a minute in a forest of tall skinny conifers. Snow melts and drips from branches to soak the shoulders of my coat. Squirrels, chipmunks and birds dart every which way disturbed by my singing. Bears won't stand a chance, move over Subway Elvis.

'You Are In Bear Country - wherever you are in the mountain national parks! Reduce risk: Make noise! Let bears know you're there - call out, clap hands, sing or talk loudly - especially near streams, dense vegetation and berry patches, on windy days, and in areas of low visibility.

Bears are naturally wary of humans, and generally choose to avoid us. However, bears may threaten and even attack people when they become accustomed to humans, when they are surprised, or when they are forced to defend themselves, their young or their food. Bears are very intelligent and complex animals. Each bear and each encounter is unique; there is no single strategy that will work in all situations.

Stay calm. Most bears don't want to attack you; they usually want to avoid you and ensure you're not a threat. Bears may bluff their way out of an encounter by charging and then turning away at the last second. Bears may also react defensively by woofing, growling, snapping their jaws, and laying their ears back.

Immediately pick up small children and stay in a group. Don't drop your pack it can provide protection. Back away slowly, never run! Bears can run as fast as a racehorse, both uphill and downhill. Talk calmly and firmly. If a bear rears on its hind legs and waves its nose about, it's trying to identify you. Remain still and talk calmly so it knows you are a human and not a prey animal. A scream or sudden movement may trigger an attack. Bears do not like surprises.

If you surprise a bear and it defends itself: PLAY DEAD! Lie on your stomach with legs apart. Protect your face, the back of your head and neck with your arms. Remain still until the bear leaves the area. These attacks seldom last more than a few minutes. While fighting back usually increases the intensity of such an attack, in some cases it has caused the bear to leave. If the attack continues for more than several minutes, consider fighting back.

Report all sightings of bears to park staff.'

I must be crazy messing about up here. 'Yes you are, man.'

Who said that? I slip my journal from my chest pocket and find a large sun-dried rock to sit on and scribble in peaceful quiet. I'm hit with more snow bombs which find the open neck of my coat and really wake me up. I've got the fingerless gloves and the parka on but it's not that cold and I'm as high as I can climb here without ingesting illegal substances. I don't think I'm going to have time for Lake Patricia as it's already 3pm and I don't want to get lost in the dark on my own, or with anyone else, its still Friday the 13th, and idea's about hitch-hiking are chased away as well.

'If a bear stalks you and then attacks, or attacks at night: DON'T PLAY DEAD - FIGHT BACK! First - try to escape, preferably to a building, car or up a tree. If you can't escape, or if the bear follows, use bear spray, or shout and try to intimidate the bear with a branch or rock. Do what-ever it takes to let the bear know you are not easy prey. This kind of attack is very rare but can be very serious because it means the bear is looking for food and preying on you.

Recent research indicates that bear spray can be effective against some bears when used properly. If you plan to carry it, be aware that wind, spray distance, rain and product shelf life can all influence its effectiveness. Carefully read directions on the can prior to your trip. The best way to live safely with bears is to avoid contact with them.'

....Stumbling and bumbling through dripping bush and spindly tree's, frightening wildlife, on the half-hunt for a glimpse of a bear but finding a gang of seemingly tame and bashful birds unbothered by my presence, birds of many colours that dart from branch to tree and back again or roost up high keeping an eye on me as I pass by; magpie impersonators do most of the brooding and small red robin lookalikes perform the darting through undergrowth as if they were winged chipmunks, and I find a hidden path that makes the climb easier and takes me higher.

'This Is Also Cougar Country. Cougars are not often seen

because they are solitary, elusive and active mainly at night. They may be more active in areas that have habituated deer, like towns and campgrounds. Avoid meeting a cougar by traveling in groups and making lots of noise. Keep children close to you. Free roaming pets may attract and be attacked by cougars. IF YOU ENCOUNTER A COUGAR: Immediately pick up small children. Face the animal, and retreat slowly - do NOT run or play dead. Try to appear bigger by holding your arms or an object above your head. Actions such as shouting, waving a stick and throwing rocks may deter an attack. BE AGGRESSIVE.

Give them the space they need. Please do your part to limit the impact that so many people have on park wildlife. Give all the animals you see the respect they deserve and the space they need. Enjoy a safe visit and ensure that future generations have the chance to see wildlife that is truly wild!'

...but not as high as the two dudes stood smoking a joint in the middle of a clearing I've just stumbled into. 'I'm getting too old for all this climbing!' They ignore me. 'Y'alright lads?' They look at each other, at me, laugh at each other and take off into some tree's leaving me stood there holding my camera and whistling, 'I'm a Lumberjack and I'm okay, I sleep all night and I wank all day.' I must have scared them off! I've finally made it to the top of the mountain with a view and I'm feeling slightly light-headed from the altitude like that climber in 'Into Thin Air' did just before he dropped dead, so I best be careful. Mist glides from a nearby mountain top to swirl through trees, foliage and my legs like a scene from 'The Fog' and reminds me of the amount of smoke pouring from that big fatty the lads where toking on before. It's getting colder up here so I snap a few more Jasper train scenes and make plans to head back.

What the hell was that?

INTERLUDE: An Encounter of the Hairy Kind! It's 5:37pm and I've just arrived back at my room sweaty and thirsty with the excitemen and will spill the beans when I return from the humming mini-fridge in the hall with a warm beer.

So, there I am snapping photos of Jasper high up in the sky, making sure not to get too close to the edge, when something makes a noise in the trees behind me. I have a sense that I'm being watched, and upon further inspection, discover that I am.

It looks to be a moose grazing but I'm not too sure as the last time I was this close to one was in Algonquin Park around twenty years ago. To be positive I do the big game hunter thing and creep slowly towards it snapping away with my camera as I get closer. I'm caught up in the hunt not believing my luck that it hasn't ran off or charged me, edging closer hoping for a full body shot and I get within yards of my prey before realising that it's not a moose but a full-grown elk with a rack on it the size of my front door, which is big, and I should know as I painted it. He stamps a hoof and blows steam from flared nostrils and kicks up clouds of snow all the time glaring at me with big beady eyes for disturbing his supper. I stop dead and back away slowly and quietly while trying to squeeze my camera back into its suddenly shrinking case, and it's not the only thing shrinking.

I make sure not to make any quick movements as he heads towards me looking pissed off. There's only saplings, scrub, and small rocks between us, so I take off down a steep slope behind me and attempt to climb a tree. In mid-climb he charges, sending dirt and snow flying. He's grunting and cursing in Elk and those horns are getting bigger as I flail at the tree, before doing the honourable thing and take off running down a steep slippery incline yelling at the top of my lungs. Yellowhead would have been so proud!

I don't know when or why he gave up the chase as I was too busy yelling and stumbling about in the semi-darkness of a forest full of dripping spindly trees, praying that the pot heads, or anyone else, weren't watching as I did a Ben Johnson down that incline.

Jumping over rotting tree trunks and foliage and prickly bushes I come to halt at a wall of moss covered evergreens stood close together like in a fairy tale and turn to face the bastard with my Swiss Army knife. But he's not behind there, the big chicken, he's stood grazing on something that looks like my wallet about a hundred yards back. Breathing heavily, I perform a quick pocket search to find everything present and accounted for except the family jewels.

I gather my wits, which doesn't take long, to discover that the easiest way out of here is back up that incline. I'm stuck in some sort of a swamp. It's getting darker and he's still up there munching and keeping an eye on me, so the only way out is through an evergreen jungle littered with felled rotting tree's, so off I go stumbling about in search of a path or human footprint.

I stop to get my breath back and sit on the least rotted tree trunk I can find in the swamp. There's no birdsong, only muffled silence. I watch a colony of black beetles feast on a tree trunk about head height. I hold my breath and my ears pop as more penny-size snow-flakes fall slowly through tree tops. A bird call echoes suddenly from up there which has me thinking it's a warning. A giant snowflake lands on my cheek and my breath plumes in the damp air. Steam rises from the shoulders of my coat and I laugh out loud, the bird does not reply. My feet are dry, I'm warm and comfortable, I feel like I could stay here all night if I can't find a way out or that elk stays put, munching.

An image of men in white coats stretchering me into an ambulance has me smiling and I give the elk the two-fingers. Come on then. I've seen Zulu. He's still up there watching and grazing, probably laughing, and waiting for me to make the first move when I hear the sound of a car engine in the distance. Saved!

I wave at the elk and force my way through tree and foliage in the direction of the engine, careful not to break an ankle. I break through and find a muddy path which I follow up a steep hill and next thing I'm sat on a mossy tree stump at the side of the road to Patricia Lake, thumb out, laughing like a demented hitchhiker just escaped from the swamps of hell. A white sports car whines past and the yellow ski jacket clad driver gives me the old I'm not looking at you so I don't have to give you a lift thing, so I flip him two fingers as well; they're all getting it today.

I can't believe how light it is out here as I retrace my steps in a downtown direction, brain going a mile a minute, coat open flapping in the wind, hat in hand, gloves in pocket, past the school, the church, imagining I'm Alexander Mackenzie snowshoeing seven hundred miles to attend a Christmas dinner.

I scale the staircase two steps at a time, fling open the door and stride into the hallway snowy boots and all to liberate that can of warm beer.

Bruno's 'Goodfellas' staccato wafts up through the floorboards along with the smell of cooking spaghetti sauce as he talks on the phone.

Mountains fade to black and the bedroom is once again reflected in the window. My stomach plays another concerto. I haven't eaten since that Grand Slam but the urge to sip beer and write is greater than the sum of Miss Italia's parts right now so I kick off the boots and strip to jeans and teeshirt, fluff up the pillows, open another beer and get to it.

1977. My sister Christine and her fiancé Eric had planned to accompany my ailing Nin to Canada over Christmas and New Year and enjoy a brief holiday before getting married but they got lumbered with me instead. Nin's eldest daughter, Martha (or Mick) and her husband Chris lived in Scarborough, Ontario, where I would stay for the first week before heading to my cousin Chris's place in Oshawa. We were following the plan that had been laid out for Nin, but somewhere a butterfly fluttered its wings etc. and I got to go instead, and after shopping for winter gear such as black eleven-eyehole Doctor Martens, a thick warm sweater and woollen socks from the Army & Navy store.

I had the drainpipe jeans, earring, and short haircut already and 'baseball boots' (Converse high-tops) didn't seem right for sub-zero temperaturs. I bought some Thomas Cook travel vouchers, made out a Will on the back of a cigarette packet, and was all set to go. I ended up having to borrow a sheepskin coat from my cousin Ronnie when I got there as my leather jacket wasn't warm enough but I didn't mind as it set off my outfit just right.

The plane journey was crying baby hell and just as hot. The stewardess was beautiful and I fell in love with her Canadian accent and sense of fun. Foil- wrapped hot food, cold cans of beer and mini-bottles of warm red wine were included in the price of the ticket and they let me smoke freely. And after a long non-eventful, overnight flight sat upright in my seat in expectation of what was to come, Wardair landed us safely at Toronto International Airport and to add to the seasonal ambience, strangely enough, it was snowing and cold in Canada. I felt like a gunfighter or rock star as we strolled towards customs which smelled of new carpet, curry, perfume, alcohol and fear, but the happy bubble was soon burst by a customs officer and I felt like a little whipped pup after she'd finished with me. It wasn't the greeting I'd been expecting from a fellow 'servant' of the Queen. She made it quite clear that she didn't like me or the clothes I stood posing in. It wasn't my fault Canada was ten years behind the times regards music and fashion!

'It's the face, lad, the face.'

What's wrong with it! My relatives made up for the welcome by making a big fuss and giving it loads of, 'Go-way, the miserable cow, what did you say to her after she said that?'....and next thing after a long journey by car, I'm ordering a hot-dog in an aircraft hangar of a grocery store overflowing with foods of the world. I had never seen so much food for sale in one place and nobody was spotted in an oversized overcoat stealing any of it. I had so many toppings on my hot dog that I couldn't lift it to take a bite. I didn't want to eat it anyway as it looked so good sat up there on a long shiny counter surrounded by napkin holders, trays of plastic utensils and condiments. I found myself humming along, me the punk rocker, to piped-in Christmas standards and carols and a big man dressed as Father Christmas stood next to a clear plastic ball full of bills and coins shaking sleigh bells without a guard or cop in sight. 'Not England is it lad!'

'Its the place uncle Chris, the place!'

On the way to his apartment in a car built like a tank he pulled over so I could buy a newspaper from a red metal box half-buried in ice and snow on the corner of a busy intersection. 'C'mon lad, I'll show you,' and he led the way from steamy smoke-filled car along frozen Canadian sidewalk where I savoured every slippery step, burning earlobe, and frozen finger.

'Stick this quarter in that slot there. Pull the handle like this, see...and its open-friggin-sesame,' and there I am stood there looking at a stack of bone-dry newspapers.

'Then you just reach in, take one out...and let the door slam like that,' and all pleased with himself at my reaction he handed me a paper loaded with flyers. 'You're only taking one, uncle Chris?' I asked him, looking around to see if anyone was watching apart from the family in his car wiping at fogged up windows.

'Am I only taking one, uncle Chris? Haha! Mick love, wait til you hear this...,' and that became my epitaph at gatherings for the remainder of my stay. He used it on everyone - even a student handing out yellow oilskins in Niagara Falls who asked me if I knew Prince Charles. You're only taking one, uncle Chris? Oh, the shame, but funny is funny and funny was expected from a lad from Liverpool.

The first morning I got to eat breakfast tucked between fresh cotton sheets on a plaid pull-out couch and watch *Happy Days* on a big solid wood console television with fake drawers. I gave myself a migraine flicking through channels using a converter the size of a baby-grand piano, as I wolfed down a plateful of eggs over-easy, strips of crispy bacon, toast, home fries and cold sliced tomatoes. Cup after cup of thick, creamy 'real' coffee went down the hatch for the first time and was way more 'coffee' than Maxwell House granules. The remainder of the morning was spent in one of three washroom's studying a TV Guide. 'Are you *sure* you're okay in there, Paul?' The afternoon wandering around a humongous shopping mall where I got completely lost and spent an hour figuring out that the money went in the slot first before dialling.

'Lost? Your uncle Chris will come get you, Paul, he'll be home from work soon. Where are you?'

'I'm in the mall across the road, Auntie Mick,' I yelled into the receiver as you do when calling long-distance, as healthy-looking Canadians strolled by giving me quizzical looks, especially the fellers.

'Haha, I knew you'd get lost. Too funny!'

'Leaving the mall now Auntie Mick. See you soon!'

'Ask someone to guide you to the front doors and cross the car park and we're in the big building across the road. Watch out for the cars on the wrong side of the road and I'll watch out for you from the balcony. I'll put a glass in the freezer!'

'Okay, won't be long!' I loved the glass in the freezer thing.

Lost and alone in the Scarborough Mall, amused at the reaction I was getting, especially from the girls, it took me a while to find the exit but seconds to cross the street and Auntie Mick was a block of ice up there on the balcony. Uncle Chris had another tale to tell.

'Soft lad got lost in the mall across the road he did. Mick froze to death waiting for him!'

On Christmas Eve I saw two Santa's read, *The Night Before Christmas,* due to too many frozen glasses, and it poured rain and washed the snow away and we got the blame for bringing the weather with us. 'Can't remember the last time it rained on

Christmas Eve, can you Mick, love?'

Cousin Chris ferried us about in his boat on wheels the day after Boxing Day and we discussed the myth about Canadian beer being weaker than English ale, as I sat up front with him smoking DuMaurier cigarettes. 'I can drink this lemonade all night,' had had been my Christmas eve refrain as we sang carols from a cheat sheet and watched partygoers dance to Meatloaf's, Bat Out Of Hell.

'That's crap that Chris, you got anything shorter?' I sneered. 'Not as short as your's limey,' and I showed him how to pogo to Paradise by The Dashboard Light as we put more glasses in the freezer. The Englishman abroad in his cousin's basement bar, pants rolled up, hankie on head. 'Wait til they hear about this one in work, Mick, the pogo, ahem!'

Niagara Falls in a snowstorm was tacky and white, like most of us in the car but not as funny. I felt like I was stuck in a snow-shaker with store window style wax effigies of Pocahontas, pirates, monsters and angels. Madame Tussaud's had me searching for a match. 'Here lie's the body of Jonathan Blake, stepped on the gas instead of the brake.'

Niagara Falls is burning! Sing it Joe.

We paid honest money to traipse under The Fall's in oil slickers and fishermen's hats like a troupe of freezing Newfoundlanders and got lost in dark tunnels and caves awash in slippery ice and sloshing, foaming, freezing water. After a short while of this shite we did the sensible thing and jibbed off the boat tour, handed in our John West specials, and took off across a snowed-in road to a warm pub big enough to seat eleven of us, and after a few rounds we crammed back into two vehicles to crawl home through a blizzard.

'Where's the road gone, love?'

'I think it's over there underneath that spinning car, Chris.' Next day, he took me to a local bar where we sat at a table full of non-English speaking old men, while dancers did their bit and we sat there trying to ignore them and smoking and sipping beer.

'The head on her, lad!'

'Which one?'

Waiters resembling Wayne Newton and Zorba the Greek showed me how to add salt to the beer and tap the glass to put a head on it. I explained that where I came from, put a head on it, meant something different and ordered another tray full of draft which Zorba delivered promptly with a flourish.

On domestic days, I learned how to play *Yahtzee* and Crazy Eights at my cousins kitchen table while bantering with friends, family and neighbours in the safety of a comfortable home with an ice-rink in the garden in the south-end of The Motor City; where gravely-voiced FM DJs read weather and traffic reports and spun Styx, Boston, and Lynyrd Skynyrd long players. Giant speakers topped with ashtrays and plants relayed it all to my amusement as rain turned to snowflakes and kissed window screens.

'Are those screens on the windows to keep people in or out, Chris?'

'You limeys always drink Molson with your eggs?'

'Yes, it's what we call tradition.'

'Does tradition dictate that I buy the Molson?'

'Only in Canada, mon cousine, only in Canada.'

I got myself arrested in Scarboro and taken home in a police car, but luckily for me the copper was an ex-pat, and finding it funny there was a scouser loose in Scarbaria let me off with an apology to the owner.

After too many frozen glasses and whisky chasers I took a fancy to a plastic menu with a portrait of Winston Churchill on it which I stuffed down the front of my jeans and hit the exit after paying the bill, whereupon a few male staff members grabbed hold of me outside and we play-wrestled for a bit until a yellow cop car, sat idling under street lights in the car park, zoomed to the rescue and a crowd gathered.

The restaurant owner demanded I be searched so a cop bathed me in the bright beam from his flashlight and asked me what I had jammed down the front of my jeans. Relishing being in the spotlight, I took one look at my bulging crotch (the menu was on a stand) and asked him how the hell that got there.

'Out with it, son!' The cockney copper advised, and knowing when the gig was up I set Winston and *Today's Specials* free. I was advised to apologise to the owner and staff, which I did, which they accepted, and the menu was taken away to be used as evidence or fumigated. The owner saw the funny side and declined to lay charges, even let me use his washroom accompanied by a second copper, a Canadian, before being driven to my uncles in the back of a police car.

'Did you think that was my weddin-tackle, like?'

'Don't push it, son.'

The cops hatched a planto tell my relative s that a shady character bearing a resemblance to myself had been spotted prowling the neighborhood and they just wanted to check my passport to make sure I was legit. And that was that, no clanging of jail guitar doors or deportations, just a farewell and a warning to behave myself from the chuckling cops as I walked them to the elevator - and Uncle Chris had another story to tell. The shame, again!

Friendly Canadians, huge clean Malls, war and peace menus, have a nice day, how do you like your eggs, ice-hockey games and NFL football watched in customized rec-rooms in labyrinth-like basements. I love your accent, is this guy ever cute, dry itchy skin, weird green toothpaste, milk in plastic bags, the CN Tower, my first blind date, all flashed by at the airport as I stood suitcase and duty-free in hand. I took three last looks at waving family members, gun-carrying cops, happy people and litter-free floors and vowed to be back. I'd had a great time and had found Uncle John's version of Canada but I wanted my own.

Back in England all jet-lagged after another uneventful flight, I lay on my bed wearing a Team Canada hockey sweater given to me by my cousin, with a forty-pounder of Canadian Club and a carton of du Maurier regular on the dressing table next to a stack of Polaroid souvenirs, when Dan Hill came on the radio singing, *Sometimes When We Touch*. I still hate that song, but alongside Patsy Gallant's *New York to LA*, it became the theme tune for my Canadian vacation. I could call it revenge when years later at a Grey Cup Final between Calgary and Edmonton I got to watch Dan warble his greatest hit from the basket of an air-balloon as it floated up into the closed retractable roof of the Skydome and get stuck, on national television, and I think the game had to be delayed to rescue him. I had to give it to him though as he never stopped singing up there on the Jumbotron. Michael Jackson played the Superbowl that year and we got Dan Hill at that 'Dome.

It's 9:41pm here in Jasper and I've survived another Friday the 13th. Somewhere an elk grazes!

Saturday, November 14th, and I exit my temporary home in Jasper's little Italy via the back door. There's not a cloud in the sky awarding me a perfect view that has been mostly hidden from view until now, and the sun smiles and anoints those mountains and surrounds day-glo orange. The big mountain I had all that fun on yesterday looks like an orange molehill from here. I head to my favourite Italian restaurant and sink into a window seat. Decide it was a good idea it to stay in and write last night instead of hanging out at a bar. Isolation was my proper destination. Melanie has the day off unfortunately, she doesn't like to work on Saturdays, so instead I'm spoiled by Miss Italia herself, the charming owner of this fine establishment. I order up the same offering but from a different pitcher with a different delivery. Yesterday a fastball, today a knuckler with a bigger crowd in attendance but the same result, baseball fans I give you a Grand Slam breakfast. I know, pretty lame, but it made us laugh.

Sinatra on repeat has my feet tapping as I finish my tea and head to the bar to pay the bill and respects to the owner before making my way to the bank for some cash. I grab a Sun on the way and the headline reads 'El Meano' accompanied by a color photo of a leather-jacketed dude with a mullet shovelling deep snow off a downtown Edmonton sidewalk. It's a good thing I thought to bring the long-johns! The elk have moved on. Too bad, I wanted to take some photos. 'Donta worry Paulo, no rush, comma back anytime!' Bruno told me, as I handed over the rent money in his kitchen, and I told him I would for sure, he's a good fella.

On official business or looking for someone to talk to, on the walk to Jasper House to report the elk incident, I notice how efficient the drainage system is in Jasper. Run off from melting snow on rooftops pours down spouts that run beneath sidewalks covered by metal grills. No ice build-up, no slippery sidewalks, no law-suits. Clever. The Park Ranger come Tourist Officer is busy chatting with a couple of American backpackers, so I take a slow waltz around creaky, well-polished wooden floors and come to a halt at a wall filled with a graph showing the latest animal sightings, weather reports, and travel schedules in and around Jasper National Park. As always, free leaflets are plenty so I take a box full. High-tech backpackers, who know I'm waiting to talk to the ranger, shred my nerves with incessant banal questions. 'Will the mountain sheep allow you to pet them?' I'm about to leave quietly, when the Ranger senses my impatience and gives me a cheery, 'Hi, can I help you?' So I snap a cheery 'Hi!' back and ask for a spare copy of the 'Elk Warning' poster plastered all over Jaspers government buildings: a classic black and white fifties-style photograph of a male elk chasing a terrified man, the spitting image of Archie Bunker, down a suburban path.

The rangerhas a look for it in a store-room before coming

up empty-handed, which is a shame as it would look ace in a frame. The American backpackers make an exit refusing to acknowledge my farewell, which I find funny, as I told them the last thing they'll need on a trip into Jasper Park is a bear behind. The Ranger laughed despite being covered in dust from his expedition into the store-room. He seems friendly and I have him cornered so I share my elk story until he develops a *heard it all before* vacant stare and concentrates on something sat upon my left shoulder. He asks if I stayed three bus lengths away from the animal because if I hadn't I was invading the elks space, and in answer to my question, no, he probably wasn't rabid.

I tell him I didn't have a tape-measure with me at the time and we chat about animals that rule the streets of Jasper. I know he thinks I'm a nut from the city, which I am, so to get a rise out of him further I tell him about the Granduc Mine incident. Upon informative and descriptive oratorical completion, he just stares at me and shakes his head, takes a deep breath, and tells me in no uncertain terms how unwise and dangerous it was to do such a silly thing totally unprepared. He tells me Brad should have known better and I agree.

'So, splashing about in bears feeding grounds and getting flat tires up abandoned mines is not recommended, sir', I ask, and he gives me the look various teachers and headmasters gave me over the course of five schools. 'No, no, definitely no young man! Mountain lions, black bear and grizzly have been all over that mine recently, harrumph!'

Do Not Feed The Bears! I thank him for the advice and leave before he loses his tripe, and I'm stood shuffling from foot to foot on the porch wondering who I can find to bother next, when he follows me outside and hands me more leaflets and wishes me a safe trip home. I thank him and that well-oiled old door closes silently behind him as I take snow covered stairs one at a time to be safe. I take a look back and he's stood waving from a window wearing a relieved smile. I do love this place. On a last slow walk around town to pick up supplies, I stop by the record/book store in search of the owner from Prince George but he's away on business. I leave a note with an associate dressed in black, *'I'm still alive, good luck with the book business. Take care – Scotty.'*

Crossing Connaught Street I arrive at the station to find that the train is running an hour late, so for old time sake I head back to the Java pub that Terry fell in love in, the tin that rin-tin-tin shit in, half-expecting the lads to be at the bar waiting to buy me a Guinness but the joint is full of strangers eating quietly.

The bartender is there though and the beer tap farts and squelches as the Guinness keg runs out, leaving my glass half full, so I make do with a local 'Big Rock' dark ale and it's not bad either. A white truck passes by with *'Do All - Painting & Plastering'* or something painted on the side. I guess that's me in a job if I should decide to come back. A little scribble and a drink to while away the time while sit here all lit up in the front window like a lady of the Amsterdam night.

Whore Frost: At thirty five below nostrils pinch and freeze shut, lungs threaten to explode, exposed skin will freeze within minutes, longjohns are a must for us mid-life, over-the-hill gang, but you just can't beat the sound of snow crunching under footsteps as breath balloons from a smiling gob with each exhalation of freeze-dried air and threatens to seal eyes shut. The sun glints off a bottle in the snow and you blink away black dots of blindness as a car spews white clouds and sewer grates spout smelly mist.

The driveway needs to be cleared again and your blood pumps after you find the shovel and start to move in straight lines. Sweat freezes on your foreheed as asphalt is uncovered. 'Cold enough for ya?,' hails the neighbour, as he extracts a newspaper from a frosty black mailbox and darts back inside like a wanted man, shivering. You smile and head inside where toques and thermal socks and boots are peeled off and the kettle boils and hot tea thaws inners as the ears tingle and burn and the nose comes back to life with a vengeance. Frost in rainbow colors is scraped from a kitchen window pane with an inquisitive fingernail to expose hungry wildlife lined up at bird feeders screwed to the deck, and a contented man carries his steaming cuppa upstairs to check for email from afar.

Aye, tis a contented man sat here waiting for the Canadian to show up as hordes of retirees appear for the afternoon train ride dressed in various eye-catching pastels and hurry inside the station after exiting cabs, to come back out minutes later wearing, 'can you believe we rushed brunch,' looks on faces and wander the main drag in search of somewhere to wait. Seven of them stop at my window to check and pull miserable faces at me and the menu taped to glass and move on. Big Rock beer is good and I have plenty of time for another but I decide I better not. Don't want to miss my ride do I. The park ranger just walked in decked out in his greens and browns and stares at me from the bar like an angry sprout. He spots me while surveying the room and gives me the nod before finding an empty seat on the other side of the room. I get the feeling he thinks I'm a nut. That's alright, he's a sprout. I order another beer.

Upon reflection, I'm glad I didn't buy a real beaver skin hat for William this morning because when one has been amongst wild animals as I have, one becomes protective of all species. I'd have no problem purchasing elk horns for the library though. Crows are huge in Jasper! A murder of them dive-bomb the station and pull crap from the eaves which has me thinking Spike Milligan, Puckoon, and Ireland. Caw, said the crow. Balls, said Paul Henry Sutton. Read the book, where's that bloody pint? The wind blows in from the east bringing clouds loaded with the white stuff, which is too bad, as I was hoping for a clear view of The Maligne Canyon and Indian Head Mountain on the ride out. Its 1:30pm and still no sign of train or pint as Fun Lovin' Criminals finish singing about Scooby Snacks and a syrupy voice warns of incoming inclement weather from another overhead speaker and segues into Chumbawamba with some Tubthumping, and my arse is bopping in its seat. I ponder performing a bit of the ol' soft shoe shuffle for the retirees as they walk past the window again, but think better of it.

Terry's muse acts shy and coy as she finally delivers the pint. She smiles as she takes my empty and darts glances at the front door as she goes. I tell her not to worry as there's a good chance he won't be on the train pulling into the station. She remembers me and we laugh.

Right then, I'm off! I pay the bill at the bar and load up my pack, nearly taking the top off a diner's head as he bites into a fajita. He pulls his head into his collar like a surprised turtle as I apologise, wave goodbye to the bartender and depart with faculties intact.

I hear that train a comin' - a comin' round the bend. -Johnny Cash

The station is rammed, jam-packed and I bump into Aussie girl who is as surprised about it as I am. I thought she'd be long gone and vice-versa. She's just bought a bus ticket to Lake Louise on the recommendation of patrons of The Athabasca bar where she's been staying all this time. Off to have a go at some sk-iing for the first time, she tells me to give her a slap on the arse if I'm ever on Quantas Airlines and she'll buy me a pint. Did I mention she's a flight attendant? There we are laughing and messing about like old times, jammed together like sardines in that hot tin of a station, and next thing we're waving goodbyes as she strides out into the cold full of confidence, leaving me to find an empty bench to park my carcass.

It's quiet for a busy waiting room. The clock on the wall can be heard loudly ticking away the day. It's humid in here and travellers are getting impatient. One old dolly stares at me from across the room. I smile and her stare turns to ice. It dawns me she's in with that retiree gang. What did I do? A member of the

Beer Coasters walks in, spots me, and comes over to make a fuss. The rest of the gang left town yesterday but he's decided to stay in Jasper for now. We chat for a bit and off he goes after wishing me well. Good fun those boys.

Train stations can be places full of sad farewells. Picture hissing steam from shiny steam engines as the hero kisses the heroine passionately through an open window while the train pulls out slowly into British fog. Whistle's shrill and chase dirty-grey pigeons from thrones of shit in rusting rafters. Our hero runs the length of the platform to greet his lover as she stands waiting at the foot of a wrought-iron stairwell. She flings herself at him with abandon as he flicks a half-finished cigarette to the track and the wind kicks it back, setting fire to the veiled hat that belonged to her mother as they kiss passionately. None of that for me old chap, just a miserable French steward stood shivering in an entranceway. 'Hello there. How are you?' I inquire with a grin.

'Cud be better!' he whines, shrugs his shoulders and blows a mottled nose into a handkerchief the size of a bed sheet. Not again. Les Miserables! I tell him I'll talk to him later, unless he's retired from life by the ague, to find an empty double seat on the left in front of a glass partition containing a model train display just like on the Skeena. My lucky spot? I settle in like I've done it all before, arrange belongings and make ready for Edmonton. Immediately, an elderly couple sit down in front of me and make themselves comfortable, all the while carrying on a loud conversation (or argument) in what sounds like Russian. A conversation started the day they met, by sounds, due to the effort and concentration elicited at every loud disagreement (or show of affection). I'm such a magnet. I swear, once again at the odds. Empty seats that surround sit silently laughing at me as we enter Jasper National Park.

To take my mind off noisy neighbours, I attempt to concentrate on a leaflet left hidden among pamphlets iin the seat pocket in front of me. Its tells me that Jasper gets its name from

Jasper Hawes who built the original Jasper House in1813 at Devona Siding just north of Brule Lake, east of Snake Indian River.

The Athabasca River meets up with the Rocky River to create Jasper Lake which, like clockwork, fills up in the summer and empties in the winter.

Henry House built in 1811 was the the area's first supply post. Mount Roche a Perdrix (2,134 metres high) south of Jasper Park gate, was once part of an ancient seabed that created the Rockies eighty million years ago. The Miette Range of mountains and its hot springs are just up the road, as is the Athabasca, Canada's seventh longest river. Which originates in the Columbia Icefields and flows 1,231 kilometres through the park and into the lake named after the Inn in Jasper that VIA staff congregate to spend their wages in.

In search of ear plugs or a translator to shut out or understand ongoing argument in the seat in front, and in all the excitement of boarding, I neglected to mention the....hold on a minute, there's a problem! The conductor is advising me, with much patience, that my ticket will take me straight through to Toronto if I want. I don't have to get off at Edmonton, he tells me. I have to make a decision, to stick twist, should I stay or should I go. Oh boy, what to do? I'm getting all excited here as passengers all around await my decision with him. I spent last night writing to save money to buy presents for the family at the Edmonton Mall. Erm...'C'mon sir, what will it be?'

'Ah, sod Edmonton, stamp the bloody thing, I'm going home!' I decide, to a smattering of applause. The conductor laughs and tells me they'll have me in Toronto on Monday night at around 9:30pm, only two days away. I can hardly hear him for the cheering from the crowd and ongoing argument between the love birds ahead. 'Erm, can I borrow your phone to call the family please?' I shout.

'Sorry sir, you'll have to call them from Edmonton,' he shouts back and takes off down the aisle after a seemingly confused passenger wearing one shoe. What a turn-up. I don't have any clean laundry. I've had the same pair of socks on for two days. Ah, to hell with it I'll wash them in the sink and dry them on the heater. I have second thoughts regards my decision for about ten seconds. Turning to a neighbour, who has been following all of this quite closely, I tell her I'll have to phone them from Edmonton. She laughs. I laugh. We all laugh.

Indian Head Mountain is glorious in a suddenly strange and weird light. Another Walker Art Gallery God in the clouds special. I've relocated to a jam-packed Dome full of passengers snapping away with camera's at everything out there with snow on it. The light is amazing. 'Sod the Edmonton Mall!' I tell a woman jostling with me to capture the same image and she agrees. 'Overpriced and in Edmonton!' She tells me as we snap away. Never get complacent when traveling folks. Get out of bed early, stay up late, see the sights, have a laugh, spend money on a decent camera.

Cold Comfort: The snow was cold, comforting, to the touch. Finger-less gloves, a gift from his wife, enhanced the pleasure. Where are you Paul? He couldn't him and he'd been searching for over an hour.

The sun was shining now. It was nice here, in the sun. He watched the shadow of a large shamrock shaped cloud cross the exterior of an ancient church set in a landscape of stone, snow and silence.

He felt rather foolish. He'd managed to find his Auntie quite easily but not Paul. He smiled and grooved on jagged memories of recycled days of youth and glory, chewy accents and DC comics. He'd loved his comics.

Orgasm Addict by the Buzzcocks had been a favourite with young punk guns who wanted to exterminate rock and roll dinosaurs that still roamed the earth. *What Do I Get?* A fitting epitaph, he thought, as he searched for his mate through England's glistening, snow white fields, the playing fields of the Lord in better days.

He made a mental note to change his will upon arrival back home in Canada and request a plain cedar marker instead with *Made in England* stamped below a serial number and date of expiry instead of all this marble and angels nonsense.

Where are you? They'd once 'played' hide 'n' seek after dark here to impress girlfriends, cronies, themselves. Smoking No.6 cigarettes, drinking cheap cider, telling daft jokes and scary stories. Billy fell down a freshly dug hole with the coppers on his boot heels. Jilted John had been going out with a girl named Julie and they all read Record Mirror, NME, and SOUNDS.

He'd left his mams early to walk and snap away with a disposable camera and tramp through streets and memories. Footprints in the snow through No-Go Zones, speed bumps, stolen cars, litter, empty streets. Shattered dreams, pigeon lofts, stray dogs, fences and walls topped with barbed wire and broken glass. Bus wheels aimed slush at row houses at a crossroads and spray painted bus stops and shop shutters, where he decided to retrace steps to visit his aunt and find an old friend. They'd loved Bob Marley, the Rasta's, Virgin, the punks outside Probe, ska, the skins at The Apple, everything about Eric's, and ignored stares from the squares at the taxi-rank on Lime Street.

Let's get together and be alright. He couldn't get anything together right now and he was being studied from afar by a Neighborhood Watcher, a Percy Sugden type pretending to check his well-waxed motor for scratches and bird shit. He had a bead on Percy in case he had to return fire but the old feller retired behind a tall well-manicured hedge that now resembled a soggy Christmas pudding weighed down with all that wet snow. He stepped into the shade of a doorway at the back of the church, shadows claimed him and he shivered into his not too great coat and watched a crow fly from a bowed tree with a crack of oily wings and echoing cackle as it swooped decapitating heads of snow from tombstones in its wake before coming to a halt atop a weathered stone cross.

See how they run like pigs from a gun...

He felt sad stood there shivering watching the crow but

halted the tear in time as he slipped on a runnel of ice from a downspout that had captured multi-coloured confetti in a mini glacier that reminded him of water or snow globes from Wales or the Isle of Man given to him by contented relatives when he was a child.

BORN
DIED
WIFE OF
DAUGHTER OF
REST
PEACE
IN

His aunt had led him into the darkness and delightful smells of the corner shop on a dank November afternoon back then when he had gathered up the nerve to ask for a battery-operated robot with red flashing eyes that had stood sentry in a shop window since September. It had beckoned him to rescue it for his birthday! Inside the shop rows of woman's magazines and assorted boxes of fireworks and packets of sparklers competed for attention with jars of hard-boiled sweets, chocolate bars and sticky things.

'You're not getting that,' his aunt had told him and laughed the laugh of her mother, my Nin. 'Not until I win the pools, so you'll have to pick something else!' and she'd laughed again and winked at the women behind the counter who joined her in the laughing as he picked out a Batman colouring book and a box of wax crayons instead and aunt had paid for them and a loaf of bread with a pound note as he ran his hand over lolly-ice stickers stuck to a warm blue metal freezer with a glass covered lid.

He'd loved his auntie Elsie, everyone did. Snow falls away and her name appears. Black marble, ice-encrusted flowers. The crow is spooked by an ice-cream van this time and *Cawwws* its way to a tree branch bereft of leaves that lay beneath melting snow at its roots.

Half a pound of sugary spice, half a pound of treacle...he whistles the next line as the ice-cream van splashes into a cul-de-sac bringing back memories of summer days and a queue of kids waiting for the man. Sugary cones filled from a whip-whirl of brilliant white cream, a stainless steel machine, a dirty tray, a gurgling sink, the jolt of a pain to the temple; frosted paper-wrappers placed on sun-burned necks, sand and salt and sea air. Peel the paper and wet your lips before you suck it but he always forgot to the amusement of adults.

Mary had a little lamb....

The tinny tune fades with the van into the distance as he walks lines of tombstones that remind him of soldiers with swelled chests, cold no more, whistling, boots soaked now, he's glad he wore the black fleece as he finds his pal. Where. Did you get that. Blank. Expression on your face. A moth-eaten canvas army tent left to rot in a Welsh field to fool the farmer, to avoid paying the bill for the pleasure of camping in the rain, a thumb sheared off in a back wheel on a scrumpified dare, the dare-devils shocked face as the bloody socket left the mark of Zorro on the white stucco wall of a farmhouse as the ambulance finally showed up and its occupants searched for the missing thumb by the light of a fly encrusted orange lightbulb; more memories of Wales.

Town called malice folk called us names and we didn't care. They had bingo on Sunday and lived on flat lager and sweaty pasties and concrete pies and had fat wifies and snooker and pockets full of change and tobacco in pouches and rolling machines and threw dole money at the feet of horses and dogs in rabbit hutch betting shops. A pub band ditching ABBA and Apache covers and cabaret pub fare to change into snarling northern Stranglers in army fatigues and spiked hair and hatchet Bowie cuts as we sat transfixed until the manager pulled the plug on them and we got thrown out and barred as well. Remember, Paul? Damp grass beneath flickering street-lights, the smell of dog shit, as we planned our escape and shared cigarettes and laughter as 'Blinded by The Light' played from an open window.

I unzip my coat as a robin pries the stalk from a faded plastic daffodil, checks his booty for ballast, and disappears into the sun. I make another snowball, no need for the gloves now, and toss it after the bird.

Oh no, it's the Beer Nazi again. He's in the kitchen being a miserable swine! He gives me the evil eye as he sells me a sandwich and a beer to take back to my seat. For a laugh, I drop Engineer Don's name.

'Ahhh, you know Don then!' I answer in the affirmative, which brightens him up, he's my pal now and I'm going to enjoy every minute.

The Canadian stops at Edson (pop 4,000) 'the gateway to the rocky mountains' to board a mother and son. Toronto, here I come! I get a regulation pillow and blanket from a smiling conductor as we climb the highest point of elevation on the Yellowhead Highway at Obed (38,18.6ft) and cross the McLeod River, Wolf Creek, Carrot Creek and the Lobstick River twice before traversing the Pembina by means of a never-ending 274 metre long wooden bridge.

The Pembina River was used as a route by prospectors hiking to the Cariboo gold fields in search of wine, women and song in the 1860s, which has me thinking about my second visit to Canada in the summer of 1979, accompanied once again by my sister Christina, who by then had dyed red hair and no fiancé.

We kicked off another two week trip at Buckhorn Lake, Ontario, where I got to drive a speedboat and try my hand at water-skiing for the first and last time because the experience nearly cost me a plum in mid wipe-out. Handle and rope whipped between my legs as I flipped, leaving me with a large multi-coloured bruise and a long rope-burn down the inside of my left thigh.

'YOU ALRIGHT SCOUSE?' Yelled my cousin Chris, now stood up in the boat the rope was attached to. 'What's it look like soft lad?' I managed, as onlookers pulled me onto the dock. I was banged up but hid the pain well like a good Englishman.

'Guess you don't want another go then?' Chris asked, as he steered the boat in slowly.

'No thanks that was enough for me like!'

'Okay, best put a cold beer on that!'

And off he went dragging the next sucker.

The following day, limping about the beach clad only in swim-shorts and an earring, drinking beer and chatting with locals and vacationes for hours, I ended up with a severe and painful sunburn, but survived a long sleepless night shivering on a cot in the back room of a trailer. Next morning, moaning in agony, I managed to stand and shuffle my way in search of help.

'Oh, Jesus Christ, Julie, will you look at the state of him!'

'It hurts. You have anything for the pain?' Was all I could manage.

'Oh my God, we told you to wear sun-screen,' Julie admonished, and went in search of medical supplies and aspirin as her husband sold tickets to view the luminous limey.

'Here buddy, lay down.'

'I can't. I'm on fire!'

'Jeez! Somebody give him a cold beer!'

The burn was that bad that I had a shivering fit in the backseat of my cousins car on the way back to Oshawa that scared my hosts into wanting to drive me straight to the nearest hospital, but I refused on the grounds that I was mentally challenged and would be alright in the morning.

'Are you sure? They'll just sink you in a bath of ice to bring your temperature down.'

'No th-th-thanks mate!' I stammered. 'Just shoot me.' That night Julie covered me in cream and placed a giant fan at the foot of a bed I was allotted to sleep in upstairs, and she and my sister brought me water and checked on me through a long and sleepless night.

The following morning I stood in a cold shower and watched skin bubble and slide down my legs to come to a stop in a white mush at my feet.

'You okay in there, big guy?'

'Yeah, gimmee some skin?'

After a couple of days I was able to walk again and accompanied family members to Ontario Place in the car on a hot sweltering day, well-lathered with thick sunscreen, where I had my portrait done by a student artist who couldn't keep a straight face as I sat all stiff and uncomfortable in a plastic chair, puffing away on a cigarette, as she put my caricature to paper in black charcoal.

'What's your name?'

'Paul.'

'What happened to you?'

'I sat too close to the camp-fire.'

'Really?'

'Yeah, mind if I smoke?'

'Go ahead.'

'Good, they've been trying to put me out for days.'

In a souvenir Polaroid of the event, my cousin is stood behind the seated artist who is laughing, I'm laughing, the seagulls are laughing, and I still have the framed portrait upon my wall.

We visited the brand new Cinesphere afterwards to watch a movie called 'Toronto the Good', and a scene with sparrows nesting in downtown traffic lights had some kind of magical effect as I smoked pot for the first time the following day.

'You sure you smoked this before, Paul?'

'Loads of times.'

'Here goes nothin'....' and I was the star of the show again as I ate bread rolls, peanuts, chips, ice-cream, un-cooked pasta shells by the handful, and performed a striptease on a picnic table backlit by a patio door. After years of being skinny I was finally putting on weight.

Buckhorn Lake: Friends and friends of friends sequestered around a roaring campfire drinking, smoking, singing and telling jokes and stories all evening long as it was summer. Later on in the early morning chill, after everyone had gone to bed, my cousin and I had the first of many bets to come: To see who could stay awake to see the sunrise. The fire burned my legs from a distance and the bugs were still out in force. Muskol on my cigarette burned the back of my throat as I took long drags and blew smoke skyward to obliterate winking stars. My cousin navigated his way around rows of discarded lawn chairs in search of beer and I leaned my head back as far as I could to become lost in bright constellations. No clouds up there made for a clear light show. Silence except for the constant chorus of tree frogs and cicadas and a mosquito that tried to move into my ear. I focused, made a vow to return to the Great Bear where I belonged, and toasted the stars. I closed my eyes and almost fell asleep but my cousin saved me by falling over a kids bicycle and landing behind a mountain of firewood, cursing a blue streak.

'Did you see that goddamn bike jump out at me?' he stage whispered, and fell asleep. I had lawn-chair-neck for days but stayed awake to see the sun rise and win the bet.

Sometimes when I'm alone at the cottage on Lake Huron and the flames from the fire are shimmering and changing the colour of tree and bush to the comforting sound of lapping waves slightly muffled by sand dunes, I think about that night at Buckhorn Lake, northwest of Peterboro, and look to the stars and wink.

Two years later I would break my cousin's leg by accident in that same trailer park as we wrestled for beers, drunk as skunks, in a sand-pit on the occasion of my first road run. *Roadrunner, Roadrunner*! Silly boys. I lay here under my blanket reminiscing while listening to the couple still babbling away in front, and thinking how lucky we are to live on Turtle Island, Ojibway land in Peterboro, all those firsts, as the rhythm of the train sends me packing again. Zzzz...

Searching, through the window of a train, it's dark outside and in but once in a while I can manage an enticing glimpse of trees and track covered in blue-white snow.

I could be in 1944 Germany or Russia, a British spy on a mission to save the Empire, or just the world, and if caught, must remember to answer questions in the correct language, and I must watch out for the Beer Nazi, I know he's trying to catch me out, of that I'm sure.

Look out here he comes, flexing his mustache.

'Spracken de Deutsch?'

'Nein, Mein beerkellar!'

'Achtung, achtung! Englisher svein on borden!'

Schnell, Schnell...I must hiden in shitenhausen and wait for the train to stop and flush myself clear onto the track, where the sound of dogs barking and the crack of a rifle shot and a bullet pings off the steel toe of my boot and ricochets off into the dark night.

'Thank Gotten for K- Marten,' I whisper before making a cat-like leap over a signal box and slide safely down a snow-covered embankment into the relative safety of the trees. I scurry quickly through inky darkness, lungs on fire from the cold, freedom is a spot-light away in the distance, but I'm stopped suddenly in my tracks by a Nazi General disguised as a male elk.

*He charges, so I take his picture and the flash blinds him and he gores himself badly in one leg. It looks like a mortal wound I'm thinking, as he screams and rolls madly around on his back as the snow turns red around him and he screams again. I pick up his rifle and take aim only wanting to put him out of his misery. I fire and the flash blinds me and he screams another terrible scream....*the screeching of train wheels torture teeth and brain and I cast aside my blanket and sit up straight, suddenly wide awake in my seat taking a long swig from a water bottle, coming to my senses as the Canadian screeches slowly towards Siberia, I mean Edmonton.

The couple ahead still argue and laugh. My Irish neighbour is smiling at me from across the aisle as I wipe drool from my chin. Other passengers are pretending not to be staring at mefrom behind books and magazines or via reflections in windows. I must have been doing the funky chicken in my sleep again.

The Canadian zips through St. Albert on the Sturgeon River, founded by Father Albert Lancombe in 1861, who lived a grand life and died in 1916. The Yellowhead Trail is close by according to a green sign below us on the Edmonton freeway. I'm told that I have twenty minutes to find a phone and call my family. I ask a kind-looking middle-aged couple to keep an eye on my pack. They agree, and off I go in search of a quarter to spend. It's cold and dark as I jog the length of the platform avoiding travelers loaded with luggage, children and parcels, some wearing panic on their faces. Some don't want to clear a path so I have to do some fancy footwork or shoulder them gently out of the way.

'Sorryaboutthat!'

'Scuseme.'

'Sorry!'

'Comin' through....Pregnant lady, beg your pardon!' I make it inside to encounter long lines of irritable people waiting to buy tickets or use the phones, and true to form, just like at the bank, grocery or beer store, I pick the wrong line and wait for years jumping up and down on my toes until the phone becomes vacant.

I don't believe it, they're home, what's the odds? They didn't go to a resort for the weekend as planned. They're all in bed and Janice is amused to hear my latest story. She is missing me and plans to be at Union Station to greet me. It's only a short conversation as I'm afraid to be stranded in Edmonton and she has work in the morning, so I promise to phone from Winnipeg, tell her I love her, love to the kids, and begin the longest mile back to steerage. The platform at this end is now packed full of first-class ticket holders waiting to board, some being transported by luggage carts to their first-class points of entry, which hampers the rest of us from reaching our destination before the next equinox, so I take my time, make a point of ignoring the well-to-do bastards and breathe in the night air as I stroll.

I stop at a chain link fence to take a photo of the far away lights of Edmonton and as I'm jimmying the camera into its case a skinny guy with long greasy hair asks me for a light. I laugh when I notice it's a joint he's after lighting. He offers me a puff and looks confused when I ask him if he has any pasta shells.

Edmonton, Alberta (pop. 850,000) is apparently Canada's Festival City. A boomtown since the Yukon gold rush, Edmonton was incorporated in 1904 before becoming the site of the huge Alberta oil discoveries in 1947. Sprawled on both sides of the North Saskatchewan River, the city covers more territory than any other in Canada; 681 square kilometres of parks, greenbelt riverbanks, Wayne Gretzky, Dave Semenko, and the Mall which rates seven mentions in the Guinness Book of Records. There you go Arthur, make that eight.

Two major fur trading forts, Augustus and Edmonton House, formed the city's roots, and the Klondike gold rush of 1897 and the hordes of 'Klondikers' that chased the dream put the place on the map, made it the gateway to the north before the railway arrived in 1905, and thusly Edmonton was established as a world class city, and don't forget the oil and the fact that I didn't visit it.

8pm, I escaped the crush to find tempers and temperatures still rising on here. The two in front must have argued themselves into the ether and have been replaced by a pleasant young mother and son. 'Danny, leave the nice man alone. Stop bothering him!'

'It's okay, he's not bothering me, honest!'

'Oh, thanks a lot. I think he likes you - don't you Danny!'

'I have two of my own. It's no problem,' I tell Danny's mom, and next thing I'm in conversation with her boy about Woody and Buzz from Toy Story. I prefer Batman, Catwoman, Spiderman and J Jonah Jameson, but I took William and Madeline to see Toy Story so I know what I'm talking about for a change. Got a kick out of the kid who tortures the toys in the movie though, must admit. Ayup! Here come the action figures over the top of the seat and Buzz bounces off my head. 'Danny!' his mom yells, 'Stop that!'

'That's alright, he's okay!' I'm off to the Dome for a bit of peace. Nice man my arse, I could lose an eye here!

It takes forever to escape Siberia. Oil tankers and all manner of freight trains stand idle as if frozen to the tracks. Long thick icicles look to be welding axles to frozen ground. Swirling powdery snow plays hide and seek with us and heavy rolling stock, as engineers play go forward come back go forward again causing passengers to tut and moan, tut and moan, which has me thinking Robert DeNiro in Boys Life. My Irish neighbour is from Limerick and wants to tell me all about it, the town not the movie. I have the time sat here eyeballing the Clover Bar Bridge through frosted window panes, I tell her, I'm all ears. She's a tiny, of indeterminate age, an ex-school teacher, witty and charming, so I invite her over to my place for a cup of tea but she wants to stay put under her blankets.

It's quiet on here now, just the sound of us two chatting. She tells me she lives alone on an island called Texada and is traveling to see friends in Saskatchewan. Once married, with a large family, she has traveled the world and shares condensed experiences as we'd be here all week she's done and seen that much. She asks if I'm a writer and if so what it is I write. I tell her

I'm just keeping a journal, no, no writer, but I would like to be one when I grow up. She laughs mischievously, comfortable in her own skin and blanket.

'So that's just a journal you're keeping, then?'

'Yes missus, just recording adventures.' You can hear a pin drop in here.

'Adventures? You must have had a lot as you've been scribbling in that thing since you got on at Jasper and it's almost full.'

'Well, I've been gone for nearly two weeks, just killing time.'

'You are a writer, Paul.'

'I wish!'

'No, you're a writer. I know you are.' I'm on stage and I usually like that, but I'm feeling a bit uncomfortable as she makes herself more comfortable. 'Eh, I left school when I was fifteen, I'm no writer, just a scribbler.' She looks at me in an irritated fashion, scowls, and tells a story about Sir George Bernard Shaw, who, when asked to teach schoolchildren a creative writing course, told the kids to go home and write.

'Simple as that,' she scolds.

'You knew Bernard Shaw?'

'No. You! I'm telling you the same thing because I...never mind, your little pal is trying to get your attention!' and she points at Ernie and Bert dancing on the headrest. 'Thanks for the encouragement,' I tell my Irish Rose and join in the fun as Danny does the business with his toys.

Bandstand Idol: My mum wanted me to take the cat but I couldn't find it so I took the caterpillar instead. I didn't mind much as Cathy was much easier to carry and didn't bite or scratch. I parked my red Raleigh bike in the backyard before setting off to the park with my sisters. They were younger than me. Three years separated us. My mum would tell everyone that. I heard her tell a woman at the fruit shop that my father only had to take his shirt off and was puzzled why the woman thought that funny. The fruit shop had a picture on the wall of the Beatles eating green apples to keep their teeth white. I liked the Beatles.

I was dressed in my best charcoal grey shorts, a white nylon shirt complete with red tie, beige knee-socks and brown, well-polished shoes. My shoes were always polished like my fathers. He learned it in the air force. My hair was kiss-curled with my mums spit and I had a three-penny bit in my pocke. My sisters wore matching white sandals, skirts and pink tops and had curly ringlets. My mum would wash their hair at night and wrap it in bandages. They looked like they'd been in a car accident. They had no money. I was in charge.

The park wasn't far away and the grass was long and wet. Lots of green chairs with yellow stenciled numbers on the back were in front of the stage. Big trees stood swaying in the wind and people sat or lay on blankets in their shade. The stage was the bandstand where brass bands played on Sunday mornings. Orchestras would play tunes for old people to dance to on Saturday nights. The old people smelled, and I hated it when they leaned down to kiss me or shake my hand. Hugging was death. Kissing was worse. The old women wore brown socks that wrinkled at the ankles and long dresses with flowers on and pearls around their necks and carried umbrella's. It rained a lot in Liverpool.

The men wore suits and shirts and ties and had badges sewn to top pockets and the non-baldy ones had greasy hair. They laughed a lot and gave me pennies. Coppers, they called them. They told me I was unlucky to have missed penny-farthings. I prefer three-penny bits. They are heavy and have portcullises on the back and are octagonal and made of brass and they shine up real good and you can throw them far if you want.

The front row was reserved for those in the show and I made sure my sisters sat next to me and I sat on the end. The

Organiser was a big lady with a shiny pin in her lapel and a big white hat. Her face was pink and sweaty and she kept wiping her forehead with a handkerchief and going, *oh dearie me, its hot!* Whe she started fanning herself with programmes some men and women made faces behind her. Children with animals of all shapes, sizes, and breeds lined the front row. The stage was a long way away. Dogs barked and peed on things and cats meowed. An older boy had a little monkey dressed in a knitted woolen suit. That can't have his. A girl had a parrot in a cage. It said a bad word and the men who had made faces and coughed. The women *tut-tutted* and pretended to be annoyed under their hats. They all smoked.

It looked nice up there on the stage with the balloons and ribbons and bunting. It looked cool and shady too. A large pad of paper clamped to a wooden easel that we use in school, said. TUESDAY: PET SHOW - PRIZES - ALL WELCOME! In red letters. It would blow away in a strong wind. Today was Tuesday and I would be brave when the man called my name. It was handy when your surname started in *M*. You were never first or last always in the middle. You had a chance to be pepared so you didn't look like an idiot.

The headmistress in our school uses a cane. She has never hit me with it. I do my homework and behave myself. I am the only one in the class of forty-eight that can spell *gnome* properly. A big boy with red hair was jealous. He was waiting for me one Monday morning and we got into a fight. I pushed him down some stairs and he never bothered me again. I was popular.

PAUL MASSAM!

PAUL MASSAM, if you please! The microphone squealed as I stood up. The woman in charge ticked off my name and pointed to the stairs and I looked back at my sisters when I climbed them to make sure there were still there. One was sat back in her seat twirling her ringlets, the other scratching herself. She had Impetigo. They were watching the girl beside her eat a toffee-apple. If I won I would buy them a toffee-apple. They didn't know I had a threepenny-bit.

It was nice and cool on the stage and you could see for miles and everyone looked at you. My sisters waved and I felt daft. The priest was sat behind a long table. He was a judge. They had a jug of water and paper cups and one was smoking. One judge had a big bracelet around his neck. He must be the mayor. I made sure to look him in the eye and he ignored me. The priest smiled. The woman judge smoked.

The St. Johns Ambulance were there on the grass. They had a stretcher and a red blanket....*Paul! Hello! Where is your pet?* The man wore a straw hat and striped coat. He had a gap between his teeth.

Hello. My pet is in my pocket. The microphone was loud. It echoed all over the place.

Well...where is he Paul and what is his name? He wiggled his eyebrows up and down and winked at the audience and they all laughed. He looked me up and down and over my shoulder and they laughed again. My sisters weren't paying attention.

I pointed to my pocket.

Well...bring him out then. Let's see him! he sang. I didn't like him. The crowd were quiet now. I wanted to go home. I pulled the matchbox out of my pocket. It was a deep pocket and I had all kinds in there.

It's a she actually, I told him.

Well, let's see her!. Right, boys and girls? He winked at the judges when everyone cheered. I wanted to poke him in the eye. The woman with the cigarette laughed. The priest smiled at me and motioned to open the box. The mayor was asleep.

I slid the outer box open very slowly until I was sure that I had the inside box the right way up. I didn't want her to fall out on the wood floor. She was delicate. The man guided me closer to the microphone stand and shouted, *Don't be shy - OPEN THE*

BOX!

Some boys shouted *OPEN THE BOX* back and the audience laughed again and I felt silly.

Cathy had pooed a lot since we left home and her lettuce was soggy. My mum said I should feed her cabbage isntead as she was a cabbage butterfly.

I picked her out gently with the tips of my thumb and first finger and let her roll down my fingers until she got a grip with her feet on my palm. She was green with lovely yellow spots.

I hope she's not vicious! the man shouted and made as if to run. *Hold her up then!* I did and Cathy tried to jump off my hand. *What's her name?* I told him and they whistled. *How old is she?* I told him I had had her for two days. *What do you feed her?* Cabbage! I answered and watched the ambulance men running with their stretcher. Cathy tried to escape up my shirt sleeve again. She did this a lot. I picked her up and dropped her back in her matchbox gently and slid it closed.

Thank you Paul Massam...and Cathy! I trust the judges have their marks? They all nodded and looked serious, the mayor was awake now and the priest said good luck as I went down the stairs and back to my seat.

The Organising Woman had a crowd around her and the ambulance man with the moustache was telling people to give her air. Her false teeth fell on to her chest when they lifted her up and a kid laughed. A woman in a blue blazer with a white armband was telling kids to sit down and behave themselves. Dogs barked and the monkey screeched. A cat hissed and scratched the girl who owned it who flung the cat at the back of a seat and started to cry. Cats have nine lives. I put Cathy back in my pocket. The woman was in the ambulance. My sisters had to go to the toilet so we went home without toffee-apples. 1 Homerton Road. We left soon after in the middle of the night with my mum. The cat stayed with father.

Back on the Canadian, North Cooking Lake and Elk Lake National Park, two wonders of the province of Alberta, are out there somewhere. Tofield (pop.900) is lit up for as long as it takes to pronounce its name by the lights from this train. Next thing we're in Holden (pop.500) sat amidst the flatlands of Alberta, which was named after Queen Victoria's fourth daughter Princess Caroline Alberta. Viking is next to be lit up and boasts a population of 1,160 all Norsemen, I assume.

We're riding the rails across plains once roamed by buffalo for as far as the eye could see from a horse, before they were slaughtered by Europeans for sport, hats, coats. A 1,000 year old carving called The Ribstones is all that is left of the tribes who hunted, lived with and relied on the buffala. Battle River's frothing white rapids are crossed by way of a steel trestle 884 metres long and 61 metres high.

A travel agent sat behind me is talking about the *New York is big, but this is Biggar!* thing mentioned earlier. 'Too bad the station's closed, guess the train crash of '97 scared them all off,' I remark, stupidly, because next thing she's sat perched on my armrest giving me a free seminar regards train crashes, rail travel and the reading of train timetables, which amuses my Irish neighbour no end. She laughs silently and pulls dying of boredom faces from safety of her blanket. After wearing a mask of awe and feigning interest for miles I make my excuses and take off to the safety of the Dome again, picking up a roast beef sandwich and a bag of chips from a happy Beer Nazi along the way.

Sat alone at the back, fed and watered, I slip off boots and socks to air out my feet. A good time for the travel agent to follow me up here, I'm thinking, as I put white cotton socks back on after drying them on the wall heater. I chase thick wool outer socks into the brown paper bag that my food came in and hide the parcel under the seat.

I'm doing toe bends for exercise while watching two

young lovers share spit and a bottle of Peach Schnapps. She chews on his bottom lip between slugs. A middle-aged David Beckham is sat at a table up front in a soccer outfit and flesh coloured pantyhose watches me watching them and pretends to write in a notebook. I'm caught! She takes time out to smile at me in the reflection of the window. I pretend not to notice and pull out my notebook in retaliation. Florescent lights are too bright to relax and lip-biter is back from the kitchen with a bag of food and I don't feel like hanging around to see how they're going to....Too late, you should see what he's doing with a tomato slice. That's it I'm off. I retrieve the bag of socks and retire back to my seat for more intellectual and stimulating conversation with the lady from Limerick, it's a lot easier on the blood pressure. It's quiet in steerage where all are asleep except for readers. The little man up front sleeps soundly at his mom's feet. Its 10:30 on a Saturday night and after some wishing my Irish friend a good night I drift off into a sleep filled with dreams of succulent peaches being rubbed into aching feet by funky devils nibbling on chocolate soccer balls.

3:40am: All hands on deck are awakened at Saskatoon by a hillbilly couple loaded down with guitars, luggage, winter coats and hatboxes. She can't find her ticket and he stinks like a distillery. He brushes my head with a suitcase as he attempts to swing it to the rack above his seat, all the time telling his partner how useless she is. 'Yeah, maybe, but at least I can do the dishes. More than I can say for you, so you better hope I find the tickets!' A conductor is stood half-asleep in the aisle. He whispers a 'Yes, ma'am,' back, and waits until the tickets are found in her coat pocket. With giggles and shushes they plonk into groaning seats and the steward makes his escape. The newcomers are fast asleep and snoring before he slams shut the door to the adjoining car.

I have to laugh even though my head's pounding, the muscles in my back are in a knot, and my legs are screaming with cramp. Aw, no, I'm gobsmacked. My Irish Rose has gone, departed in the night. Her ticket is gone from the bulkhead above her seat too. When and where did she go? She didn't wake me to say goodbye! Was she real? I didn't see her leave her seat or indulge in conversation with anyone else. Did I imagine her? Nah! If you're out there reading this missus give me a slap on the arse next time you see me on the Canadian.

False Teeth Lady and husband are gone as well. Departed at Biggar as promised. A large frizzy-haired redhead, she sat and talked the ear off her beloved all the way from Jasper and had a habit of removing her false teeth to examine them as he looked longingly at her as if he couldn't believe his luck. The best scene was when someone asked where they were going while she was in mid-inspection. 'BIGGAR!' she shouted, and sat up straight as her bottom lip upped and slapped her unibrow and flapped back again to slap her ample bosom with a loud thwack. Love is... sharing your teeth!

Saskatoon (pop. 185,000) is the largest city in the province of Saskatchewan. A city of bridges, centre of economics, historic heart of its province, home of the Riel Rebellion and Wendel Clark. Located on the banks of the South Saskatchewan River - which in summer, I'm told, is lush with dark green vegetation - the original 1882 Saskatoon settlement was a temperance colony founded by the most Reverend John Lake and flock who wanted to escape the evil influence of alcohol, the daft sods.

The name Saskatoon is taken from the purple Misakwatomin berry that grows in abundance along the river. Wanuskewin National Park boasts indigenous archaeological findings that date back 8,000 years. The plains tribes knew Saskatchewan as 'Kisiskatchewan' which means swiftly flowing water. Fur traders used the Kisiskatchewan River as a major trade route and when things started to get out of order regards booze n' women, the Northwest Mounted Police were formed to bring law and order to the prairies, and as you know, the Mounties always got their man, especially after the railroad showed up and settlers flooded in like water from a burst dam. Saskatchewan is still the bread basket of Canada and home to over a million people with roots mainly in Russia, Scandinavia and Europe.

The North West Rebellion unfolded here in 1885; the last armed conflict on Canadian soil (unless you count the Oka conflict of 1989) when Louis Riel and Chief Poundmaker were defeated by the militia. Depending on what you read or who you're talking to: Riel, a Metis descendant of white fur traders and Cree-Ojibway parents, was either a founding father or treasonous crook. To the Cree and Blackfoot the rebellion was about language and culture. Some historians reckon that Riel's intentions were more on the profitable side by selling whisky to his people

'The white settler coming into the country to farm or raise cattle cared little about what became of the poor Indian. If a cow was killed or a horse stolen, the Indians where to blame. Their land was looked upon with covetous eyes and they were regarded as a nuisance and an expense. The right of the native red man was not for a moment considered or acknowledged.' - *The Law Marches West,* by Cecil Denny, a veteran of 'The Long March' undertaken by the Mounties in 1874.

Denny left the Mounties to become an Indian agent on the Blackfoot reserve east of Calgary, to resign in protest when his political bosses ordered him to cut daily rations as part of a government attempt to reduce spending.

In *Blood Red Sun,* William Cameron, a Hudson's Bay fur trader, recorded an interview with captured warrior Wandering Spirit, shackled and imprisoned in a jail cell in Battleford, Saskatchewan, on November 26th, 1885, the day before he went to the gallows with seven members of his band for their part in the Frog Lake Massacre: *'Four years ago, we were camped on the Missouri River in the Long Knives land. Big Bear was there, Im-*

asees, Four Sky Thunder and other chiefs of the band. Riel was there, trading whisky to the Indians. He gave us liquor and said he would make war on this country. He asked us to join him in wiping out the Canadians. The government had treated him badly. He would demand much money from them. If they would not give, he would spill blood, plenty of Canadian blood. Last fall, Riel sent word to us that when the leaves came out the half-breeds would rise and kill all the whites.'

Heavy reading, horrible times, no urge to sleep after reading, so I lose myself in the dangers of crossing the Skeena Pass with Sir Sanford Fleming. Some favourite quotes from 'Poor Richard's Almanac.

'Dost though love life? Then do not squander time, for that is the stuff life is made of. The sleeping fox catches no poultry...there will be sleeping enough in the grave.

That's it then, I'm up for the rest of the night. Watrous, Saskatchewan, is like the grave at 4am. A cold, bleak burial ground of prairie dogs, coyotes, farting and snoring passengers, and chickens. Little Manitou Lake is around here somewhere: A salt water lake used by the Cree as a healing source long before the arrival of the Vikings. Manitou means god or spirit to Cree and Ojibway by the way. At 6:16am the sky is a sliver of red horizon on a black-blue background. I'm amazed by how many people snore. Some general observations regards the train-locked: The first thing female travellers do upon waking is to fix their hair with a fluffing-teasing motion with clawed fingers while checking to see if their partner is still breathing. Men rub eyes with clenched fist or open palm and cough before standing up to tuck shirt or sweater back into trousers, blow their nose and check to see if their partner has buggered off during the night, or gone to fetch coffee, while attempting to flatten bed-head hair with spit.

I've not met anyone who's done the Alaska thing yet, just

a few Prince Rupert's or on the way home from Churchill and the Polar Bear thing. It's desolate up there in Hudson's Bay according to a nice fellow I spoke to while purchasing a sandwich last night. No roads for two hundred miles, he told me, just railway tracks and open space. Travelers usually catch the train home from Winnipeg to points east or west from Churchill, but he was using up his Rail-Pass to Vancouver and back to wherever he told me came from. Morning sun brightens 'The Plains' slowly but not enough to read location signs. Where are we? I miss my Irish Rose! Greybeard with hockey-head hasn't stopped coughing all night. It must be easier and faster to die by smoking than to get comfortable enough to sleep on a VIA train. You can turn off the overhead light and use a sleeping bag or rolled-up coat for a pillow. You can pull footrests all the way up to make a level platform, hide valuables in a seat pouch or shucked footwear or under the seat in front and conceal further with your backpack. You can wrap a VIA blanket tight around your lower body or snuggle in a sleeping-bag and place your pillow or bag against a window or arm-rest. You can lay sideways and pull up your feet, bend your knees, say your prayers or sit up all night. It helps to crack a bottle of rum before any of the above but if none of that works you can join hockey-head and his mates in the smoking car for the slow death or banter.

The Badlands slip by like a Springsteen anthem as pale bodies rise like zombies to make their way slowly to the washroom. Tall church steeples, buzzing power lines and rotund grain silos signal the arrival of Melville (pop.5,000) and frozen prairie ponds for as far as my eyes can see. It looks mighty cold out there, as man who worked on railroad and knows everything and wants to tell all within earshot about it for two days, escapes the heat of the Canadian by disembarking accompanied by his lovely, still paying attention spouse. He's stood there fastening his overcoat and sucking in cold air and yacking with obvious delight, with train station as background, as she listens intently beside him. He spots me watching him and smiles, gives me the nod. I smile and wave and he waves back. These are the nice couple who kept an eye on my backpack in Edmonton when I ran off to call home. His jaws still flap and his batteries refuse to run out as hot air billows from his mouth as he walks toward a car followed by a wife lapping up every word. He starts the engine and is lost to sight by exhaust clouds added to his billowing. It does look cold out there!

'I fearlessly announced that the so-called arid country was one of unsurpassed fertility and that it was literally the 'garden' of the whole country.' - Captain John Palliser of the British North American Exploring Expedition of 1857-60

'In the central portion of the continent there is a region, desert, or semi- desert in character which can never be expected to become occupied by settlers...although there are fertile spots throughout its extent, it can never be of much advantage to us as a possession...'-John Macoun of the Sanford Fleming Expedition of 1872-75

The explorer and the botanist! While at Melville waiting for an elderly couple to board, I was entranced by a large flock of Saskatchewan Sparrows as they dipped and darted around and between the legs of a tall skinny chap wearing bright blue running shoes as he shoveled snow and meticulously carved perfect square corners and straight edges along the platform, seemingly oblivious to a train load of passengers admiring his skill. The birds eventually left him alone to command a bush growing up the station wall, where they settled quietly to watch me curiously. I sat still and watched them watching me. Draw birdies! Was a good old-fashioned prairie standoff until the engine kicked into life and left them behind tweeting away in the bitter cold.

Second call for breakfast, second call for breakfast, squawks from the intercom at 7:30am. I didn't hear the first call as I was engrossed in prairie life while reading a map which alerted me to the fact that we passed through Eldon sometime during the night. My sister-in-law, Smellaine, has a ginger-red cat named

Eldon. My son sold it to her for two dollars. It should stay clear of chiropractors and five-gallon pails of blue paint or varsol he has a habit of falling in. I love cats!

We're not due in Winnipeg until around 12:15pm, so I decide I best eat breakfast. This decision is thwarted by a self-important sombre bastard in a blue uniform who tells me that it's 9:30am and I have missed breakfast...and besides, the breakfast car has been moved back four cars since the last time I used it, blah blah blah...I don't hear the rest as I tune her out and stride back to steerage chasing away comic-style images of Eldon and his adventures in my basement.

'Sod it!' I say to no-one in particular, grab a coffee, and take it with Saturdays Globe Arts section up to the Dome for a slurp and a read, which is a bit of a treat as it's been two weeks since me last Globe, father! A large herd of deer run free on a sun-drenched frozen prairie. Run deer, run deer, run, run, run, here comes the farmer with his gun, gun, gun. It was rabbits afraid of the gun during afternoon story-time sessions with my mum and the wireless as we sang songs of sixpence and birds baked in pies back in black and white television times.

A Poem from the Dome after spotting a little house on the prairie: *'Oh lone house upon the hill, is it quiet up there, is it still? Must be peaceful, no fear, no ill...does solitude include a wave from that distant windowsill?'*

Rolling across spectacularly high bridges to the Assiniboine river to cross Saskatchewan and its Manitoba borders and skirt hundreds of frozen lakes in the Qu'Appelle Valley, through Rivers and its tall grain elevators, exiting via an extremely long bridge over the Minnedosa River or 'swift water' to the Cree, all the while playing peek-a-boo over the back of his seat with my pal Danny and Woody from Toy Story, I can't make my mind up which was more fun. During a lull in play, while Woody is substituted for Ernie from Sesame Street, Danny's mum tell's me that Winnipeg was only an hour away, she's wrong, but I'm not arguing as I'm having too much fun battering Ernie with my notebook. Danny laughs and tells me proudly that his dad buys him toys at Value Village, and asks would I like to take him to the Dome, to the amusement of the crowds that surround. 'You get real good toys there you know!'

'In the Dome?'

'Noooo, silly...Value Village!'

'I know someone who shops there all the time.'

'Who? Your mom?'

'No, Isabel.'

'Who is Isabel?'

'Is a bell necessary on a bike?'

He doesn't get it but his mom and the traveller in the seat behind me do and they laugh.

'C'monnnn, Paul, let's go for a walkkkk!'

'I'm writing, big man.'

'Awww, pleasssse! he pleads, jumping about on his seat.

'Come on then. Let's see if we can find Value Village...' I suggest, laugh, stand, stretch and decide to take my water bottle in case we get lost.

'There's no Value Village on this train, silly!' he shouts, jumps over his mom and lands in the aisle next me. 'Come on then Superflea,' I tell him, and the crowd laughs, but halfway down the aisle he tells me he doesn't want to go to Value Village.

'Well, let's go to the Dome, then.'

'You mean the Skydome?' he shouts. 'Mom, I'm going to the Skydome!'

All excited, he skips down the aisle as smiling faces beam at us from all sides like we're at a church wedding. We make it to the Dome without incident but as he's climbing the stairs he realises it's not the baseball Dome and he wants to go home back to his seat. So, we stroll back through the realms of the Canadian and I deliver him safely to his mom. She's over the moon regards the short breather and thanks me profusely. She's happy to see him, vice-versa, he's back with his toys, all quiet, I can read my book. Only a day and a half to go until Toronto....

Golf: Hunkered in along the banks of a polluted stream nicknamed The Ratty we await the chance in silence to a soundtrack of trickling water, fighting crows, and the occasional far away car engine. We listen for the sound of male adult laughter thought private. Bodies tensed we crawl deeper into the undergrowth, make like a tree, no breathing, just like in the war comics. To be caught is to be tortured, or worse, they might take us home to our mothers.

Snake belts glint in the sun and we become one with the earth as laughter increases in volume. Someone giggles and The Ratty takes it away to the ends of wherever it goes, the Pier Head, someone said. I think it goes on forever like the summer we spend navigating, hurdling, and falling or being pushed in that smelly rainbow colored Nile.

Clunk! one hits the ground beyond the fence. *Clunk*! another. Crows fighting, birds trilling, water trickling. *Clunk*! three of them! With luck there might be four as sometimes there are stragglers.

Men shouting and laughing. It's a go. We jump into action there's not much time. The laughter is carried closer by the wind. I rub my lucky stone and follow John who is leading us into battle today in honor of his brother who fell out of a tree and broke his arm, the first casualty of the summer.

I'm third through a hole cut in the wire fence, and have time to look around as I crawl to the lip of a sand bunker where water sprays from a sprinkler making trees behind it shimmer in the heat. We are Commando's. John removes the flag, reaches in with one hand and unzips his jeans with the other. The jeans are cheap 'Bobby-washables' from the market. We all wear them. They shrink after one wash. Mine have no back pockets because they're stitched to my knees. Not literally but my mum says she'll do it one day if I don't look after my clothes.

Nothing in the hole but earwigs, John whispers, and does the business as we scurry about on our bellies looking for trophies of war. The bunkers hide us well. The flag is replaced and we retreat back through the hole hidden by doc leaves, brambles and stinging nettles, back to the safety of our lines; mission accomplished, no casualties yet.

I lay on my back in long grass juicy at the roots that stains my windcheater. Peering up at blue sky, white clouds, black birds, a lone seagull, a flock of starlings performing bird ballet in unison. The Crows have stopped fighting for now and have retired to an old tree that touches buzzing power lines with branches. We'll find the nest later. Crows are hard to get. Robin, blackbird, song thrush, sparrow, starling and magpie eggs are easy. One of each nestle safely in cotton wool in a chocolate box hidden under my bed. We only take one egg from a nest so the species won't die. Skylarks put on a show of aerodynamic antics and a pheasant hurries from its nest in the long grass. Brambles on the banks of 'The Ratty' rustle and sway urgently; there's no wind,likely a fox, probably a cat.

The dimpled white ball in my hand is almost new. One scuff-mark above a red *SPALDING* and a grass stain below a black number ***3***. Billy gives me the thumbs-up from behind the trunk of an old oak tree and holds up his trophy with a smile. I pull a funny face and wave my ball in the air. He laughs and I lay back down in the grass. A frog calls, another answers. I collect frogs as well. I keep them in an old bath tub in the cellar. Toads give you warts, frogs don't.The sun burns my face, it feels good. To open your eyes to the sun will end in blindness.

We all know this. The Navajo did it to the 7th Cavalry when they caught them. Ant hill, honey, four pegs, rawhide strips, a sharp knife and off with the eyelids. What a way to die. I stave off blindness by half-closing both lids until the kaleidoscope show starts. Wavy lines and black dots dancing, I could do this all day. The ball in my hand is comforting like a lucky stone. The blade of grass in my mouth is bitter but gets rid of the thirst. Never chew grass with frog spit on it.

Someone laughs.

SHHH! No need, John, they can't see us we are invisible. I roll over into a hollow and listen hard. Someone meows like a cat, probably Billy, another giggles. John '*SHUSH*'s' us again and we are silent.

Ahhh - will you look at this!
Bloody hell!
Who would do that?
Little bastards!
JUST YOU WAIT! DON'T LET US CATCH YOU!
It's all over my trousers!
What?
One of them shit in the hole!
ANIMALS!

A whistle, I whistle back, another from behind the oak tree. John gets to his knees and points and we retreat as one across a field keeping low, no cover, it's a danger spot, they can catch you here! We make it back to the safety of a half-demolished farm house with a stained mattress, newspapers, broken bottles and the smell of tramps in the cellar. Home is across the road. They never cross the road. We're safe, they didn't chase us. They must be scared of us.

Sat along the top of a wall in 'The Garages' laughing and taking turns acting as posh golfers reaching into holes and wiping hands on pant legs and spearing poo with a flagpole and chasing us with it. Next time we'll stamp the balls into the green with the heels of our baseball boots, but now its time for a scalping.

To scalp a golf ball the knife has to be sharp and you need lots of patience. You quarter it like they did to Guy Fawkes and peel the outer layer away like an orange to reveal black elastic wound around another ball, the core, that looks like the planet Venus. Then you find the end of the elastic and unravel it in one go because if you don't and it breaks you get knuckles from the gang.

Powder on the elastic makes your hands soft and smooth and we save the elastic for catapults or flicking at girls. You can play football with the rubber ball or bounce it off walls and bus stops like a Super Ball and stray dogs like to play with them as well when they're stealing ice-creams and biscuits from the hands of kids.

You can make a tiny hole in the rubber ball with the tip of your knife but make sure not to get the white fluid on your hands because it burns like acid. Sometimes we squirt it at each other. Billy's brother told him you can get pregnant from what's in the balls. It will last forever if you write your name with it.

I wrote *PAUL MASSAM* '68 on a lamp post and went home to play with the frogs.

I spot a magpie sat on a fence-post just outside of Brandon North. Half buried in frozen mud in front of it juts a vinyl long-playing record that looks to have been flung from an open train window. It glints in the sun which attracts the bird. I wonder who the record is by and can't think of an appropriate band name that may be funny. Stone the Crows? Black Crows? The mood is lost when I spot a tough-looking dude in army fatigues stood in a field holding a long rifle. He's focusing a telescopic sight at something in the distance, face half-hidden by a hood. I hope he's not aiming at the magpie and give him the finger. Someone should drop him off on a mountain in Alaska, the wildlife would love him. I'm overcome with the urge to sing 'Train, traaainnn...' Elvis style, as coyotes chase each other, their tails, and launch themselves skyward to land and roll in prairie grass all the time aiming silent barks at us as we chug past.

Three million eager pigeons peck, peck, pecked at grain piled next to a pregnant silo as we passed through *Portage La Prairie (pop. 21,000)* a major meeting place of the Voyageurs as they rowed canoes between Lake Manitoba and the Assiniboine River back in 1738, I'm told by a passenger named La Verendrye sat behind me, his English is pretty good. I set out on a voyage of my own in search of the elusive exclusive dining car which is empty of all human life when I find it. Absolutely no one about in First Class either, so I chance a look, a walkabout la dangerouse into a strong smell of vomit.

It's deathly quiet in here and I'm thinking Miss Marple films as I tip-toe about expecting to trip over a body with a knife protruding from its back, but nothing murderous of note except for the drip, drip, drip of water from the showerhead in an empty shower stall. No Vivien Leigh or Anthony Perkins in there, unfortunately, so I carry on my investigation through empty berths bereft of anything sinister except for a single white running shoe hanging by its laces from the handle of a window blind to keep it closed. Where have they all gone? I'm game to investigate more but the smell drives me back towards the relative safety of steerage. I'm wandering the aisles pondering the fate of the moneyed classes when a jolly chap armed with a camera, a smile and three days growth on his face catches my eye and hits me with the old, 'Excuse me but are you from....' thing, but I'm not in the mood to play or divulge, so I tell him, all wide-eyed and breathless, that, 'they've all gone in first class, not a soul about, go take a look for yourself while I go off in search of help!...and sneak back to my seat to batter Ernie and Bert for the last time before Danny and his mom depart the show at Winnipeg.

Winnipeg: Danny's mom thanks me for making the trip easier. He thanks me too. I return the compliments, load my pack and pretend to steal Ernie, say my goodbyes and head for the exit door.

The St. Paul's of Manitoba, designed by those who created New York's Grand Central awaits me. Stone walls faced with local Tyndall limestone loaded with prehistoric fossils, seaweed, crab-shells and ammonites from ancient sea-beds that once covered the prairies. Built in 1911 at the forks of the Assinboine, the Seine, and the Red River situated dead centre of the train universe; ladies and gentlemen, I give you Winnipeg's Union Station!

Again, I don't take much time to take it all in as I need to grab a burger and fries at Veejays before I die of the consumption. I bump into the Edmonton truckers outside sharing a smoke while admiring each others cowboy boots as traffic roars by sending slush flying to the kerb. 'Fancy meeting you guys here!' They just chuckle and look me up and down, at each other, back again, each other, laugh throatily as usual and resume their architectural viewing.

It's minus 7c according to a clock on a building, Caw, said the crow. I rest my pack on a bus stop bench to dig out the camera and spot Danny walking down the street with his mom and a miserable man, and he sure is happy to see me. Danny waves and points me out, the man scowls and ignores me. Must be his dad. I think about asking him if he knows the way to Value Village but don't want to cause a scene. Danny tries to get him to look my way but he won't as they disappear around a corner, Danny and his mum waving. Wonder what was wrong with him? Miserable shite. I take a shot of a big multi-colored banner advertising the 2000 Pan-Am Games of 2000 hung on the side of a building, load my pack, and head back across the road to St Paul's of Minnesota to eat my food in peace.

A gang of native kids are hanging around the station dressed like Crips and Bloods. I've been warned about gang violence in Winnipeg so its invisible cloak time as they mess about and act hard. They remind me of us lot back in the 70's only we were skinny and had better style and didn't smoke weed or worse. I want to walk have a chat with them about Tomson Highway and William Least Heat Moon and the film, Dance Me Outside, but they'd probably just laugh and shoot me. I'm not comparing growing up where I did and what they've had to deal with but I used to be in awe and fear of gangs as well and had to join one to save my neck from other gangs.

Merseyside, England. It was freezing cold but we didn't care as we clung to metal grills with frozen fingers. The grills were vandal deterrents fastened tight to wooden frames to protect glass that brought light to the local Community Centre sat in the middle of a housing estate built in the 1940's.

To beat the cold we concentrated on pulling funny faces at dancing girls inside as plumes of breath escaped from mouths and multi-colored lights blinked through marbled glass to light us up like time travellers on Star Trek or Doctor Who.

'Eh! Piss off. You're not old enough to get in!' yelled the Les Dawson look-alike in the slack-arsed flares who guarded the front door from real and imaginary foes. So we did, round to the back door which we knew would be open to let air in or the heat out.

Snuck across a courtyard of broken glass, cigarette butts and old newspapers, to be punched in the face by ska guitar and throbbing bass from speakers on a small stage beside a spray-painted door we hid behind to watch regimented dancers leap about as if on puppeteers strings in a jam-packed dance hall.

Too bad we weren't old enough to get in as you had to be sweet sixteen. Three more years, I told a mate as we shivered in jeans, Ben Sherman shirts, Harrington jackets and Doctor Marten boots.

Saturday night on a council estate. A 'No Go' area with nowhere to go and we were definitely going nowhere but here tonight. Dave & Ansell Collins had the mob in the palm of their hands with 'Double Barrel.' *Uh, Uh, Uh's!* echoing as lads dropped to the floor on cue to bounce back up again in Air Wear boots some sprayed gold or silver or hand-painted in Union Jack colours. Skinhead or bootboy trademarks along with the close-cropped hair; a working-class appearance promising violence and mayhem.

Painted girls preened and posed like cigarette-smoking peacocks as they tottered about in platform boots and shoes.

'Wan' alllllllll you skinheads to get-up off your seats, put your braces together and your boots on your feet. Get ready...' Symarip had them dancing with their smooth Jamaican reggae as I hid mesmerized by it all, the stomping boots, long legs and mini-skirts, a ritual as old as football playing itself out before us.

The DJ with the Elvis sideburns switched gears and couples got close and in unison to the sweet soul of Al Green as he urged everyone to stay together, which they did for a short while, but it didn't last long as a fight kicked off between suedeheads and the Clockwork Orange brigade. Pandemonium ensued, girls screamed, glass was smashed, the lights went on, the music died, its throat cut by a panicked DJ - and the fight poured into the street.

I threw an empty milk bottle from across that street and we watched it arc through the air and shatter against the screen we'd clung to earlier and took off running, laughing with the gang as police sirens got closer, homeward bound through freezing fog, heart pounding, dogs barking....and that's all I'm saying, but when I got my first motor bike....nah! Gangs, bangs, shangalangs.

I find a seat in a quiet corner of the lobby to savour my burger, fries and banana milkshake while flipping through a well-thumbed copy of the Winnipeg Sun left behind on the table. The Leafs are winning, Everton are losing; same old, same old. 'Hey Englishman, did you know that Winnipeg was known to the Cree as Winni-nipi and the rest called it '*The Chicago of the North*' and that its laid out in a diagonal street plan like spokes on a wheel with connecting rivers as hub? '*If there ever was a fool's paradise,*' wrote George Hamm, '*it sure was located in Winnipeg.*'

'*The new Eldorado,*' the Winnipeg Times dubbed Winnipeg in1881." I tell the man cleaning tables that I do and the burgers are good too.

The night train to Toronto is packed to the rafters, bursting at the seams as eager faces new and old pile aboard. I find myself in another conversation about Churchill and its Polar Bears in the crush with a guy from Collingwood, Ontario, which convinces me that I must contact Boston Eric about a trip north when I arrive home. No doubts he'd like to give it a shot.

*I do, and he did, and he was making plans with Rail News with me to accompany him as photographer but personal matters on his side of the border scuppered it.

It's a mad rush of bodies searching for seats when a confused steward sends passengers the wrong way towards reserved seats, which causes a traffic jam, and panic ensues when some passengers realise they are in the wrong car and turn back to find their way blocked by reserved-seat ticket-holders trying to get to their seats, and I'm stuck right in the middle of the crush as babies cry and legs are battered by luggage.

'Like sardines in a tin can.' I tell a bright pink face jammed against my chest and it agrees. 'Excuse me...coming through!'

'Sorry.'

'Excuse me!'

'No problem.'

'Excuse me...argh!' I'm glad to be wearing these boots with all the toe stomping.

'Christ, who's got hold of my pack!'

Mimi from the Drew Carey Show has me jammed against a locked washroom door. Her chest, poured into a bra two sizes too small, slowly squeezing the life from my body as bony knees and sour breath inflic torture. I'm overcome by sweat mixed with Odor deToilette or whatever she splashed all over herself last week and come very close to using chasm of cleavage as receptacle for not quite digested burger and milkshake.

'Is this first class, dear?' she inquires throatily, rouged lips centimetres from my nose.

'Not bad but last night was better!' I wheeze back, which causes her to laugh like a vibrating bed in overdrive that starts at my groin and work its way upwards, as her pickle and nicotine breath begins to remove the first layer of skin from my face like a puckering sand-blaster. But luckily for me she slides sideways an inch or two and I manage to pop free like a bar of soap into the arms of a shocked steward, who gives me a 'Zorry, zir!' and heads into the carnage to save lives.

Glad to be alive, back in my seat, I find books and magazines intact where I left them before disembarking at Winnipeg, and this time I took my backpack! The seat in front has been taken over by an Italian Princess and two slinky slaves, or girlfriends, who are attempting to stow king-sized luggage into queen-sized compartments above their heads, which makes for great entertainment after what I've just been through.

These attempts at stuffing things attracts the attention of the spiky-haired steward who almost got me crushed by Mimi. Smiling and giggling with much flickering of eyes did the trick and in the time it takes for him to turn to silly putty they have him dead in the water, and order him to turn their seats around to face each other when he's finished stowing their luggage so a cozy wine-swilling party of three can commence and now. 'No problem ladies!' He gushes, stopping short of bowing, but after several attempts, realises he hasn't the strength or know-how to perform the task and takes off down the aisle, red-faced and sweating, in search of help.

I'm not getting involved, for a change, and settle in for the party when he shows up with another young steward, who eyeballs the situation and informs the ladies that it will be an easy chore to perform, no problem, so I put my feet up, pop a bag of chips and open a bottle of water in anticipation. Half-an-hour later both stewards have removed coats and rolled up shirt sleeves and argue animatedly in French as heave and sweat their way into the pages of my journal.

I reckon this is what they were after, all that heaving and sweating, me too, but the fun is cut short as the stewards retrieve coats and dignity and take off in a huff blaming 'VIA maintenance for not maintaining!' Hillbilly Fiddle Player and his wife are slapping their knees and guffawing at this. They look like they haven't had this much fun since they raided their neighbour's moonshine still. Most passengers are in some stage of contained hilarity as Simone and Poombah return with a conductor elder all ready for action, who after a few knowledgeable manoeuvres rearranges the seats to satisfaction before retiring down the aisle and into a rear car to a scattering of applause, as the Canadian crosses the Red River Floodway at Transcona using a viaduct 275 metres in length leaving Winnipeg far behind.

We speed through Elma (pop. 81) and slow down enough to just meander through Whiteshell Provincial Park and its two hundred lakes of wild undeveloped glory, situated at the edge of the Pre-Cambrian Shield, the vertebrae of the continent. The couple to my right, The Pringles (named after the snack they prefer) are Australian. I ask if they know Aussie Girl and offer them a read of my newspaper but they don't want to converse or interact, so I return to 'The Great Railway' as flatlands morph into bushlands leaving me to go in search of a phone booth and a change of clothes.

Hillbilly fiddle player has no teeth, you should see him eat a ham sandwic, his face collapses with every chew. I would have loved to have seen him and Miss Biggar have a go at a foot long hotdog from different ends. What a double act, especially when they met in the middle, but that's too much for me to think about in my present state, as the Canadian pounds away at an endless Canadian Shield with wheels of steel.

'The land that the railway builders set out to conquer was beautiful in its very bleakness. At the western end of Lake Superior it was almost all rock - the old, cracked rock of the Canadian Shield, grey and russet, striped by strata, blurred by pink lichens, garlanded by the dark vines and red berries of kinnikinnick and sparkling, some-

times, with the yellow pinpoints of cinquefoil. From the edges of the dun-coloured lakes that lay in the grey hollows there protruded the spiky points of the spruce, jet black against the green clouds of birch and poplar. Sometimes there where tiger lilies, blue vetch, briar rose, and oxeye daisies to relieve the sombre panorama; but in the winter the land was an almost unendurable monochrome of grey.

As the line moved west, the land changed and began to sparkle. Between the spiny ridges lay sinuous lakes and lesser ponds of bright blue or olive green from which the yellow flowers of the spatterdock glittered. The lakes became more numerous towards the west, the bright sheets of water winding in chains between the broken, tree - covered vertebrae of granite, with here and there a chartreuse meadow of tall, rank grass. This lake country, smiling in the sunshine, gloomy in the frequent slashing rains, would one day become a tourist mecca; but in the seventies it was a hellhole for the contractors who saw their fortunes sink forever in the seemingly bottomless slime of the great muskegs.

The muskegs came in every size. There were the notorious sinkholes over which a thick crust of vegetable matter had formed. In such a morass near Savanne, north of Fort William, so legend has it, an entire train with a thousand feet of track was swallowed whole.

Worse than the sinkholes were the giant muskegs, like the Poland Swamp or the Julius Muskeg, the most infamous bog of all - a vast bed of peat six miles across, its depths unknown. From these deceptively level, moss - covered stretches the naked trunks of dead tamaracks protruded, their roots weaving a kind of blanket over a concealed jelly of mud and slime. The road was carried over them on log mattresses floated on top of the heaving bog - unwieldy contraptions of long, interlaced timbers, which would sometimes run for eight hundred feet. Later on the muskegs were filled in.'

Brilliant from Berton. More? Okay then:

'Then there where the apparently placid lakes that seemed so shallow, whose bottoms consisted of unfathomable muskeg which swallowed up tons of earth and gravel fill, month after month. The

real lake bottoms were concealed by a false blanket of silt which had never been properly probed during the hasty surveys. Lake Macquistinah, for instance, devoured 250,000 yards of earth fill; and on Section Fifteen the hapless Joseph Whitehead saw his dreamed-of profits slowly pouring into the notorious Cross Lake in the form of 220,000 yards of gravel at a cost of eighty thousand dollars. And still the line continued to sink.

Cross Lake was to prove Whiteheads undoing. The contractor began work on it in 1879 and was still pouring fill into it when the government relieved him of his contract in March, 1880. Ton after ton of sand and gravel vanished into that monstrous gulf without appreciable results. Sometimes the embankment would be built up five or six feet above the water; then suddenly the lake would take a gulp and the entire mass of stone, gravel, and earth would vanish beneath the waves.'

A train swallowed whole! I'm wondering if there are life-jackets aboard this train as I'm not a strong swimmer and we are in the vicinity of all that vanishing. Rain-spattered windows allow me a view of rock formations that surround the town of Hoctor. Serious blasting must have happened here by looks of boulders scattered about like fossilised mounds of orange-brown elk shit or giant marbles scattered amidst tough scrag, muskeg, dank lakes and tall spruce. I cannot imagine surveying or dropping a rail line out there, man, no way!

The rail station is closed in the village of Minaki (pop. 350) situated just north of Gun Lake. Sealed up tighter than a duck's arse in cold water at this time of year. Teeshirts in the window might be for sale though. Minaki boasts a world-famous ski lodge accessible only by plane, so we'll give it a miss this time. Its 4:40pm, according to a suddenly conversational Mel Pringle, who tells me that we're not far from Lake of the Woods. The man is an oracle of information. He's been immersed in a battered Star Wars paperback since he boarded, stopping at every town to take a breath and a peek over to check if we're all still here. After some prodding and cajoling he divulges that he's been living in Guelph, Ontario for the past two and a half years working as a landscaper and retires back to his book. His wife remains silent. That's it, I realise that I'm losing my touch. I sip on a beer and search high and low for that red pen in my bag but can't find it. My pen has gone the way of my social skills. Let me out of here!

The sound of a baby suckling at the breast of its mother asleep in the seat behind sounds like a high pitched can't believe it's luck and its not gonna stop till it's had enough tune, which soothes and transports me back to a rented house in High Park, Toronto, in the early-nineties; sat there in the dark on a striped couch feeding offspring bottles of Enfalac while watching late-night television when late-night television was a non-stop sales pitch for work-outs hosted by muscled men and anorexic women dressed in day-glo gym gear and matching big blonde hair. *Last call for dinner,* crackles from the intercom. 'Last call for dinner? Its only six o clock!' Pringle exclaims, in my direction.

'It may be but my watch says five. Don't worry, the rest of the country is catching up!' I tell him, which appears to soothe him too, and that's two of us sorted.

Just wanna get off this train and get on home to you. I got da blues baby, dem ol Travellin Man blues. Bring it on home momma! - Paulie One-String

SIOUX LOOKOUT: An eiderdown of crispy twinkling snow covers Sioux Lookout and appears to soothe ancient troubles, as shadowy figures in the distance pool in the moon-light. I'm stood track-side watching my breath freeze and soar up and away above the roof of the Canadian towards bright stars on a night made for demons. I feel like I'm an extra in Dr. Zhivago. 'This ain't Russia, this is Siouxiside!' Hits my bonce in Bowie fashion before chasing after breath dragons.

Top of a hill sits Sioux Lookout and its population of

three thousand mostly native souls. Before me sits the largest community till Sudbury, located on the English River in Sunset Country. A recreational centre for summer fishing and canoeing it may be but tonight it's deserted and spooky, outlined by a dark and dangerous looking forest of silent tree's.

I'm under orders, the keepers of the train tell me I have only twenty minutes as I take a stroll up a hill towards Sioux Pizza, Sioux Bar, Sioux Movies and Sioux Variety, where several figures huddle around something in a darkened doorway safe from a bright moon. I cross the road until a bedraggled women pops up from the huddle and points me out to a gathering of shadows that spread out and shuffle towards me sniffing and snorting the night air, breath pouring from babblingmouths. At this point I'm thinking *Night Of The Living Dead* and that *Thriller* video, and remembering the finale of both I cease my exploring. My intention was to hit the bar for a quick beer but my radar is up, so I turn and head back down the icy slope towards the train, belly tingling.

'Hey buddy. Hey, come back!'

I want to but my feet won't let me

'Hey buddy…Come here...you got any change?'

'Sorry lads, I don't.' In the shadowy half-light besides the engine I scoop a handful of snow and sculpt a hard snowball. A guard tells me to board the train as we're leaving. No way have we been here twenty minutes,' I tell him, and he nods his head yes.

I mumble an 'alright mate, you're in charge,' and climb the steps, snowball hidden in my hand.

I smuggle it past more guards, stealthily like an assassin and stop and raise my hand silently above my sleeping victim - and dump the snowball down the back of Mel Pringles sweater.

'*WHOAH! BLOODY 'ELL MATE!*' he yells, and jumps about three feet in the air. He whips out his shirt-tail and hops about in the aisle like an Australian Michael Flaherty. The remains of the snowball land on his seat and melt in the tropical heat of the

Canadian. Laughs all around from those still awake but his wife doesn't miss a snore. I escape down the aisle to the washroom where I lock the door and sit quietly. Mad at myself for not having the guts to enter that bar.

When we assert that they are steeped in ignorance, debased in mind, and crushed in spirit, that by the exercise of an illegal claim over the country of their forefathers, they are deprived of the natural rights and privileges of free born men, that they are virtually slaves, as absolutely as the unredeemed negro population of the slave states of America - that by a barbarous and selfish policy, founded on a love of lucre, their affections are alienated from the British name and government, and they themselves shut out from civilisation, and debarred from every incentive thereto - that the same heinous system is gradually effacing whole tribes from the soil on which they were born an nurtured, so that a few years hence not one man among them will be left to point out where the bones of his ancestors repose - when we assert all this in honest, simple truth, does it not behoove every Christian man to demand that the British legislature should not continue to incur the fearful responsibility of permitting the extinction of these helpless, forlorn thousands of their fellow creatures, by lending its countenance to a monopoly engendering so huge a mountain of human misery? For the honour of this great country, we pray it will not be; and, sincerely trust some few voices will respond earnestly, Amen. - Alexander Kennedy Isbister: Caesars of the Wilderness

The son of a Hudson's Bay Company clerk and Cree mother, Isbister served in the northern-most outpost of Fort McPherson. Angered by the Company's reluctance to promote 'Mixed Bloods' like himself, he resigned and enrolled in the University of Aberdeen and went on to write numerous speeches, articles, and books on the subject of the treatment of his people. He died in London in 1883 and a trust fund was set up at the University of Manitoba in his name. Bloody fine writer!

The native peoples had succumbed in dramatic numbers to the 1837 smallpox epidemic, he wrote. That summer the dreaded in-

fection spread up the Missouri from St. Louis carried by crewmen of an American Fur Company supply ship who spread the virus at every stop. The Indians who went south to trade brought the disease back into Rupert's land, and the virulent plague wiped out about three-quarters of the Plains people in one wave. A frightened traveller noticed there was no smoke rising from the Indian lodges.

'Not a sound can be heard to break the awful stillness, save the ominous croak of the ravens, and mournful howl of wolves fattening on the human carcasses that lie strewed around. It seems as if the very genius of desolation had stalked through the prairies, and wreaked his vengeance on everything bearing the shape of humanity.'

And here's me worried about getting mugged in Sioux Lookout. I return to my seat and apologize to Pringle, offer to buy him a beer, which he accepts. Hillbilly laughs and claps like a hungry seal when he spots me and I think the truckers see me in a different light; the guards didn't notice.

'I never heard you coming, mate, you must be in the forces!' Pringle tells me. He's wearing quite the smile when I present him with his beer. 'May the force be with you more likes,' I tell him, and drain half my beer. We spend time in hushed conversation of Sioux Lookout and immigrants and the immigrant according to two immigrants and marvel at stewards Simone and Poombah as they sashay down the aisle handing out pillows and blankets to passengers asleep and awake.

'Anyboddeee for a mashmellow?'

''ere comes santa claws wid ze blankettes!'

'Wood you like one madam?' Simone asks a long-haired guy fast asleep in his seat. He winks at me and drops pillow and blanket in my lap before mincing down the aisle, laughing at Poombah following behind loaded down with pillows and blankets wrapped in clear plastic – two packets of which he drops and boots after Simone, leaving Pringle and I in stitches. Funny guys. Much-needed laughs.

It's my final night on the Canadian and my last supper consists of a cold turkey sandwich and a Molson Canadian purchased at the snack bar where the Beer Nazi no longer plots Adolph's revival, having escaped us at Winnipeg. I think he's gone back to Brazil. Last I saw of him he was sat next to Gregory Peck in the back of a black limousine outside of Winnipeg station.

Longlac, Ontario (pop. 2,400) sits on the northern-most tip of Long Lake (ah, Longlac!) Longlac is quite the sight at 3:37am, all frozen and white like an ice-cream wedding cake. A fur trading route left behind a town split fifty-fifty between French and English speaking inhabitants of Longlac, and all lakes and rivers connect here on their way to Lake Superior. I love Longlac, it rolls ever so gently from the tongue!

Respite from Berton:

In the dismal land west of Lake Superior, nature seemed to have gone to extremes to thwart the railway builders. When they were not laying track across the porridge of the muskegs they were blasting it through some of the hardest rock in the world. Rock that rolled endlessly on, ridge after spiky ridge, like waves in a sullen ocean. Dynamite, patented in the year of Confederation, was as new as the steam shovel; the major explosive was dynamites parent, nitroglycerin. This awesomely unstable liquid had been developed almost thirty years before the first sod was turned on the CPR but was only now beginning to replace the weaker blasting powder, being ten times more expensive not to mention more dangerous. It had never before been used as extensively as it was west of the lakehead in the late seventies.'

Good stuff on a frigid night like this, eh. Too hot to sleep in though because Bert and Ernie complained about the cold and a staff member relented and turned the heat up full blast. They snore, I bake. The lights are out in the Dome so I'm back in my seat reading and watching Northern Ontario flash by. The mother behind feeds her baby again. I smile, she growls. Ah well, I was only going to ask if she had any baby powder for my feet. I'm the smelly white man come for your children, *Wahhhhh!*

'The technique was to pour the explosive into drill holes, each about seven feet deep, and set it off by a fuse. In less than two years some three hundred thousand dollars was spent on nitroglycerin on section fifteen, often with disastrous results. There was among the workmen an almost cavalier attitude to the explosive. Cans of Nitro with fuses attached were strewn carelessly along the roadbed in contravention of all safety regulations, or carried about with such recklessness that the fluid splashed upon the rocks. Whole gangs were sometimes blown to bits in the resultant explosions, especially in the cold weather, because the chemical was notoriously dangerous when frozen; the slightest jar could touch it off. Under such conditions it was kept under hot water and at as uniform a temperature as possible.

It could not be transported by wagon along those corrugated trails but had to be carried in ten-gallon tins on men's backs. The half-breed packers and the Irish navvies remained contemptuous of it. Armstrong the engineer saw one packer casually repairing a leak in a tin by scraping mud over it with his knife, oblivious of the fact that the tiniest bit of grit or the smallest amount of friction would blast him heavenwards. Sometimes the packers would lay their tins down on a smooth rock and a few drops would be left behind from a leak. On one such occasion a teamster took his horse to water at just such a spot. The horse's iron shoe touched a pool of Nitro and the resulting blast tore the shoe from his foot and drove it through his belly, killing him and stunning the teamster.

The number of men killed or maimed by accidental explosions was truly staggering. In one fifty - mile stretch of section B, Sandford Fleming counted thirty graves, all the result of the careless handling of nitro.

Under such conditions the only respite was alcohol. Prohibition was in effect all along the line, but this did not stop the whisky peddlers who had kegs of liquor cached at points along the entire right of way. Since a gallon of alcohol, which was sold in the cities of the east for as low as fifty cents, could, when properly diluted, return forty-five dollars to an enterprising peddler on the line, business continued brisk in spite of the vigilance of the police. The peddlars hid out in the bush or on the islands that dotted the swampy lakes, moving into the work camps in swift canoes of birchbark and darting away again at the approach of the law. If caught the peddler generally escaped with a fine, since these where the chief source of income for the struggling towns and villages that were springing up at the end of steel.' - The Great Railway

These towns and villages are your Armstrongs, Longlacs, Gogamas, Capreols and Hornepaynes, all struggling to survive cutbacks on anything to do with railroads by various governments. Canadian governments that would rather see clogged highways and roads than rail lines. Why? Beats me.

Cripes, this sleep-depriving heat is getting to me. I'm back in the Dome, bare feet up on the dash with a window to the world providing quite the view as engine lights filluminate the track ahead and anything trackside, all lit up like a movie set. It appears as though we're gliding through a never-ending tunnel like the scene in *The Shining* when Jack chases his family through the maze. I can lean back in my seat and look straight up at the stars above as if the Dome were open-topped, and those stars are bright, not a cloud in sight. I'm alone but not alone, awestruck in a solitary cinematic scenario. Ayup, what brought that on!

Unfortunately, solitary stargazing and interactive trainspotting is interrupted by a large lady from Newfoundland who proceeds to regale me with scatter-gun stories of family and how much she loves to visit such characters by train. We discuss the death of Pierre Trudeau's son by avalanche last week. Young lives lost in youthful exuberance brought to mind a shrine in the window of a store in Jasper, dedicated to a young skier doing what he loved best, with photographs of him with family and friends and heart-breaking written tributes; another reminder of our mortality.

She was one to talk all night, the Newfoundlander, and after a bit the stories began to run into each other. 'Didn't you just tell me that one missus?' 'No!' So I gather boots and socks again and cheerfully bade her a good night and retired back to my seat. Along the way I had a peek and discovered that those sleeping in the baggage car are not, according to rumour, rock stars, actors, acrobats or porn stars, just trainee VIA employees billeted in there due to lack of seats. Poor sods are worse off than us great unwashed in steerage. Speaking of which....There was no time for sentimentality in 1980's England as Maggie role-played with Ronnie Reagan and England didn't swing like a pendulum anymore. More like a dead man from a noose and immigrants were taking the blame from fascist mobs in pubs and streets, dole queues were still never-ending and the people in them angry or beaten. Uncle John's Revolution was afoot or ahead depending on where you stood and The Specials were sending a message to Rudy. The political and social climate told me to take a hike, so I did, back to the Great Bear. Elvis was dead and John Lennon was about to be and I didn't want to be next in line despite not being in the same league when it came to performing.

My cousin found me a job with a crew of painters, the boss and his brother being natives of Clydebank, Scotland, and I got to meet them at a neighbourhood party.

'He looks like a painter the way he swalleed that beer, eh Bob!' sang brother Alec.

'Aye, when can you start son?'

'Monday any good?' I suggested, and opened another can of Newcastle Brown, as someone murdered 'Flower of Scotland' on an off key piano in the basement.

'Aye son, good enough, don't be late, four bucks an hour plus time and a half for travel.'

'Sounds good to me, Bob!' We shook hands and my future was sealed as a painter. Next thing I'm on a six month tour of

Ontario and Legions in Oshawa, Pettawawa, Ottawa, Algonquin Park, Wawa, Bobcaygeon, Windsor, Tobermory, Arthur, Kingston, Toronto, Sudbury, Sault Ste. Marie and Thunder Bay. Bob's van drove its way around and across the province, it could steer itself in direction of any bar, legion or motel, and I got to stay in motels and hotels of all description, drink gallons of Molson Export, smoke cartons of DuMaurier cigarettes and learn how to paint anything that didn't move. Sat next to an old town cop one morning at the counter in a Smiths Falls diner as a waitress poured me another coffee and Bob ordered the breakfast special twice, I felt as if I were in a Norman Rockwell painting, and when the cop stood to pay his bill and wish me a good day he paused to hitch up his pants and check out my tattoos, the gun on his hip prominent. 'Nice tatts, don't be sticking up any banks around here now,' he joked, winked at Bob and the waitress as he pushed open the door and strolled off into a glorious sun-baked country morning. 'Definitely not Liverpool, eh Bob.'

'Definitely not Glasgow either, son, but you'll get the hang of it.' He asked if my dad was alive because I only mentioned my mum in talk of 'back hame.' I told him he was and he wasn't and that Frank was a good man but we didn't really get along and I hadn't heard from Harry since I don't know when, and that was good enough for him.

The plan was to work our way towards Petawawa and meet up with Alec before making our way into Algonquin Park to paint a CN Rail hotel. I was excited at the prospect of spending a week in the bush with such characters and the chance to be among folk not infatuated with beating England at Wembley in 1967, but first we had to stop at the Legion to discuss the event further.

A week later we were heading into the bush after spending a morning in a greasy-spoon waiting for Alec, who eventually showed up cursing traffic and slow painters. The weather was perfect for painting but that would soon change and I got to learn just how fast. Checking in to the hotel after a long bumpy ride into the 'park', we were shocked to find that alcohol was banned from all CN property.

We would have to improvise so the first night found us four painters out of sight sneaking cold beers hidden in submerged five-gallon pails in a lake. Just one of many hide-the-beer tactics we would use over several years, especially when painting the interior of St. James Cathedral in the humidity hell of August in the big city of Toronto as the 1982 World Cup went on around us. 'Right son, lets get that "paint" up on that scaffold,' and up it went tied to a rope, eighty-six feet to the toppermost of the poppermost among angels with gold-leafed faces.

Back in Algonquin Park, the week was spent waiting for breaks in the rain so we could dash out into clouds of biting bugs to slap brown Sherwin Williams latex paint onto faded aluminum siding. ' Make it cover, son!'

'Right Bob.' No chance of a one-coat job there, a wanner, as the siding was faded almost to pink. Exposed skin was lathered in insect repellent I convinced myself had to be flammable, so made sure to smoke cigarettes outside in case of instant combustion; but for some reason the 'mozzies' never really bothered me, and still don't, but the blackflies devoured me like an English steak, leaving welts the size of dimes on my skinny white frame.

One rained-out morning I left the guys playing pool with engineer Casey Jones and headed out for a walk in the bush. It was amazing to be out there alone experiencing the smells and sounds of Canada at its finest. Warm moisture from clouds and trees dripped down my neck and I was too cool for a hat which allowed biting flies to dive-bomb my head which had me walking faster, trotting along a trail, as a hidden insect world played humming tunes and sudden wild crescendo's just for me. A green snake slithered across my boot when I stopped to light a cigarette and a helicopter-sized dragonfly hovered inches from my face and next thing I was stumbling down an incline into a thorn bush which hid a large wasps nest. Good thing it was raining or they would have stung me to death on the spot, I was told later.

Consumed with the wild itches I strayed across a dirt road to find an old log building that advertised itself as a convenience store and went in thinking I'd buy some groceries. The fellers would surely be impressed with big brave me out in the bush on my lonesome buying groceries for the crew. I shook off rain like a wet dog and hailed the old man behind the counter. He hailed back in a friendly fashion so I asked for two pounds of boiled ham, a loaf of bread, and a packet of smokes for starters, and he ripped me off by pressing on the scale with his thumb as he weighed the meat, the bastard. Two pounds became two ounces but I wasn't saying anything about that, no sir, are you kidding me, a killer may have lurked beneath that greasy head of white hair, blue flannel shirt and well-worn oily jeans. He asked me what I was doing out there in the rain in the middle of nowhere dressed the way I was, as he robbed me blind, so I told him about the CN job. 'Oh yeah! You wanna be careful out there young fella. Don't stray from the path on the way back and watch out for bears, you hear!'

I thanked him for the sage advice and paid for four tins of baked beans, a loaf of hard bread and 'two pounds' of still breathing ham, pretending not to notice a beady-eyed man watching from behind a multi-colored fly curtain hung in the doorway behind him. Hmmm, bears and perverts, I thought, and headed back the way I came to be chastised by pool playing painters and rail guys.

'Yer mad, son, bloody mad, you could have gotten lost so ye could!'

I just laughed and told them I knew what I was doing, the bush was nothing compared to the streets of England, and after a bite to eat strolled down to the lake for a smoke and a beer.

Later on, I was involved in a game of pool with a big ol' railroad feller from Prince Edward Island dressed in pinstripe overalls, plaid shirt, and a red well-worn ball cap. I mentioned the walk to the store and he frowned and tutted and gave me a lecture from behind the eight-ball. 'You want to be careful out der on your own young fella. Da bear will eat you up even if you are tough from dat Liverpool,' and he laughed and pocketed my two dollar bill. I laughed along, racked the cue, and headed back to the lake to watch a beautiful sunset and get hounded mercilessly. 'Fuckin big game hunter so you are!'

'Take your slap brush with you next time.'

'They'll be scared of his Doctor Martens.'

We finished the job out of beer, behind schedule, but still alive. I was headed to Thunder Bay with Bob, the other two back to Oshawa. We packed clothes, tools, empty pails and equipment into vehicles before heading back into the bush using the same road that was now resembling a mud gulch. Branches laden down with moisture bowed in the wind to lash windows and scrape paintwork from mud-covered vehicles as we played follow-the-leader with Alec and Joe up ahead in an old blue Ford that spewed black exhaust whenever we got too close.

The windshield of our van resembled a distorted ocean of wiperblades fighting a losing battle to clear the flood. Bob had his head stuck out of the window in order to see and smoked furiously. The radio was useless, nothing but static and moans from an airwave grave. I twiddled the knob back and forth one last time before turning it off with a resounding click.

Tired and sleepy from the tropical heat, the rhythm of rain drums on the roof, and sick of cigarettes, I leaned my head against a steamed up side window scarred with a solo game of X's and O's and nodded off into the ether.

'Jesus Christ, son, look at the size of that!'

I jumped, opened one eye, and followed Bob's finger which pointed in direction of a big brown monster escaping from the bush. 'What the fuck is that?' I yelled, wiped the window, and sat up straight in my seat as it ran alongside the van. A humongous eye stared from a great head as it ran. The beast looked to be in a panic and frantically overtook us, almost colliding with the truck up front. It slipped and slid in the mud, corrected itself, pulled up slightly and ran alongside Alec's truck, mud flying in great clumps from its hooves.

'Is it a cow, Bob?'

'That's not Coo in its life, son, it's a fuckin great Moose. Look at the size of it!

He's stood up in his seat working the steering wheel, head touching the roof like he's riding a bronco. I can see Joe up ahead panicking in his seat. He's bouncing about and pointing and trying to put as much distance between him and his moose-filled window, he's almost sat on Alec's lap. Alec takes a look at what Joe's pointing at and jams the stirring wheel hard. His cap flies off with the effort and the truck skids for a bit before slipping into a muddy ditch. The terrified moose, eyes still bulging, keeps on running as if its about to win the Grand National.

'Aw, fer Christ's sake son, what he's done now!' We pull up slowly, marveling at the dripping arse of the truck reaching for the sky. I can see Alec searching for his hat as Joe pushes open the passenger door and escapes like an Apollo astronaut. The air turns bluer inside before the door slams shut with a muffled clump, causing kernels of rust to flutter and glitter and settle in oozing mud. Silence, except for rain beating on leaves and the van that we sit quietly in that gives a sudden slide and tilts a bit but stops short of following them in. 'Has it gone, Bob?' I whisper, scared to add extra weight to our predicament

'Aye, son, mooses are more frightened of us than we are of them. It'll be at the main gate by now! But let's not tell that to ma daft wee brother.' He whispers back with a big grin.

A plan is drawn up to go off in pairs in search of rescue or a Ranger Station, and after arming ourselves with telescopic aluminum roller poles, 'Fe the beasties,' and drop sheets as oilskins for protection from the rain, off we went.

'Are ye scared?' Bob shouted, revelling in the excitement, as I took a leak against a mossy tree bent over like an old man beneath the weight of another sudden downpour before catching up to Rommel tramping through the mud.

'Scared? No. You?'

'Nae bother son, not exactly Bengazi is it. Aye, the desert was the place to be...shoulda seen the flies,' he shouts above the roar of torrential rain, flapping about in some tree's, almost losing an eye to a swishing branch, 'Eh, be careful there, Monty!' drowing trees that we are having to crab-crawl under to cross the road.

'Did you have roller poles in the desert, Bob?'

'Aye, right, would have been better than the guns they gave us,' he spits, and laughs, and acts out a stabbing with a rifle and bayonet thing when we stop to light a fag in the shelter of a sagging spruce covered in spider webs.

'What was that? Fucksakes....'

Another rustle in the bushes.

'It's the moose, run!'

'Could be a bear!'

'Argh!'

'RUN, son!' and off we went, running, ciggies jammed in mouths, drop-sheets trailing behind in the mud, laughing like school kids and tripping over each other's sheets, slipping and sliding and brandishing roller poles at imaginary foes.

Back at the slightly tilted van, soaked to the skin, the smell of varsol somehow comforting as we dry off with paint rags and get cozy under dry drop sheets and ready ourselves for a much-needed doze, but a sudden pounding of hands on metal and glass scares the crap out of us and ruins the moment.

It's only Alec and Joe, back with a park ranger who is busy attaching a big hook to the chassis of Alec's half-drowned truck.

'You two bastards are sleeping while we're runing around in the rain saving yis!'

'Shut it you, numpty, we got chased by a big bastardin beastie back there, didn't we son!' I concur, but Alec is not amused and demands cash to pay the ranger, who looks to be having a grand time.

Bob and I sit at the side door, bare feet swinging in the sudden sunshine, bantering with the ranger about bears and moose and spiders and football, while Joe and Alec watch their ride being winched out.

'Should have seen this wee Englishman running...a right Roger Bannister he was!'

'Fuck off.'

Have brush will travel!

Monday, 16th of November. Mel Pringle's wife snores pretty good for a woman of no words. She belts out a tune with unknowing gusto from across the aisle, in complete harmony with Hillbilly Fiddler's wife who gives it loads from just a couple of seats north-west of here. I'm thinking of joining in with some bowel percussion when from the depths of smoking car hell pops ol' Hillbilly. He staggers up the aisle and raps his wife on the forehead with a big hairy knuckle, and just like that she stops snoring. He laughs, makes himself comfortable in his seat, falls into a deep sleep and hits us with a double bass snore of his own. His wife joins in on cue with a viola vibrato and Mrs. Pringles got the well-practiced bugle going. Where's Mickey Rooney when you need him? Buddy Rich? I want to join the band but can't because a smiling bald man in new white running shoes is wandering down the aisle with his eyes closed tight, shirt unbuttoned exposing a hairy chest and stomach enough to make Burt Reynolds blush. No way am I going to sleep with him on the loose. He looks like he's auditioning for Sleepwalkers II. I wish I had a pellet gun. Ping! Fairground attraction.

Ohhh...across the country back and forth, went the lad not from Liverpool North. Pins and needles he did have, from sittin' all day on the friggin lav.

Ohhh...across the country he went twice, jammed on a train like sardines on a slice. And next time he tries it he'll be forty twice.

Ohhh...finding out quickly that he's not eighteen, up a moun-

tain in Alaska he has been,

You're reading the memoirs of a travelin' man who copied his outfit from Desperate Dan. Dan, Dan, that dirty old man, who washed his face in a frying pan.

Paul, Paulie, travelin' man, headin' home as fast as he can, and he runs real quick cos he eats All-Bran.

Thank you, thank you very much!

I eventually fell asleep to wake up in Hornepayne of all places. I was having a lovely dream about singing to a full house in a smoky Labour Club. Everyone was there and a strobe light lit a full dance floor and, no I wasn't naked.

Hornepayne (pop. 1,800) who gave you that name? A railway town with a pulp mill hidden amongst immense forests lit up by a big and perfect moon as white as a cue ball. To my left sit rows of worn out CN rail cars and a thin line of white smoke wisps from a rooftop chimney on top of one. Billets for rail workers or homes for the temporary homeless? To my right sits Hornepayne, a town that has seen better days like its cousins along this route. We've been stopped here long enough for me to have sneaked off and taken a walk around town, but hang on, people are climbing aboard and they are right noisy buggers. A woman settles into the well-documented seat in front and tells me its 6:15am by her watch. She's joined by a long-haired male who proceeds to wake up steerage as he makes a clumsy attempt to stow his luggage whilst whistling a weedy rendition of YMCA. Upon completion of his task he makes himself comfortable, stretches like a cat, and snaps his seat all the way back with a loud CLUNK! nearly crushing my right kneecap. I curse quietly and plan his fate, within minutes they are both fast asleep. I stand gingerly and hover above them with an imaginary blunt spoon gripped tightly. They don't know how close they come to their own Wounded Knee, man.

These wakers-of-the-dead are railway employees. Gangs of co-workers dressed in assorted tough-guy clothes follow them aboard and surround me in small groups. I'm trapped, but it's too late to jump as the doors are closed with a loud bang and the engine warms up causing the train to shudder, lights to flicker, and off we go into the Ontario dawn as a Jean Chretien imitator in greasy overalls informs those unable to sleep, 'Dat der are lot of lodges and tings for skidoo types here in dis 'orn-epayne. Der is a lot for dem to do in de winter,' at the top of his voice. Someone near the front shushes him and he shouts, 'Fook dem!' and laughs along with his pals like a big old French bear.

I want to shout something clever, but I'm outnumbered.

Outskirts of Liverpool, England, 1971. The weather was abnormally warm for the time of year. Afternoon sun played hide-and-seek from behind large white cotton-wool clouds as stray dogs and children tried to catch the shadows as they raced across the shopping centre square. A gritty wind whipped up tornadoes of discarded newspapers, chip papers and sweet wrappers. Tornadoes of trash. Keep Britain Tidy, stickers glinted from lids of unused rubbish bins.

A new decade in England had been ushered in by unrest both political and social. Strikes, blackouts, and poverty went hand in hand with terrorism both urban and national. Football violence and riots, factory closings and long dole queues were the norm. I sat on a wall wondering what to spend my hard-earned pocket money on, not knowing that I was about to begin a love affair and it didn't involve a girl.

I hadn't been in the new record shop before, the one on the corner with the black and white hand-painted smiling ram's head above 'Ram Records' in block letters. Music blasted from a doorway as I hurried across the road to enter into teenville and rock and roll. Alan Freed, Soda fountains, poodle skirts and duck-tails were a thing of the past as Marc Bolan lisped and growled through 'Jeepster'...'You're so sweet, you're so fine!'

Alice Cooper, David Bowie and Sweet posters were pinned to the ceiling and fought for superiority over David Cassidy, the New Seekers and Donnie Osmond on the wall. Idols of the day grinned, posed, and leered from other vantage spots, among them Peace signs and rows of iron-on patches telling possible buyers to 'Keep on Truckin' or 'Rock On' or make some bacon.

I found an empty space at a long wooden counter, leaned across its black cigarette ash dusted top and studied the latest record charts hung up on the wall above a shiny metal till adorned with Hendrix, Animals and Steppenwolf stickers. Those charts were as important to us as a bookie's board to a punter in a betting shop.

'Tokoloshe Man' by John Congas had been getting air-play on BBC Radio, and I liked it, but I couldn't make up my mind and the owner was too busy lining up a single on a fancy record player to get his attention or help me in my decision what to buy. Rod Stewart was singing about Maggie May as I glanced discreetly around the store full of booted and suited tribes searching through record bins. Cool girls with feather cuts and bright-colored eye shadow danced on the spot.

The owner, the Record Man, was a short, portly character clad in flared jeans and a pink Ben Sherman shirt, both a size too small. He had a wrinkled face framed with frizzy mutton chop side-burns and a non-filtered cigarette stuck in the corner of his mouth, the smoke from which was burning away at his left eye.

He was on form as he performed on his tiny stage, obviously a veteran of many a hard crowd to sell to and this lot, by looks, was easy pickings for him. Maggie finished making a fool of Rod and the Record Man shouted, 'I promise you,' and paused to shush those in the back and suck another inch off his cigarette, 'I promise anyone who buys this record that they'll get their money back if it doesn't go to number one. NO MESSING!' And with a flourish worthy of a magician, placed the vinyl 45 onto the turntable and deftly guided the needle into its groove.

Giggles and catcalls broke the silence as a choppy guitar intro and a violin brought the place to life and then there it was, the voice of 'Noddy' Holder, one that would send chills up my spine for years to come, and as if by magic, a copy was on the counter in front of me as the Record man dealt out singles as if he were dealing playing cards in a casino.

The record spun to a halt and someone shouted, 'play it again mister!' and he did, and it was still playing when I headed out into the late afternoon chill, my new found treasure safely hidden from marauding gangs beneath my windcheater as the sun started its disappearing trick behind an old church on the hill to the clanging of graffiti-covered metal shutters that signalled the closing of shops. Those spray-painted shutters always reminded me of multi-colored pirates eye patches.

I ran home only stopping to avoid the half-starved mongrel that hid in the bushes of the Catholic Church. The mangy beast always knew when I was about to pass by before I did and off it went with the barking and snarling but I made it home safe and sound in record time. I snuck in through the back door and straight up the stairs into my bedroom, locking the door behind me: Bright pink paper bag, shiny black vinyl, stark white sleeve, band name 'Slade' and song title etched in black on a dark red background.

My heart skipped a beat when the three pointed star in the middle fell out and disappeared under the bed but I found it hidden behind a Subbuteo box, a Roy of The Rovers annual and some dusty old Action Man gear. For days my family had no respite from that song as I played the arse off the 'Coz I Luv You' on a portable record player to moans and groans.

'Not that again!'

'Bloody racket, I'm gonna make an ashtray out of it!' but he didn't and Slade went to number one on my birthday and a bond was sealed.

All hail the *Record Man!*

The function of music is to liberate in the soul those feelings which normally we keep locked up in the heart. -anon

Meanwhile, back on the Canadian...a matching Japanese couple just wished me a 'Good Morning' on their way to a seat in the back that they've made into a comfortable home. They look like twin pro-skiers or figure skaters topped with short blonde streaked hair. I return the greetings as we follow the moon eastward before taking a sharp right into a likely head-on collision as it appears to be sat on the track ahead. It waits like a throbbing bulbous eye, then appears to mock us by floating up and away to resume its rightful place on the horizon to be replaced by a sun that rises to blind us with a red explosive glare. 'This alone is worth the price of admission,' I tell the Japanese couple, who giggle and smile back as if to an idiot. They have a point. I aim two six-gun index fingers at the orange orb and perform rising sun actions. Hey, we're all smiling!

Note, dear reader, for the privilege of experiencing these strange and wonderful tales from the Dome, each missive I relay to your home, facility or jail cell, I sometimes risk death by evil eye from the likes of Big Mama Melons who is sat glaring at me from her 'never sit here or I'll kill you' roost in the smoking section as she lights up her third cigarette on the bounce as I stand here waiting for the steward to fill my thermos mug with hot water. To break the spell and save my life I nip back to Steerage to tell The Pringles that Deliverance, the movie, was made in Grand Valley, Ontario, using locals as extras, and if they ever get round to making a follow-up they could film it on the Canadian.

Small pockets of water are frozen over on the five billion years old Canadian Shield; a single blood-red cloud curves eastward through purple skies like a sabre from the gods as menacing black thunder-heads rumble slowly from the south. The sky is a vibrant video game as we, the players, glide through Oba, a small ghost town of the highest calibre.

It is a land where nature started to say something and stuttered a thousand times, an extraordinary region where there is one small landscape constantly shifting...'- Journalist William Hard (1909)

I just found a few crinkled bank notes hiding in a lint-filled corner of a pocket in my ratty jeans (I thought Queen Victoria was dead) and have decided to spend them in the dining car in celebration. I know it's hard to believe but they let me in without a fight and eggs Benedict is served prompt and hot by a nervous but friendly waitress who hands me two tea-bags to soak in a silver tea-pot because, 'you're English and you like your tea strong.'

Everything rattles in this car, teeth, silverware, the china, my wallet. Miniature jars of assorted jams and honey are placed on a bone-white china plate to rattle next to a tiny vase of fresh flowers.

Silver milk and sugar bowls compliment the presentation laid out on a starched white cotton tablecloth on which I spill my tea while pouring.

Rattled, I'm trying to hide the stain with an elbow and slip miniature jars of jam into my shirt pocket when the waitress sneaks up behind me to tell me that breakfast includes yogurt, cereal and fruit juice all for the same price, would I like more tea?

'Yes please!' I order the works and in no time the table is overloaded with edibles. I play a game of 'I see' with a Seminole Warrior sat shyly at the next table as I munch. He's removed his hat, mine's still on and I think it bothers him. I try to make eye contact again but he's not interested in talking.

The sun lights me up through a well-polished window and its blinding rays warm my face. What a feast this is after living on sandwiches and Pot Noodles! I'm a big fat roasting pig and I don't care. An inner chill has evaporated completely and the waitress attacks me again from out of the sun like a Japanese Zero to offer more tea and light me up even more with witty banter about my type allowed to eat in first class. I tell her to behave or I'll steal the flowers. She tells me they're fake. I smell them to see if she's lying and she's not. She curtsies and tells me to take my time, there is no rush, and takes off to the kitchen for more hot water as a gaggle of large, macho, railroad guys enter and sit at a table across from me. At this the silent Seminole places a few bills on the tablecloth and takes his leave.

The railroad guys are tougher, dirtier and smellier than me and only want to talk among themselves, so I follow suit carrying my full belly in a wheelbarrow, sporting a slight sunburn, a contented smile and several jars of jam in my pocket. I aim a classic wave at the waitress who chases me down the corridor calling my name. Look out, I'm in! No I'm not. She just wants to tell me that I forgot to pay the bill. Oh boy!

Upon arrival back in steerage I make as much of a racket as I can. I whistle loudly and out of tune, bump and bang the backs of seats in front in guise of trying to find my toilette bag in my backpack, but it takes a while to wake both rail workers in return for last night and I retire laughing to a washroom in the next car for a good scrub. Where I stand naked as the day I was hatched to watch the country zip by as I scrub and brush and soak and dry. On goes the deodorant, the moisturizing cream, a red teeshirt I've been saving since I washed it in Terrace. It still smells of the family Pretty's laundry detergent which has me feeling sad for a second but I'm a happy man again when I check the mirror for cracks and find only one in the glass. I'm ready for that date with Janice. I gather belongings and open the washroom door to a line-up of glaring, fidgeting walking on the spot, totally irritated and not-very-friendly passengers. I smile and wish them all a good morning as I take off down the aisle feeling like a million dollars; you know, the full belly, the clean teeth and all that, but something's not right, something's missing, which I can't put my finger on until I sit down in my seat and realise I left my boots in the washroom.

It's a humble man who waits in line to collect his boots, and to get over the humiliation I take off to the safety of the Dome where I enter into conversation with two well-dressed elderly chaps from Painesville, Minnesota. Turns out they don't live far from Fargo and are astonished that anyone bothered to make a movie about the place. They had no idea, they tell me. This revelation leads to talk about the wonders of Canada and the railroad and they hit me back with something astonishing about America which leads to a right old pissing match without the pee. I have them interested in *The Great Railway* and the history of the country they are traveling across and spending their money in, when like a switch being turned off they forget which country they're in. I'm reminding them when the elder of the two (I've got the years he's got the money) leans across his seat and eyeballs a lone native passenger sat at the back watching the world go by, something he's been doing for days and he's made it obvious he wants to be left alone while he's doing it.

'Excuse me, miss.'

No reply.

'I said, excuse me miss!'

Not a peep, the old guy looks about the car wearing the look of a man not used to being ignored, especially by foreigners.

'ERMM, EXCUSE ME MISS!'

His eyes are bulging behind his glasses now and his friend starts to fidget in his seat. He appears to be praying for an immediate reaction from the guy in the firing line because the look on his face tells me he's been in this situation before.

'Excuse me yourself, ASSHOLE! I'm not a fuckin MISS,' the lone wolf hisses with pure venom, which gets everyone within striking distance immediately interested and silently awaiting the outcome.

'OH, I'm sorry! the old guy sputters and sinks back into his seat in shock after doing a triple take at his quarry. He looks to his partner for help but he's busy staring intently out the window at something he's suddenly found fascinating. I'm on the floor here laughing and hiding behind the seat while trying to write this all down. Help! I'm chewing on a knuckle.

Pretending to have found my pen, I resurface to find the American as white as a sheet and still looking uncomfortable. In one motion his partner makes a big show of checking the time on his wristwatch, taps it twice, looks like he's forgotten something and abandons ship down the stairs to safety.

It's that quiet in here even a pack of prairie dogs stop gambolling outside to await the outcome. Smokers find their seats and passengers pretend to sleep or read and a few sit and stare or smile at 'Miss' as he combs his long black hair with an oversized pink plastic comb. It dawns on Mr. America that he's on his own and he jumps up suddenly as if shot, and bumps his head on the bulkhead, catches his falling glasses, grabs his coat, and casts an exasperated angry glare at an audience most of whom are pretending not to be paying attention (me in particular) and slinks off down the stairs rubbing the top of his head.

At this the theatre cracks up. Rail workers are in stitches. I can't breathe, I'm back in school and the headmaster has just swallowed his tongue while reciting the Lord's Prayer. 'Miss' is having a hard time holding back a laugh as he brushes his hair into infinity watching me laughing in the reflection of his favourite window. I can't help it I'm back in church and Father has just dropped baby Jesus on the red carpet. In order to hang on to what's left of my sanity I stand slowly, gauging distance between head and bulk head, stretch dramatically, gather my things, and stroll off nonchalantly to the sanctity of a washroom.

Unfortunately, it's occupied and I'm stood there between cars with the door window open bobbing for fresh air, when the carriage door slams open and Miss glides on through. He looks my way and smiles. I give him the nod and smile back. 'Excuse me,' he says. 'Certainly, miss,' I reply, and he takes off into the next car laughing, hips swinging, flicking his hair like a model on a catwalk to the astonishment of several rail workers. The washroom door flys open revealing a tiny old lady stood holding a well-thumbed copy of National Enquirer in one hand and her glasses in the other. A loaded handbag dangles from the crook of one bony arm and she feigns shock or heart-attack at me stood there holding my belly wearing a pained expression.

'OH! Terribly sorry! Have you been waiting long?' she giggles, and escapes in the same direction as Miss. That's it for me, man. I'm gone, solid gone. I nip in and sit down with both hands clamped to my head and laugh that hard I think I might break something inside. The mirror is above the sink and when I catch a glimpse of myself sat there I fear I'm about to die of laughter in a little washroom on the prairie. Later on I'm stood in another carriage waiting to fill my plastic bottle at a water fountain when Miss pops out of his seat, lays a hand on my arm, and stage whispers, 'Can you believe that,' laughs out loud, and sits back down with much flourish and drama.

'Guess, you made their day, mate,' I reply, aiming water into my well-used bottle. 'Take it easy. See you later,' I tell him, and look up to find a population pretending not to be looking at me. The stroll down the aisle is a hoot.

Back in the Dome, which is as hot as a greenhouse and I feel like an over-ripe tomato as Mr. Collingwood yaps my ear off about photography and polar bears as he snaps away at all and sundry with his fancy camera. 'Don't mind if I take your photo do you!' I tell him I don't and he does. I don't think he's lost his mind completely yet but give him time, he boarded at Vancouver. He must be getting some amazing photos though, as we glide through winter scenes accessible only by plane, train, 4x4, dog-sled or snow-shoe. The time is 11am and unfortunately the bloody camera refuses to comply again, as eiderdowns of ice that blanket streams and rivers melt slowly in the heat from the sun.

A teenager wearing a Mohawk haircut and fatigues marches by scowling. He's been wandering up and down aisles and corridors playing the hard man all morning. His teeshirt tells us he's '*Independent*' but he doesn't look very happy about it. Another guy wearing a similar teeshirt follows him and he doesn't look too pleased either. Wonder whats going on? I don't think they work for the newspaper.

My mind is working overtime and I try to send it home to bed. It's high noon and I'm thinking of renting a dog-sled as we sit waiting again in another siding on a windswept Canadian Shield adorned with sundrenched undisturbed frozen lakes, unclimbed trees and endless blue sky.

Unfortunately, after that feast of a breakfast I've been up and down like a blue-arsed fly for over an hour. It's getting harder to be inconspicuous using the conveniences. I feel like a coke addict and have taken to using a different point of disposal on each trip.

Help!

The toilets, and this is no joke, the toilets have now run dry of water. I overheard a conductor bemoaning the fact in hushed tones to an engineer while I stood in line again. *'I don't know where it's all gone. We loaded up at Winnipeg!'*

'Are you sure the pipes haven't sprung a leak? Best radio ahead to Capreol, we can fix it and load up there,' an engineer whispered in his ear - and almost swallowed his can of Coke as Miss strolled on by.

I wanted to tell them that it was all my fault but thought it best to keep my gob shut for a change.

And now the washrooms are off limits.

Oh dear!

To keep clear mind and trousers, I focus and recite Elvis songs in my head until we pull into Capreol (pop. 3,800). The Canadian smells like a three week old meat pie found in a dead tramps boot when we finally stop, and I'm off this train in search of a fence, wall, hill or hole in the ground but the terrain is as flat as a witches you know what, but I'm a veteran of such situations, and I'm feeling much lighter and well-exercised upon my return and find a quiet spot on the platform to recuperate and thank the Lord for hidden hidey-holes. I'm enjoying the fresh air and silence when Bert the trucker strolls over. 'Have you seen that!' he barks, nods and points at Miss who is leaning on a split-rail fence staring off into the distance enjoying a furtive smoke.

'Ah, he's alright,' I tell him, smile, and perform knee-bends to help the circulation.

'Yeah? He doesn't know if he's a man or a woman!'

'I think I know how he feels right now but what's that got to do with the price of hockey pucks?' I ask him, as Miss preens for the cameras, he's a natural.

The look on his face tells me he's even more suspicious of me now. Ernie strolls over and they stand there smoking like two mulleted soul brothers. Bert tells me he'll see me later and takes off to board the waiting Canadian shaking his head and mumbling with his pal. I'm not sure what his problem is and don't really give much of a shit, not that I have any left in me at this point in time, but I follow them aboard.

The Dome is rammed with rollicking, rambunctious rail-guys, so I retire to steerage for a nap where I make sure to make a hell of a racket while making myself comfortable.

'Oh, I'm sorry, did I awaken you?'

Jean Chretien, that rugged old railroad guy who boarded at Hornpayne, wakes *me* up with his latest tour guide sermon at Sudbury (pop. 89,000) and, no, he's not from dat Liverpool.

'Deez treez are midjet treez, undreds of years old!'

'Over a million year ago, de Zudberry Bason, a groun de-presheeon fifdy kilometres long an twenty severn kilometres wide dat woz probabalee creeate by an eerupting volcanno or a larche meetyoreye crashing to Eard, with de resulting force twisting de groun forsing mineral rock to de surfass, bringing to Zudberry an abundence of diverse ree-sauces an' a lanscape that is trullee a bizarre contrass of barren black slag eeps an white birsh bark treez.

He nips off for a quick smoke before resuming class.

'This is de INCO world, de world of de ardee miner an de sauce of de famuss INCO song aboud de drinking an de fighting on a Saturday nigh while de wives are safely ow de way at de bingo all.'

Big laughs all round. He should be on stage alright, a landing stage.

'Zudberry as de worls largesse nickel mine an smelter complex, gardead by a tree undred and eighty won metre eye smokestack zat loom ovher all it surfhey. De luner gardon zat as rezulted from all dis mining, along wid de ravages of assid rain, as denuded de immeedeeate landscape of veshetation an creeated moon-like ills.'

More laughs, some claps.

'Thank yoo folks!' he shouts, and heads off to hang with his compadres in the Dome. It's true though (Trudeau?) Sudbury does have an Apollo moon landing look about it. Barren as barren can be except for the midget tree. Acid rain damage slowly being repaired by extensive reforestation projects that have created protected woodlands in and around Sudbury, I believe, which has me in the mood for a bit of a read:

'When Andrew Onderdonk (Engineer, Railway contractor, monied, mysterious, respected and aloof, with a degree from the Troy Institute of Technology, born in New York, responsible for work on The San Francisco Seawall, The Trent Valley Canal and the New York Subway tunnels, 'very popular in local society circles' according to the Victoria British Colonist of the day) arrived in British Columbia, there were only thirty-five thousand white citizens in the province."

I know we are in Ontario but it makes the same bang anywhere does nitro-glycerine. More from Berton...

"He would need to employ at least ten thousand men (actually many more, because of the turnover); from the very outset, there was a kind of terror that he would solve his labour problem by importing and employing Chinese. As soon as he arrived in Victoria, in April, 1880, Onderdook was met by a deputation from the Anti-Chinese Association. He assured them that he would always give white labour the preference. When the white labour of the province was exhausted, Onderdonk said he would, if necessity compelled him, fall

back on the French Canadians of eastern Canada. Should that be not sufficient, he would reluctantly engage Indians and Chinese.

The first Chinese had come to British Columbia from California in 1858, attracted by the Fraser's gold. Anti-Chinese feeling had been rising steadily since that time. By 1878, when their employment in public works was banned, there were some three thousand Chinese in the province. All were prepared to work for lower wages than any white labourer and that was the chief cause of the discontent. It was considered political suicide for a public figure to take any stand other than an anti-oriental one.

The feeling elsewhere in Canada, though less intense, was also generally against the Chinese. Almost all newspapers were editorially opposed to Oriental immigration. In Winnipeg, where Chinese were all but unknown, the Times published a fairly typical series of opinions about "the beardless and immoral children of China," as it called them; they possessed 'no sense whatever of any principle of morality" Their brains were "vacant of all thoughts which lift up and ennoble humanity" and "it is an established fact that dealings with the Chinese are attended with evil results."

The Prime Minister himself agreed that the Chinese were "an alien race in every sense that would not and could not be expected to assimilate with our Aryan population," but he was far too pragmatic to exclude Orientals from Canada until the railway was built. He put it bluntly to Parliament in 1882: "It is simply a question of alternatives: either you must have this labour or you can't have the railway."

Onderdonk was operating on a tight budget. He had been forced to accept four contracts at bids that were more than a million and a half dollars lower than his own tendered price. He had paid out an additional two hundred and fifteen thousand dollars to buy up the contracts. He was trying to get men to come all the way to British Columbia for lower wages than the Northern Pacific was offering - as little as $1.50 a day for labourers.

Chinese coolies, on the other hand, could be employed for one dollar a day. In addition, they did not require all the paraphernalia of a first-class camp. The coolie was prepared to move about in the wil-

derness, set up his own camp, and pack all his belongings, provisions and camp equipment on his back. Michael Haney, who went to work for Onderdonk in 1883, discovered that it was possible to move two thousand Chinese a distance of twenty-five miles and have them at work, all within twenty-four hours.

The same task could not be performed with a similar number of white workmen in less than a week. It is small wonder then that almost from the outset Andrew Onderdonk began hiring Chinese in spite of a volley of protests. The Chinese would not work in the presence of death, which they considered bad luck. Haney once came upon two thousand Chinese, all sitting idle; one of their number had fallen off the bank and his corpse lay far below, spread-eagled on the rocks. In vain, the walking-boss argued and swore. He pointed out that it was impossible to reach the body. The bank was a sheer precipice and no boat could approach it through the boiling waters.

"Well," said Haney, "what do you propose to do? Can't have these Chinamen standing around until that Chinaboy disintregates." The walking boss scratched his head. "There's an Indian who promises to move that body for ten dollars. I've tried to make a deal with him, but he won't budge on that price and it's too much."

"Never mind how much it is," Haney retorted. "Pay it and get those men back to work."

During the evening, a sharp explosion was heard in the canyon. When Haney returned, the Chinese were back at work and the body had vanished. The Indian had stolen some dynamite and caps, lowered them with a smoldering fuse down the canyon wall, and blown the cadaver to bits."

Nickel & Dimed at the Nickel Mine: 3:20pm above the largest nickel mine in the world. Tiny gnarled Bonsai trees that resemble overgrown roots sprout among boulders, rocks and shingle. Beaver River runs through barren landscape unmolested and unchanged and is littered with felled trees as if from an explosion. Stephen King's *The Stand* comes to mind, as a dead-ringer for Benny from *Crossroads* stands grinning, alone in the wilderness. He waves at us as if he's been waiting there all day for the chance. Iron bridges straddle streams, rivers and gravel roads that criss-cross the desolation. Rocks in shades of purple, brown and orange nestle among wicked trees that appear to have been scorched by a rocket as it took off for safer planets not inhabited by lawyers, politicians, weathermen, priests or Spice Girls. Cue X-Files theme.

Rushing-rapids empty themselves viciously into a still lake the color of mud, where large ugly tree stumps peek from small lakes like drowning swimmers. A dam appears as if in a dream or oil-painting as we round a bend in the track. A fine dusting of snow attempts to cover a grey film of powder that covers everything except moving water. No foliage here at all. Another muddy lake filled with tree stumps that resemble necks sheared of heads. Rounding another bend we enter a stand of silver birch that look to be guarding a more familiar Ontario landscape, and it's at the town of Mowat that I receive a jolt to the gut in sudden recognition that this Yellowhead journey is almost complete. Mowat, by the way, consists of two shacks. Not a Farley in sight.

At 4pm I purchase another $1.50 Pot Noodle from the giggling gourmet in the kitchen and sing him a song from the heart, with apologies to M:

POT-POT-POTNOODLE!
POT-POT -POT -POTNOODLE.
Hot water and noodles in a plastic cup.
Hot water and noodles will fill you up.
Prince George-Jasper-Winnipeg-Poodles....
Everyone talking about POTNOODLES!
POT-POT- POTNOODLES.
POT-POT-POT –POTNOODLES!

He loves it and, once dancing subsides, I find myself surrounded by happy hunter types and conversation about my song writing abilities turn to encounters in the bush with wild animals, so while savouring my hot noodles I swap elk and bear tales to kill time. An elder reminds me of Robert Shaw in Jaws, sat there all quiet and alone minding his own business, until he pipes up to advise that I take someone I can outrun next time I head up an abandoned copper mine in Alaska, which brings forth laughs but ends all conversation, so I head back to bug the neighbours.

It's snowing gray snow out there, I kid you not. Toronto must be close. Do not go gently into that dark gray snow. But first the French and Pickerel Rivers must be crossed to reach Parry Sound (pop. 6000) named after the Arctic explorer Sir William Parry. The Sound basks calmly in a lake region riddled with thirty thousand islands. The Muskokas or 'the Lake Country' is also famous for the invention of the Muskoka dinner jacket, much loved by hunters, construction workers, grunge fans and hillbillies.

We train-portage rivers that where like the Trans-Canada Highway for explorers Brule and Champlain, La Verendrye, Mackenzie, and Thompson, who lived for fur, fame, fortune and infamy. Talking of which and whom, Hudson Bay Company boss George Simpson once took his new bride Frances on a honeymoon trip across the country by express canoe, and he had no problem hiring a crew of Iroquois to power them to their goal using the Voyageur route from Lachine, Quebec, and up the Ottawa River across the Mattawa to the Nippissing. The French River led them to Georgian Bay and Lake Huron, where they went north to Sault St. Marie and across Lake Superior to Grand Portage and onward through Rainy Lake to Fort Frances for fun and frolic. Governor George and his beau ended up staying at Fort Garry at the junction of the Assiniboine and Red River where they built a big house known as The Stone Fort, which went through numerous guises such as army barracks, prison, asylum, the North West Mounted Police training school and the Manitoba Country Club. The place is now known as Lower Fort

Garry National Historic Park.

Voyageur routes from Hudson Bay to Vancouver were established, of course, by native peoples for thousands of years before fur traders appeared, but I thought this quite the venture for an old white guy, especially as Simpson was rumoured to have fathered seventy children before meeting Frances and must have had quite the J-Stroke!

The Muskoka's is also a recreational playground for the city dwellers of Ontario, according to VIA's *Log to Western Canada.* Torontonians escape the heat and humidity of the big city by traveling north in droves on each given Friday during the summer months. Columns of vehicles full of happy folk head for sanctuary of beer, black-flies, mosquito's and barbecues; where they mess about in boats and boat shoes. Tilly hats are worn to ward off the sun and Sunday afternoons are spent stuck in traffic jams on the way back home to make more money.

I prefer Lake Huron. Where rain falls in sheets exposing secret webs of spiders and holes in the cottage roof, and the wind attacks tall trees and cracks in walls. Where waves reach out to dunes with tendrils of foam as a deer hides among young pines, unmoving, as snippy sand-pipers dart from morsel to morsel tirelessly, forever children. Where black, rain heavy clouds caress the Huron waves, seeming to quench never-ending thirsts, and an umbrella decorated with bright images of passion fruit modifies the scene as a strong wind propels it across wet sand.

It was a wilderness scene owned by us for one week at a time when the sun winked from a chink in a cloud's armour and bought a slice of blue to split the horizon with shadows. The lake is hungry when we leave and cool breezes sing a Fall tune. Waves erase footprints, steal shells and pebbles, tree limbs, and sand from dunes that refuse to bow to thoughts another oncoming Winter. Iroquois war canoes pass in the night and whitecaps carry them south to Ipperwash.

I smell wood burning in campfires, the lake as it laps at hot sand. I hear seagulls pester children for a nibble at their sandwiches. Muskol irritates the burn on the back of my neck. I hear a chipmunk as it darts through undergrowth in eternal quest to fill its belly and my lungs burn after a walk up a steep ravine. Fames crackle as children in summer pyjamas fry marsh-mallows. The wine is warm, heat from hot embers chase bees to bother a garbage bag hung high in a tree instead of me. I smell fire on my clothes, sweat, my skin, the morning mist, as I fill a kettle full of tap water and put match to stove in the pre-dawn chill.

This train has tried to keep a-rolling all night long but at this moment in time we're stopped dead in Parry Sound, where I'm having a conversation with the woman who woke me up in Hornepayne, and we've swapped photos and tales of families missed. She had me laughing when she told me she thought, 'I had to be a musician or something.' I assured her that I'm just a house-painter on the rails and asked her if she knew that 'Water squeezed out' means Lake Couchiching to the Huron.

'I do now,' she answered. 'I thought for sure you were writing songs,' she said, and handed over another photo. I tell her if my journal morphs into a book I'm goint to call it 'The Yellowhead Papers' and she tells me she likes the title and wishes me good luck with it all, she'll look out for it on the best-sellers list. I share a last photo from the album in my wallet and we shake hands as she gathers belongings and makes ready to depart the train at Washago. I wave and she waves back from the platform before being greeted and hugged by faces she showed me from her wallet.

My heart is warm with friends I make, And better friends I not be knowing; Yet there isn't a train I'd rather take, No matter where it's going. - Edna St. Vincent Millay

The Canadian is almost bereft of passengers as the VIA

double-act from Quebec retrieve blue ticket stubs from above empty seats. I ask politely if I can keep mine as a souvenir. 'Sorry sir we have to count them all!' Poombah tells me and shrugs his shoulders as he breezes past. I stand up, shrug my shoulders like a gangster and tell him to keep it. At this he stops in his tracks, turns, looks me in the eye, smiles, and hands it over. 'A souvenir, huh! Okay, take it to keep.' I thank him, shake his hand, and slide the stub between the pages of The Great Railway. It seems appropriate. 'You're a sweet talker, mate,' Mel Pringle tells me as he finishes his Star Wars epic, tosses it at his wife playfully, and sits back with a contented look on his face. She laughs, and tells him that was quite the accomplishment. She spoke!

The Hillbillies entertain with their lack of respect for Toronto and its inhabitants by pointing and laughing at signs, vehicles, buildings, the sky, anything Torontonian.

The Canadian is moving at a fair clip now and I'm thinking it's not going to stop in time. Ernie and Bert ready themselves for big city action. *Girls, Girls, Girls*? Ernie walks towards me slowly from his seat up front and hands me a paperback book. He tells me someone left it behind on a seat and he thinks I'm the only one on the train clever enough to read it, which gets a big laugh, mainly from me. I thank him, and he tells me it's no problem. The book is a brand new copy of *A Time To Kill* by John Grisham. Poignant, but I've read it so I hide it in a seat pocket. Nobody notices as they're busy gathering belongings, excited as Toronto draws closer. Mrs. Pringle arse-dances in her seat (she spoke and now she dances) and her husband tells me not to forget about them in my book. I tell him I won't, as I finish tidying up, zip up my backpack, check my pockets and head for the exit door.

Last train tip: Pee from a distance and fast as the toilet seat doesn't stay up long unaided and the washrooms aren't soundproofed.

The BIG City: *Toronto is Canada's commercial heart and Ontario's capital. Dramatic office towers built by large financial com-*

panies have created a striking skyline, but the hundreds of thousands of new Canadian's that have made Toronto their home have also given the city a vigorous, multicultural air.

The best way to see the layout of the land is with a visit to the CN Tower, at 180 stories, the world's tallest free-standing structure.

It seems fitting that Toronto also has Canada's most impressive railway station. Union Station was built in 1927 as a cooperative effort between two great railways, the Canadian National and the Canadian Pacific. The massive hall, with its arching coiffered ceiling and pillars, (and spelling mistake) *is a fine example of the 1920s style of architecture. This multi-modal terminal provides access to an extensive railway network and is the heart of VIAs intercity services between Quebec City, Montreal, Ottawa and Windsor.*

Union Station is symbolic of the glorious adventure of a transcontinental train journey across Canada. The sounds of luggage wheels and the clicking heels of people rushing through the terminal resonate from the floors and walls, to become hushed in the high spaces between the arches. As passengers embark, they see the bright reflection of lights in the stainless steel of the Canadian, poised for its westward flight. - VIA's Log to Western Canada (liberated from First Class.)

Whistling 'the old town looks the same' I step from the train and make my way towards the concourse. My hands are shaking. Floors and walls really do resonate and I find myself buried in a crowd of happy, smiling, hugging people. Escaping the crush I spot my family to see relief on their faces when they see me. Smiles appear as they run to greet me. My daughter presents me with a crushed flower she found on the floor and holds my hand tight all the way to the van. My son hugs me shyly and greets me with a 'Hi Dad, how was your trip?', and asks if he can carry my pack. Janice tells me I've lost weight, wants to know if I'm hungry or thirsty, and if I have any change for the parking meter, and she's sorry but she had to park miles away as they were running late. Home.

White Heat: The last thing I see as we exit Union Station is Miss talking animatedly into a pay phone, he looked sad. When we found the van and drove off into the noise and organised chaos of big city streets, I doled out presents and snuck glances and gauged reactions. It was a strange feeling to be back, and my family were obviously happy to have me back, and I was glad. I loved them so much and I'd been away far too long. I thought of my Nin as we hit Highway 10 at a junction that comforts me by fact that I really am homeward bound. I see her in her prized fur coat sat next to my Granddad at a reserved table in the front window of the Oak Tree public house in the sky and I thank her. A black and white photo of the two of them at their fiftieth wedding anniversary party hangs on a wall at home. Another posing with thirty grandchildren in various stages of evolution taken by a photographer from the Liverpool Echo sits in a photo-album.

I spent most of that party serving drinks from behind the community centre bar with my best mate Steven John James Bullock, between nipping outside for furtive smokes and enjoying the shenanigans of my relatives. We had been warned not to give Grandad whisky to keep him from boxing with imaginary contenders for his title but we still slipped him a couple of shots in a Coke can to the chagrin of my Nin. An uncle took them home in a cab and the photo of Nin stood next to Grandad in front of a white French door appeared in the paper the following week. She's wearing her fur and a quizzical look, as granddad leans in eyes on his glass, a half-smoked cigar in his left hand, knuckles scarred and swollen from battles won and lost. They seem amused and a little bit lost.

Shot in the knee at Dunkirk, French polisher by trade, boxer, goalkeeper, warrior, Grandad arrived home from the war carrying more than the weight of a German bullet, and Nin made do with what she had like most brides of the war-damned.

I kept her company, talking in front of a coal fire in her living room as Grandad lay dying in their big old bed carried downstairs by his sons. She had made me a cup of tea spiced with dark rum and we smoked unfiltered Woodbine cigarettes when she showed me three one-pound notes hidden behind the mirror hung on the wall above the fireplace. A mirror Granddad had scraped the silver backing from in shapes to fit photos of his grandchildren so he could look at us while he combed his hair, he told us.

'He doesn't know I know, Paul.'

He'd been secretely, he thought, taping money behind that mirror for years

'You should buy a ticket to the south of France with that lot Nin,' and we laughed at the thought of her over there in the heat in her fur coat.

'No, I'll buy him a nice pork-chop for his tea instead, he loves his pork chops,' she told me, suddenly serious.

He passed away in a veteran's hospital not long after. 'Suffered in silence' engraved on his tombstone. Funeral blighted by an argument in a pub which escalated into a family fight after closing time. After the dust settled, I sat with Nin by the electric fire in our living room, having another ciggie, and she asked me what had been going on out there as nobody would tell her. I told her there had been a fight and she told me I was better than that but Grandad would have enjoyed it. She spent her last days searching for her husband and told visitors that he'd just left, they must have passed him in the hallway. She joined him four weeks before I boarded the plane to Canada.

Snow hits the windshield hard and I remember a game of football with Grandad in the yard behind the big house on Tarbock Road, when I smashed a cellar window with the perfect volley and he took the blame. 'Leave him alone Sally, it was me.' No one messed with my mum! James Cagney in White Heat he was and that was the end of that. and I'm proud to have been given his gold watch and chain, the watch made in Canada, the chain a mystery.

'Na Bother Ata' is the motto of Orangeville, Ontario, high up in the hills of Headwaters Country, where the Ojibwa fished and hunted until settlers and founders like Robert Dodds and Orange Lawrence staked their claim. Wipers swiffer the windshield and I tell Travelin' Dad stories as the van takes the gradual incline that snakes through the heart of Caledon. Taillights lead the way as if we were on a runway. William wears his beaver-skin hat with pride and Madeline fusses over the rabbit she has named Jasper. I ask William what he will call his hat, as Janice catches me up on the latest gossip and drives carefully as is her want. I shoot glances at my backpack propped up in the back of the van as we chat - as making sure it's still there has become a habit. The new hospital looms into view nestled among shells of identical homes waiting to be snapped up by disenchanted city dwellers.

An over-sized Canadian flag lolls from a flagpole soaked and lifeless like a hanged man on castle ramparts. McDonald's neon playroom rears its ugly head. 90 billion served now, 89 when I left. Blockbuster Video sleeps halfway up a cobbled, truck-battered Broadway and its sentries of turn-of-the-century buildings. The Town Hall and newly renovated theatre on the right, the lit-up Library we love on the left.

A sharp turn at the light onto First Street where traffic parts like the Red Sea and just like that I'm sliding across a slick, snow-covered driveway to turn the key in the front door.

I'm home!

Who moved the friggin furniture?

'When you wake up in the morning and you can't remember much about the night before. A small reminder of the state you were in all the tattered clothes across the floor. Your head still keeps singin', your phone still keeps ringin'. Remember just exactly where you've been, 'cos there ain't no doubt about it there's no better things to see than what you've seen.' - Slade

‘September 27, 1999

Paul,

I was planning on sending you a note from The Halibut Capital of the World, but I didn't have time to write anything worthwhile there. This message finds me gazing from a train window in Shelby, Montana, 25 miles south of the Alberta border. There is "Dancing" in Shelby, according to an electric neon sign above the Oasis Bar & Casino. There are drinks to be had at the Oil City Saloon around the corner, and of course, you can furnish your trailer from the selections at the Western Furniture Store. That's about all that is here except "...there is a train every day leaving either way..." to borrow a line from "My Opening Farewell".

I am on Amtrak's Train No. 8, the eastbound Empire Builder from Seattle to Chicago. For the next 1000 miles to Minneapolis, there is nothing but high prairie and the faint outlines of distant hills. From my window I can see north to the Sweet Grass Hills of Teddy Roosevelt fame. They straddle the Canadian border and bring back thoughts of the week I have just spent in British Columbia. I managed to see moe of the province than I ever thought possible. I rode the most spectacular train in North America, if not the world. I visited the haunting Charlotte Islands and came face-to-face with death. All of this happened in the course of seven days.

First, I'll recount the Charlotte Islands. I took a float plane from Prince Rupert to Massett on the north coast of Graham Island. I was one of five passengers on the Harbour Air Dehavelland "Beaver". There was a Sheriff from the mainland escorting a handcuffed "First Nation" prisoner, a man who repaired heating boilers for the school district, an insurance salesman and, seated next to the pilot, a man on the cusp of middle age looking for new moments in a routine life. His first new recollection would be the slow motion smoothness of the float plane as it left the water among sleeping freighters in the harbor and gently touched it once again 45 minutes later on Massett Inlet.

I rented a car and drove 65 miles south along the island's only paved road to Skigigate Reserve (read "Reservation") and Queen Charlotte City (Pop.1,000). The road traverses the broad flat-forested plain that is the eastern half of the island. Every few miles, I would encounter a solitary pick-up truck or 4X4. Fog, drizzle, sun breaks, and rain showers constantly shuffled around me. The haunting nature of the island is at first suspected and then made palpable, when I pass a cedar tree stump that has been carved into an eight foot high seated raven. Then a wooden bear peers out of the shadows followed by a wooden carving of a women shrouded in a veil. Someone (a Haida) took the time to create these figures. The resistant cedar of which they are made, will last for decades before it slowly rots back into the soil. I am told that on remote parts of the west coast of Graham and Morsby Island to the south, one can discover ancient totem poles among the trees.

The Haida Arts and History Museum is located in Skidigate. I explored the exhibits, talked with the (white female) director and bought a black argillite raven statuette by a Haida artist named Edgars from Old Massett Reserve. (I'll call it a modest "investment" in a rapidly appreciating art form. It remains to be seen what Kathy calls it, when I get home!) I met and had coffee with the town's leading business man (another non-Haida), whose daughter I knew from e-mail correspondence. She sells Charlotte Islands smoked salmon. (I found out from her grocer father that the salmon actually comes from Vancouver, but what the Hell? It's delicious anyway.) The young people, native and white, are leaving the island he told me. The fishing and lumber industries are producing fewer jobs. The education system is poor in his opinion. (He was a former member of the local school board.) Even the few government bureaucrats on the Islands want to send their children to school in Prince Rupert.

At the Alaska View Guest House (where it is claimed on a clear day one can see Alaskan islands), I met the other registered guest, Agnes Krantz - the Provincial judge from Prince Rupert, who will preside over the trial of the prisoner on the plane. The prisoner's predicament involves domestic abuse, assault, robbery, and driving without a license. It was such a familiar litany to me. I asked Agnes (off the record, of course) if she thought the defendant was an alcoholic. "Without question," she answered. "It is the scourge of the native population and there is little or no infrastructure to help them." I told her I spoke twice a month at a substance abuse unit in a medium security prison in Massachusetts. We agreed that the prison population would drop by 80% if there was a solution to alcohol and drug addiction.

The Charlottes also constituted the Discovery Channel nature adventure part of the trip. The two and a half days on Graham Island were about as authentic an encounter with the unspoiled natural elements of the Pacific Northwest as I care to have. I loved it, but there were moments when I wasn't sure going to the Charlotte Islands was the best decision. A fierce Pacific storm, which resulted in the cancellation of all flights and ferries, forced me to stay another day. The 110 kilometer winds made me feel vaguely vulnerable, as if my freedom were being taken away by the spirits that haunt the history of the Island's Haida peoples.

Although Graham is the most inhabited of the Charlottes, it is desolate and wild. It lies 80 miles west of Prince Rupert and 30 miles south of Alaska. My guess is that it is about twice the size of Rhode Island, but only the eastern coastal area is accessible by car. The principle town of Massett has barely 1,400 residents. It has a hospital, but I wouldn't want to be in need of its services. There is little wealth on the island except for unseen remote fishing lodges reachable only by chartered float plane. The Haida natives are poor, in spite of their rich artistic talents. The two main "Reserves" where they live (by choice, I think) have an eerie beauty caused by the presence of their totem poles. The impressive monuments cannot, however, hide the unkempt ugliness of abject poverty.

The Island's rain forests have all the mystical qualities that are ascribed to them in the literature. It is the moss which most impressed me, as I walked over a trail to a small mountain on the north coast of Naikoon Provincial Park. Under foot, the moss cover is 15 inches deep. It is an effective way of keeping a hiker on the narrow trail. On the wood of the branches of the Skita spruce, the moss swells in diameter by three or four times. From the branch ends, a lace-like cousin of Spanish moss drapes down in yards of translucent silver-green tinsel. The moss seems to absorb all sound. The silence is at once pleasing and disturbing. A raven flies low over my head, heralded by the increasing sound of its rhythmic wing strokes. Then it is gone, and the silence returns. Even the tiniest sound overhead, behind or out of sight gets my attention and then instantly vanishes into nothingness.

At the base of Tow Hill, I decided that there was enough light left in the day to climb to the top. The base of this 500 foot basalt outcrop is in the ocean. The trail is elevated on wooded planks coated with a non-skid adhesive. The storm had ended two hours earlier and water is cascading down the flanks of the hill as if it were a sponge that had been lifted out of the sea. (That's another role the moss seems to play.) About half way up the hill, three small Columbian blacktail deer cross in front of *me* and stare. They have no fear, only curiosity. There is a small platform at the summit.It is perched at the edge of a cliff that plummets straight down into Dixon Entrance. This 30 mile wide strait of water is all that separates British Columbia from Prince William Island, Alaska. Finally I get a glimpse of the one state I have yet to visit.

There was little time left to spend at the top. The clouds were closing in once again and it was nearly six. I decided to make a brisk walk of it back to the trail head and the car. I was concentrating on negotiating the narrow wood planks of the trail, when I heard a crash and looked up. Ten or twelve feet in front of me, straddling the trail, was a black bear. He was as tall as I was and on all four feet. He was easily 6 feet long. I froze. The terror that went through me is indescribable. We stared at each other for perhaps 10 seconds. It seemed like an eternity. All I could think of was that I hadn't met another individual since I left the guest house 15 kilometers back from the end of the trail. The bear began to move very slowly and deliberately across the trail to my right. He stopped again, looked at me, and then continued into the forest. I was still paralyzed with fright. Although he was out of sight, I had no idea how far he had gone. I broke into a run, trying not to slip into the wet ooze of the forest floor. Thank God, I didn't see him or anything else again.
In case you are wondering, the answer is "Yes". I had peed in my pants. Bears are meant to be seen from observation cars of trains with Diet Pepsi in hand, Discman ear phones on head, and laptop computer booted. That's what I will be doing right now but, alas, the only wildlife today in north central Montana consists of cattle, sheep and penned horses (the latter destined for Canadian packing plants, since Americans don't eat horsemeat.) Prince Rupert is a much more interesting place than you seemed to convey when we talked about it. I wanted to spend another day there, but it was lost to the storm delay on the Charlottes. It seems much bigger than its 17,500 population. I'll bet that is because of the large area it services commercially and juridically. I'll get into that and the train part of the trip in a later note.

Best regards,
Eric

PS. I hope I can send this to you tomorrow between trains in

Chicago.'

Thanks Eric, wish I could write like that (you're not the only one: Editor.) A journalist pal, Steve Payne, interviewed Pierre Berton recently for a newspaper article regards a century of trains, planes, and automobiles, for the millennium edition of The Toronto Sun and had him sign my well-traveled copy of The Great Railway.

'To Paul with best wishes - Pierre Berton, Sep '99'

Thank you Steve, Pierre, Brad, Quint, Terry, Don, VIA, elk everywhere, and all who appear in, contributed to, and championed this bloody book; especially Shells, Mrs M., Janice, Madeline, Sandra, Cousin John, Writers Fderation of Nova Scotia, Anne Nothof, Barbara Lange and the Somervilles; Slade, Beatles, Elvis, Liverpool and Scousers, Canada and Canadians, family, friends, loved ones, lovers, teachers and sensei's; animals passed and present, frogs, newts, turtles, hamsters, mice, Ringo, Noddy, Sammy, Catherine, George, Lenny, Juno, Fanny, Fred, Merlin, Murphy, Ambay, and Milo: The Mick, the best dog in the world, champion recycler of hockey pucks.

Paul Henry Sutton

Made in the USA
Middletown, DE
11 January 2020

83018097R00158